The Homesie Kids

Joyce Shurmer

First published in 2007
By the Author

A catalogue record for this book
is available from the British Library

ISBN 978-0-9556617-0-9

Printed and bound in Great Britain by RPM Repro

Please note: This is a work of non-fiction. The events it recounts are
true: as detailed by exact reproductions of actual letters and reports.
Most   names   outside   the   family   have   been   changed.

This book is dedicated to Lydia,
who never gave up.

I would like to thank

Mark who pushed me to DO it, helped me with it and finally brought it to fruition.
Andrew for believing in me and encouraging me to tell the story to the world.
Scott for reading my dossier and expressing sympathy.
Shireen for her greatly valued editing skills which has made this a better book.

I am also grateful to Eric for sharing his memories, no matter how painful and helping me so much with technical advice.
Thanks to Bob and Bernard for their memories, too.

I must mention a lovely lady named Pearl that we met, who was very helpful on all things Cornish, especially the speech.

And thanks to Linda, my 'agent'.

Contents

First Thoughts

At last I have made it and the story is told. It has been in my heart forever. Sometimes, I felt like a detective uncovering a crime, for I had to research what I thought I *knew* inside out. There were lots of surprises, shocks and pain. I have coped with it in the end because I have lived with the telling of it for so long.

Much of *this* story revolves around large self-contained children's homes, run by the L.C.C. They covered many acres, and contained 'cottages' in which damaged children lived with unmarried women, who had little or no training in childcare. It's small wonder that sometimes things spiralled out of control. All these places contained shell shocked children with backgrounds of heartbreak.

And that wasn't all. Behind these children were inadequate and ill educated parents thrust into circumstances beyond their control. This is their unbelievable story, too.

There was also the untimely birth of a boy child, during an air raid. The war would bring sadness and pain enough for most families. But it wouldn't end there.
For some, that was only the beginning.
By the time this boy reached seven, he was bewildered, sad and very angry. His incredible tale will be told, too, because it is very definitely linked to mine.

I can still see those rooms at the top of the house, as clearly today, as I could then. They weren't much, but to us they were home. In my innocence, I could not know that even this would soon be lost. By the time, I was six years old, life as I knew it would fall dramatically apart. As if that wasn't bad enough, the people that I'd known in the years I've been on this earth would be gone, too. I would be alone in a terrifying place called Birch Cottage, under the 'wing' of a cruel 'housemother'. All the members of my family will be scattered. My mother would be in hospital. My older brother Bernard would be gone, too. These things were painful enough. Even after all these years, I can still feel the pain of the loss of my little brother, Bobby.

Only my father would remain in the place we called home. He would be alone. I knew without seeing that he sat at the plain wooden table by the window and painstakingly took a small pinch of tobacco from the silver tin with the flip up lid. Holding his tongue between his teeth, he would transfer the pungent smelling stuff to a wafer thin paper and spread it into a thin line. With surprisingly deft fingers, he would flick the edge of the paper into a tight roll, which he would place in his mouth. I have sat on his knee many times and watched him flip up the lid of the silver cigarette lighter, which he told me over and over again, once belonged to a German

What I couldn't know was how often he sat at the table and sobbed on his forearms for the hand that life had dealt him.

I first began to notice that things weren't quite right when I was four years old or thereabouts. Lots of years would pass before I could build up a complete picture. Or answer the inevitable questions.

WHY ME? WHY US? WHY? WHY? WHY?

NOW, I know, that these questions have followed me all my life.....................

And I also know there *IS* no answer.

I couldn't know either that the events I encountered during my childhood would colour and influence my whole life.

PART ONE: SUITABLE TREATMENT

Chapter One: Knee Hill

We lived in the second house next to the alleyway that ran alongside the railway line. It was really a paved pathway, despite being known by all and sundry as 'the alley'. It led to the station and the few shops that were Abbey Wood. Our street was Abbey Terrace; we lived upstairs in four rooms in a small terraced house.

The railway line continued its journey to Plumstead and Woolwich, across the end of the street, just a few houses away. It was a great magnet of attraction for all the boys. The dead end would have been a great safe play area, if only the boys would remain on this side of the high wire fence. Of course they didn't. I can still hear my mother's cry. "Bernard's on the railway line, again."

At the mouth of the street, St Michael and All Angels stood guarding the way into our wicked world. It was a nondescript red brick church, without any frills, built in 1907 for the princely sum of £8000. It squatted squarely on the corner, surrounded by a narrow skirt of scrubby, weedy grass, staring balefully at the new world unfurling rapidly before its pale, stained glass eyes.

The vicar that presided within its midst brought little comfort to the troubled lives of his immediate 'flock', for they were mainly a godless lot. They only ventured inside his church to exchange wedding vows, if they could raise the necessary 'readies' to put on a show for the neighbours.

An R.A.C.S 'cheque' usually sorted this problem. My mother always referred to it as a 'stores' check. An agent would call to collect the weekly (with interest) payment, wearing a thinly veiled superior smile and sporting a shiny suit.

My mother would have been one of the vicar's followers, if it had been allowed.

It wasn't.

My father and his family were non-believers.

The vicar DID get to christen every child, though. Beliefs were immaterial. This was done as soon as possible after birth, even in those harsh times. (I still have my tattered certificate to this day). It didn't matter that parents couldn't afford the lacy finery or the 'do' afterwards. It was a tradition and they managed. The next time they saw inside the church would be to attend Sunday school. The vicar's wife and her helpers, who were brave enough to deal with the likes of my brother and his friends, drew the short straw to run this. The children didn't have a choice, anyway, for their parent's needed a bit of peace on a Sunday afternoon. It was a long-standing tradition to have a 'lay down'!

And even non-believers needed burying!
On these occasions, the church was full.

Most of the people wouldn't have even been here if it wasn't for the Royal Arsenal. This was a secretive government armaments factory surrounded by a tall, grey brick wall. The main core of it was in Woolwich, but it stretched from there to Plumstead and on to Abbey Wood and in the other direction to Charlton. Beyond the Arsenal were uninhabited marshes and the murky River Thames. In front of it was the railway line. It was no-man's land. The towns of Charlton, Woolwich, Plumstead and Abbey Wood grew up around the Arsenal. It was responsible for building rows and rows of terraced houses which stretched as afar as the eye can see to Charlton.

Of course, I didn't know anything about all of that. Nor did I know my Dad worked in the Arsenal. I knew he went somewhere called work, every morning, very early. I knew Bernard went to school. I wasn't big enough to go to 'big' school. I did go to the nursery. Bobby didn't. He was only a baby. My Mum didn't go to work. She had what my Dad called 'turns'. Since the war's end, more and more women were starting to work. But she didn't.
I loved all my family. It wasn't something I even thought about, it was just something you knew. I also always realised that we didn't have much money.

The four rooms we lived in were poor. There were two bedrooms, a living room and a scullery. My dad's brother, Lou and his wife Rose lived downstairs with their five children. (They had four rooms, too). The lavatory was outside. I can still see the tin bath hanging on a nail on the grey brick wall. We all shared this. On bath nights, this would be hauled up the stairs and filled with hot water, by saucepans, from the copper. The lucky person got to bath first!
On the whole, we managed better than them.
My Mum and Dad had the room at the front of the house. This one was big with a bay window. There was little furniture, except a spring bed with a solid wooden headboard, a dark wardrobe and a dressing table with three mirrors. Bobby's cot was in there, on a homemade rag rug, at the end of the bed. The other bedroom had two single beds in it. Bernard slept in one and I slept in the other. He was a terrible tease. He was always climbing up on the big, old chest of drawers by the window and playing with the gas mantle to frighten me. He would turn it down until long shadows formed in the room.

The main room where we spent most of our time had a coal burning range with a high metal fireguard in front of it. There was a table, under the only window, and one armchair, by the range. A homemade wool rug was in front of the fireguard. I can still see the scullery, too. I remember a mottled iron gas cooker and a copper just inside the doorway of what seemed a very narrow room, even then. I can see a brown draining board and a chipped enamel sink under a small slit of a window. There was also a narrow table pushed against the wall. An old chair was wedged in between this and a cabinet with a drop down flap. There was worn lino everywhere.

My mother complained about the furniture. Scornfully, she would say it was only second hand rubbish. That was when she was having a 'turn'. At other times she would be very, very quiet. Most of the time, she would stay in bed and leave us to fend for ourselves. I often looked after Bobby, carrying the heavy baby everywhere I went.

I knew there was something wrong with my Mum. Grown-ups talked about it at Auntie Elsie's in hushed whispers. She lived just up the road. My mother never seemed to be present.

My Auntie Elsie, Cousin Rose, Peggy and Cousin Bill lived in a hut!

So did my Granny and Granddad, my Uncle Ronald and Cousins, Pauline and Joanie.

They lived at Knee Hill.

It was a magical place. Opposite, a sloping field and a thick wood made it a very popular playing place. All the little girls, including me, were scared stiff of the woods. Everyone knew there were gipsies in there and that they took children away.

There were about a dozen huts perched on a hilltop. They were not to be confused with prefabs. Originally they were built for munitions workers in the Royal Arsenal Armaments factory. Since, they had been taken over by the local council. As old as they were, they were better than our four rooms. All the huts had an inside lav and a proper bath. It was iron, I think. It was in the scullery, with a board over it. But it did have taps. Bernard turned them on once, when the board was in place. He got a clip around the ear from Dad. I can still see Auntie Elsie sitting by the board, in her dressing gown, eating her breakfast, even though it was past noon.

We spent a lot of time at Knee Hill.

It was awkward, even then.

We felt like piggies-in-the-middle.

It depended on the situation where we spent our time.

Mum and Dad's family DID NOT GET ON.

When Mum was in her quiet phase, we would visit Gran on a Sunday for tea. I can't say I ever enjoyed it. Even by the standards of the day, it was old-fashioned. Inside it was dark and gloomy, with the curtains drawn almost all the way across the window. There were large pieces of furniture fighting for space. Over the chairs, dark green crocheted antimacassars hung. And it smelled musty, although it was neat and tidy. Grandad was a strange man. He sat in a striped collarless shirt, by the open coal fire, which was alight even at the height of summer, smoking his pipe and spitting phlegm into the flames. He rarely spoke. Occasionally, he grunted an answer to a question put to him by Gran. We always dreaded Uncle Ronald being there. We hoped he would still be at the pub. He was a nasty individual, always making snide remarks and goading Cousin Pauline, until she was in tears. It was little wonder that his wife had left him for another man, lumbering him with two small children. Out of politeness, we had to eat Gran's dry meat paste sandwiches, watery jelly and stale homemade cake. She was a quiet, gentle, old-fashioned lady with neat clothing and tidy pinned up hair. On our departure, she always pressed a sixpence into our palms with knobbly, arthritic fingers.

When Mum was 'high', we never went near Gran. Not even for Sunday tea. What was strange is nobody ever asked why.

At those times, Dad would make for the sanctuary of Auntie Elsie's place, with us in tow.

This was daft!

Gran's place was at the front, next to the road, immediately behind it was Auntie Elsie's hut. It was necessary to climb a rough pair of stairs cut into the hillside to get to it. These led to a narrow pathway liberally filled with cinders, which crunched noisily as we shamefacedly crept past Gran's garden into Auntie's Elsie's gate. We always hoped Spot, her dog, wouldn't start barking at the top of his voice and give us away. It mattered little because we would soon have to 'go out and play like good children', anyway.

But not before we heard father call someone a wicked old bitch. I had the uncomfortable feeling that he was talking about Gran.

I felt bad about that.

Always!

Sometimes Joanie or Pauline would sidle up to the fence at the corner of their garden and call me over. They were always properly dressed in print dresses, white socks and white sandals. I wore only a pair of grimy knickers and I was barefoot, with my white skin coated with the dirt of Auntie Elsie's garden.

(My Dad was an advocate of the natural way of life, of which Gran highly disapproved.)

None of that mattered to me, or them.

I would carefully put the big brown rabbit back in his hutch and join them gladly. I think I thought it made up for the mad actions of grown-ups.

And I liked them, anyway.

Pauline was a year older than I was and Joanie was a year younger. They would squeeze under the stranded wire fence and we would all escape to Knee Field. Usually, I took Bobby, too. Spot was a willing accomplice to our 'crime', racing wildly across the road to the field, ahead of us. Of course, Bernard always wanted to go into the woods to look for 'buried treasure', which was reputed to be in Lesnes Abbey. Us girls didn't. He normally got his way, though.

Auntie's Elsie's place was a sanctuary for a lot of other people, too. Big cousin Pat came to see his mother, with his wife Eileen, who was 'a bit of a looker'. They brought Raymond, who was Eileen's illegitimate son by another man. A shadowy figure never referred to in family circles. Pat took him on and was a good father to him. They would eventually go on to have two more sons, and a long way into the future, Eileen would leave Pat for another man.

Auntie Nell also came with her brood of children. Her husband Albert never came with her. She lived in Croydon, which was two tram rides away. She also had a child 'born out of wedlock'. It had happened while she was 'in service' and caused her to lose her job. This was a shocking occurrence, which made her go back home with her tail between her legs, and face her father, who was a formidable man.

He married three times and used his children like workhorses. My father told me that he had a vivid memory of his mother dying horribly in childbirth, without even the benefit of a doctor, when he was eight years old.

Auntie Nell soon escaped by marrying Albert and having five children. Cousins Bill, Peggy, Rose and Pat were Auntie Elsie's children, born of a marriage to Pat an Irishman, who died young, leaving her with four school children to bring up on her own. She was diabetic. I often watched her stick needles into her flowing folds of flesh with horrified fascination. Bill had a horrendous time in the war, he was blown up and had steel plates put in his head. He had no other choice than to go home to his mother. Peggy escaped to the Land Army as soon as she was old enough and would, later, marry drunken Maurice in haste and produce a daughter, Sandra.

Rose would never leave her mother, eventually marrying twice in the twilight of her life.

My memory of their hut is that it was muddled and untidy. There were beds in every room. In Elsie's room, visitors sat wherever they could find space. There were two armchairs. These were brown and bulky, and set at right angles to the bed. A big treadle sewing machine was by the door. There was a wooden chair beside it and a pile of unfinished sewing. Auntie Elsie and her two daughters were accomplished needlewomen. The treadle often worked overtime.

Mostly we enjoyed our time at Knee Hill where the sun always seemed to shine. We had many, many adventures on its green and brown mantle and returned home, filthy, but happy. It was only once we let ourselves into the dank passage of Number 6, Abbey Terrace, and climbed the worn stairs to the upper floor that the sunlit happiness would drain instantly away. It was replaced with a sad despair that we all knew and accepted from an early age, was our lot.

Chapter Two: The Convalescence

The state of my health didn't help matters much. I was thin, sickly and I think I was born with a cough! There was a suspicion that I had tuberculosis, which was rife at the time. Even in later life, as an early teenager, I can remember having to go to the visiting X-ray unit. I never knew if they found anything wrong. No one ever told me of the results, and it wouldn't have occurred to me to ask.

I wouldn't exactly say I was my mother's favourite. I think she just preferred me because I was a girl and so little trouble, being very quiet, shy and scared of my own shadow. It didn't matter much *who* she preferred. No one took any notice of *her*. It was either as if she didn't exist, or her existence was lower than any human being could possibly be, therefore, her opinions about anything didn't matter at all. All she could do when the chips were down was to hang grimly onto me.

They fought over me, all the time. They pulled me back and forth between them. My mother howled, hot, angry tears, and often was unable to control herself, usually resulting in her wetting herself. Sadly, I inherited her weak bladder. My father would alternate from desperate pleading with her, to yelling abuse at her, calling her a dirty bitch, amongst other things, which would make her round on him, clawing at his face with her long fingernails. He would stare worriedly at me, clacking his tongue agitatedly against the roof of his mouth. I just cried in terror, praying it would stop. Although, he had contributed to my obvious traumatized state, he would leave us all in no doubt where the fault lay.

Bernard would look on, through a crack in the bedroom door, in a state of distress. This would show itself by the way he wound his forefinger around a lock of hair, which as a result always stuck up like a thatch, despite the copious amounts of water applied to it, daily.

A neglected Bobby was in his cot, crying with indignation. He was the apple of my father's eye and had his brother's name. He had been lost in the war and had taken on almost legendary qualities since his demise. There were a lot of 'Bobbies' around at that time!

Ours liked to be the centre of attention.

And if he wasn't, he let everyone hear all about it.

As it was, he had been luckier than both of us, for Dad had always been around for him. He had been in the Army for all of Bernard's childhood. They never did see eye to eye. He was also away for a lot of mine. But it was different because I was a girl. So, I suppose we *did* have a kind of bond. And I could be useful. I could do things to help the situation, despite my young age. I could keep an eye on Bobby for a start. He didn't trust Bernard to do anything.

It was an extremely bad situation when the doctor decided that I needed a spell in a convalescent home. I was about four at the time. The chest infection I had hung on relentlessly. Dr. Holt had shaken his head in despair. He explained carefully to my mum that I needed special care to shake it off. She sat quietly and listened. Her agitation only showed in her badly cracked hands, which trembled and shook in her lap. He was asking her politely if she could manage to pack my clothes. My Dad never did give her time to answer. He always chipped in first. Even at my young age, my face burned with humiliation for her, in between my bouts of savage coughing. But, I was powerless to help and so it was all arranged. I was to travel with my Father on a tram and two trolley buses. My Mum was invisible as usual. I saw something like pain flit across her face. Then it was gone, and her usual expression was in its place.

At that moment, my heart swelled and filled with an all encompassing love for her, which would last a lifetime, no matter what.

Of course, I was sick on the tram. It went all down my new coat. I was always sick. We had to get off and wait for another one. I expect my father hoped that was it! He was wrong. I was sick all the way.

I had a cream bed in a long white room. Sunshine streamed though the large windows, which were open. A soft breeze blew the brightly coloured curtains. Sunbeams danced on the yellow counterpanes. The food was specially prepared to tempt poor appetites. How, in those austere times, I'll never know. It was such as we could never have in our own poor homes. No child refused it for long. Outside there were toys I had never seen before. Although I was away from my family, I was happy for the experience. Nothing seemed too much trouble for the smiling nurses.

A blot on the sunny horizon appeared in the shape of my father, who wore a desperate expression on his face. All was not well and it was *my* fault! There is a limit to the responsibility a four-year-old child should have. Because, I was missing, she had gone into a terrible frenzy. Of course, she was taking it out on him. Life for them all was unbearable. It was time for me to go home.

By some stroke of a miracle, I wasn't sick on the homeward journey.

My stomach churned as we let ourselves in the door, but I need not have worried. It actually looked lighter and smelled freshly of soap.

Auntie Rose and her family stood expectantly in the downstairs passageway.

Several of the children gave me homemade presents. Rose managed a gracious smile and offered her cheek for me to kiss. (She always DID have ideas above her station). I meekly pecked at her. She shooed her children back into their rooms. Her raven black hair swung in a sheet. She trilled sweetly.

"You'll want to be alone, Harry, with your family. We shan't disturb you."

What she didn't say was that she considered us beneath her anyway! She NEVER had ventured on one stair tread all the while we'd lived there. Dad knew that, too. Still, he raised his hand in salute and ushered me up the stairs.

Familiar loud crashes came from the scullery. A barefoot Bobby crawled around the floor. Dad tutted in annoyance at the sight until his eyes lit on his oldest son. Bernard guiltily dropped the poker he had been playing with *inside* the fireguard.

Dad swooped on him.

"You little beggar. What have I told you about playin' around with fire?"

He clipped him across the head. Bernard howled loudly.

Mum shot out of the scullery. Her eyes were icy blue shards. High spots of colour stood out on her white skin. Her lips made a very thin red line. This was *not* a good sign.

She flew at my father.

"Leave 'im alone," she screamed, gathering Bernard to her. He clung to her filthy pinafore, sobbing. (This meant she had been peeling potatoes. She always got it all down her front)

Dad backed wearily away to the door, as if a resigned escape was his only option. Bobby toddled to his side and hung onto his leg. He patted his head fondly.

I stood awkwardly in the middle of the room. She hadn't taken any notice of me. I wasn't sure if she had even seen me. A familiar feeling bubbled up in my chest. I fought desperately to control it, but the cough escaped into the room. Her head shot up.

"'Ello love," she said simply. "Still got that rotten cough, I see."

I grinned, taking small steps to her side. I am not sure what I expected. A hug and a kiss of welcome, I suppose. I was disappointed. Instead, she fussed over removing my coat, straightening my dress and tightening the loose ribbon in my short bobbed hair. Dad was watching the attention she gave me with narrowed eyes.

"'Ere, Joycie," he said. "Look what your Auntie Elsie has made for you. Come and have a look at it."

Reluctantly I left her and crossed the room, feeling like a traitor. I was amazed to see a dark brown teddy bear dressed in tartan clothes. He sat on top of the wireless. I couldn't contain my excitement. Hating my betrayal, I reached out for the Teddy. Smiling, my Dad placed it in my arms.

"Look," he said. "His clothes come off, an' all."

"Say that to me would you," she screeched at the top of her voice. "That's it, go off. Bugger off to your sisters. I'll come up there after 'er, 'ave no doubt about it. I'll give 'er a piece of my mind 'an all. Yeah, you will, won't yer. Don't you dare raise your 'and to me, man. I don't think so. Pills, you say. I will take the bloody things. I'll take the lot in a minute. Don't you get that doctor down 'ere, now then. I don't wanna see 'im. I'll give that Doctor 'Olt a piece of my mind an' all. You see if I don't."

The loud tirade continued, interlaced with my father's voice pleading with my mother to calm down. His words and actions only enraged her more resulting in the sound of an obvious physical scuffle coming from the living room. A loud wailing came from the front bedroom, which added to the din. Bobby was screaming loudly at the indignity meted out to him, once again. I cowered in a tight ball on the little bed with my hands pressed over my ears. `

Bernard's flushed, round face loomed over me. He pressed it close to mine.

"S'alright," he said comfortingly.

I stared up at him, watching the black frond of hair bobbing up and down on his forehead. My eyes filled with tears.

"She's not shouting at you, is she? She's shouting at Dad."

Then a door slammed. I heard my father's footsteps on the three stairs, which led to the bedrooms.

I sniffed miserably and whispered.

"Bobby's crying. Can't you 'ear 'im?"

Bernard's bright, apple pink cheeks creased into an earnest smile.

"S'alright," said cheerfully, "Dad's gone up there. He'll be alright."

I stopped sniffing and listened. There was no noise coming from the living room, now. It was quiet. Dangerously quiet. Bobby was quiet, too.

My lip puckered. I fought to control it. We sat on the bed with our arms around each other. The brass doorknob began to turn and the door opened. My father appeared in the doorway with Bobby in his arms. He passed a weary hand across his forehead. The living room door opened with a crash. We heard feet stomping loudly up the three stairs. Dad staggered violently back from the doorway still hanging onto Bobby.

"You," she said. "You get away from them."

"You bitch," he countered. "I'm holding the baby."

She lunged at him.

"Give 'im 'ere," she bellowed, trying to forcibly pull him from Dad's arms. We shot alarmed glances at each other as we heard the struggle on the landing.

There was a loud crash and a succession of thumps. My mother burst into harsh sobs.

I heard Dad mutter under his breath.

"Serve her bloody well right. Now look what she's made me do. Tut! Tut. Tut."

We both shot off the bed and poked our heads out of the door. We were shocked to see Mum lying in a broken heap at the bottom of the three stairs. Her bare legs were twisted at an awkward angle, the skirt of her flowered dress bunched around her waist revealing the long legs of her pink knickers.

Dad shooed us back inside the room and warned us.

"Get your shoes and coats on sharpish."

He dumped Bobby on the bed.

"Get 'im ready, Joycie," he shot at me, shaking his head. "I've got to see to your mother."

Bernard and I looked at each other mutely.

At five years old, I was very capable.

I stood Bobby on the floor and checked his underpants. They were dry. I held up his fleecy pram jacket and pushed his arms into the sleeves. Holding my tongue between my teeth, I struggled with the pearl buttons, until at last they were done up.

A spasm of coughing caught me unawares. I sat down on the bed and struggled for breath. Bernard banged me on the back. Mum and Dad were struggling past the door into their bedroom. We heard her say in a slurred voice.

"Is that Joycie coughing again? It's not my fault man. I've rubbed Vick on her chest. I don't know why she keeps coughing. I suppose it will be my fault."

"Hush, woman, never mind about that, now," cautioned Dad. "Let's get you into bed."

We heard slow feet past the door and muffled talking. Then the bedroom door closed and we could hear nothing.

Seven-year-old Bernard lunged swiftly after Bobby, who was trying to escape.

"No you don't, chubby chops," he said. "You gotta 'ave your shoes on."

He plonked him on the bed and shoved his feet into brown scuffed sandals.

We sat in a line on Bernard's bed and waited obediently for our father to appear.

The door opened. He poked his head in and beckoned to us with an extended

fore-finger. Then he raised the finger to his lips. We tiptoed out of the room and down the stairs.

"Let 'er sleep it off, now," he said, pulling the peeling brown door shut behind him.

Mum sat in the only armchair. Her thick, black hair usually had a good sheen to it. Now it looked fluffy and fine, with a large matted area on the crown. The front of her flowered dress was stained and grubby. She scratched her arms continually. An angry red rash crawled up the length of them. The skin on her hands was rough, chapped and peeling. Looking at them was a painful experience for anyone. I couldn't bear to touch them. I wanted to cry for her.

But, it was easy to forget the state of her hands and arms when you looked at her face. Her skin was soft and clear for no makeup had ever marred it. Her bright blue eyes would alternate between a mischievous sparkle to a vapid blue simple stare that seemed to see nothing. Not even the scathing remarks my frustrated father shot at her could reach her.

For this was the quiet part of her mental cycle.

She hummed under her breath to the music on the wireless as she stirred the steaming contents of an enamel basin perched on her lap. I sat on one arm and Bobby sat on the other, perilously near the fireguard. She ate from the basin, dipping the teaspoon into the sweet bread and milk, occasionally offering us some. Laughing, we vied with each other for her attention.

Bobby had just had his third birthday. Soon I would be six. We were both May birds. Bernard would be eight, in July.

It was after school, and after the nursery had closed.

There was no sign of Bernard. He had done his duty for today, which was to collect Bobby and me and steer us home to Mum. She never came for us in this part of her cycle. I never knew why. I just accepted that, too, along with all the other strange things that made up our life.

That was just the way it was.

Usually she would appear from the bedroom, singing to herself. She would have a distinctly dishevelled appearance as if she had gone to bed in her clothes. At this time, I always had the feeling that she didn't really care about us at all. She was beyond feeling anything about anyone. It was immaterial to her if we came home from school and nursery or not. I always hoped that she would rally round and do all the things that normal mothers did. But, she didn't. Not ever. And even when she tried she never seemed to know how to do them right. My father told her she was useless. And of course she believed it, utterly. Why wouldn't she?

Bernard would escape as soon as possible and leave us to it. He would clatter down the stairs, holding a large lump of bread smeared with jam in one hand. The front door would bang loudly and then there would be silence. He would stay out until night forced him to come in. He and his mate Patrick Hillman always got up to mischief. Mum couldn't cope with his antics. She let him get away with murder. He was always in trouble with Dad, too. His behaviour was beyond him, too. We struggled to regain our former positions, without calamity. She picked up three small brown medicine bottles from the mantelpiece.

"Better take my tablets," she announced.

We watched her unscrew the bottle tops and tip coloured pills onto the surface of the dusty mantelpiece. She picked them up and shoved them in to her mouth. Several bounced off into the grate.

"Sod it," she said mildly.

She didn't pick them up.

A silver-coloured companion set hung by the side of the black range, inside the fireguard. It comprised a small brush, a shovel and a poker. With a chuckle, she unhooked the brush and swept the spilt pills under the ash pan.

"Don't tell the old man," she warned.

We chuckled, too, at being in the conspiracy, although we had no real idea what we were agreeing to, especially Bobby. He was a bright three-year-old, nevertheless. Dad always said 'there were no flies on him'. He was right.

Mum unscrewed a large jar also on the mantelpiece. She dipped her hands in it and rubbed the greasy contents on her poor hands. She yawned suddenly, revealing large horse's teeth that were a surprise. There were quite a few gaping holes where the rest of them had been. Not many people could afford to visit the dentist. My mother was no different.

"I'm tired," she said. "I think I'll have a lay down."

We looked at her in alarm, knowing full well she had not long got up.

"Why don't you come up with me," she suggested. "We could all lay down together."

She smiled vacuously, liking the idea of that.

For me, going to bed at night was bad enough. I didn't want to do that in the day as well. I did have my reasons. *That* pastime was *not* a luxury for me. It was more like a nightmare.

I shook my head.

"Me an' Bobby want to play in the garden. We want to play with the rabbits, don't we Bob. An' I want to go to the lav'."

His face lit up. The front of his checked shirt was stained and grubby. So were my clothes. There was a pile of dirty laundry already gathering dust in the scullery. I suppose it didn't make sense to add to them.

"Yesh," he lisped. "Bobby wan' a lav."

The outside lavatory was a new and an exciting place for him. Negotiating the steep stairs and running into the garden and climbing up on the big wooden seat was an adventure. It was so much better than sitting on his tin pot until it stuck to his bottom.

I wish I felt the same. It was dark and grimy with spider's webs in the corners. I carried out my visits in a tearing hurry.

The rabbits were a different matter, for they were my favourite. I loved their soft fur against my skin. I couldn't possibly have known we would be eating them someday. There were also chickens pecking around in the small garden. I didn't care much for them.

Mum yawned sleepily.

"I'm going to bed."

She sauntered up the three stairs to the main bedroom.

We looked at each other.

"Come on, Bobby." I said.

We held hands and climbed down the stairs. The front door was open wide.

I turned to my little brother.

"I know what. Let's go for a little walk instead!"

"Yesh," he agreed.

"We'll go to the lav first," I said sensibly.

We were startled to meet Dad halfway up the road. Our 'little walk' had got out of hand. We had gone nearly as far as the Rec! This was almost to Belvedere. It was a familiar haunt of Bernard and his cronies. It was quite a way for them, being a long walk up Harrow Manor Way. Luckily, Bernard *was* there that day. It didn't do him any favours, though. He got the blame of course. His eyes blinked rapidly and he twisted his hair non-stop. When we all got back, Mum was still in bed. She was fast asleep, knocked out by the strong antidepressants she had taken.

Dad shook his head and muttered under his breath that *something* would *have* to change, mark my words.

Chapter Three: Harry and Lydia

I always got up really early, unable to stand my steaming bed any longer. I would wake up with a start and feel my nightdress expectantly. But my hopes were always dashed before I had ventured further than my waist. It was always the same. Dad was the only one up. He was always first.

"Wet again?" he would ask anxiously.

I would nod my head shamefully, unable to form words in my throat.

What I desperately needed at that time was a reassuring cuddle.

But, sadly, it didn't happen. Such an open show of love seemed beyond him.

The nearest contact we ever had was when I sat on his lap, or when he cleaned me up. He would always drop everything to do that to make me comfortable before he left for work, washing me down with a hot, soapy flannel and helping me to dry myself. Bobby would appear next, then Bernard. It wasn't unusual for him to attend to us all before he left. I wonder how often it made him late. It never fazed him; in fact, he seemed to accept this as normal.

Dad had a very poor start. The family came from Maidstone originally and then migrated to the Old Kent Road, in South London. It was the law to register a baby then as it is now. He fell on his head, soon after his entry into the world. It was reputed to be the fault of one sister, who was helping with the birth. His father ordered his mother not to register him, in case he didn't live. When he showed remarkable signs of survival, it became urgent to register him. The time limit allowed had run out, so his mother lied about his age. All his life, we celebrated his birthday on October the 8th. Goodness only knows when it *really* was. By his own admission, his education was poor. His father had a barrow and plied his wares at various markets. It usually meant his sons hardly went to school. As a result, my father could never catch up with his schoolwork. He had one hope of salvation. It was his dream to go to a cobbler's school to learn the trade. He spent all his spare time hanging around the local shop, whose owner, a bent old boy, tried to exert pressure on his father. But he wouldn't budge, scoffing at the idea that his son could make something of himself, adamantly refusing to fund it. He never ever forgave his father and remained bitter about the trade he could have had.

His mother was a shadowy figure he had little memory of, except that she died in childbirth when he was eight, without the benefit of a doctor. A succession of stepmothers followed who were too busy producing yet more children, to care for little Harry and his brothers and sisters. He grew up quickly, leaving the family home at the age of fourteen, when he could no longer stand the beatings or the lack of any home comforts at the hands of his father and stepmothers.

He spent the next eighteen years travelling and working on farms, deep in the countryside, as an odd job man.

Occasionally he would return to visit his sisters.

He was a shy man with little self-esteem and a marked stammer. His success with the opposite sex had been minimal, although he could talk easily to people, once he had broken the ice. No woman had ever taken him seriously as a prospective beau. At the age of thirty-three, he, too, felt the pull of Knee Hill.

At this time there was serious talk of war. Harry's fears were the same as any other man, for on every ones lips was talk of national call-up. Rationally, he told himself they would take the youngsters first. Still he felt he had to walk along the cinder path to collect the mail from the postman. That was his first sight of Lydia. He saw a woman with shiny jet-black hair, cut in an old-fashioned way, hanging washing on the line. Like him, she didn't seem to be in her first flush of youth. In fact, she was 28 years old and considered to be 'on the shelf '. He noticed that there were no rings on her finger, so he plucked up the courage to speak to her. He questioned his widowed sister, Elsie about her, but unusually, she knew nothing. The family hadn't been in the front hut long. The talk was that they came from Hertfordshire. They kept themselves very much to themselves.

On September 3rd, 1939, Prime Minister Chamberlain told the nation that all negotiations had failed. England was now at war with Germany. This news struck fear into the hearts of every man and woman and child.

The Randall family, however, were bemused and preoccupied by Uncle Harry's romance, which looked serious.

The British people waited for a war that only seemed to happen in the newspapers. Then September 30th, Hitler struck. There was a massive air raid in East London, devastating everything in sight. War was finally here, with a vengeance. The Blitz had started. What had begun in East London could easily spread to Woolwich and Abbey Wood, was everyone's inner thought. For here, they had the Arsenal. And wasn't a lot of the ammunition made just across the railway line.

On December 25th, 1940, Harry and Lydia married in St Michael's and All Angels church. Lydia wore a white wedding dress and lacy veil, which made her look almost beautiful for once in her life. Harry's nieces, Peggy and Rosie were bridesmaids. Members of both sides of the family were present, each keeping to their own side of the church hall. Curiously, according to Peggy, there were no photographs taken.

Harry had found work as a labourer, in the Royal Arsenal, which would in the future make him a civil servant. He had a job for life, which even carried a pension. In his pocket, he carried the rent book of the upstairs rooms of number 6, Abbey Terrace, for which he had paid one week in advance. He had been to Handley's second-hand furniture shop in Plumstead and made some purchases.

He rubbed his hands with glee, when he thought of the surprise his bride was going to get when it arrived. He was looking forward to his new life, which he intended to enjoy before this dratted war took everything away. Life was good, indeed.

By 1942, everything had changed. For a start off, poor Harry *did* get called up.

But that wasn't all. There was something else very wrong. Lydia's behaviour was strange, to say the least. Harry put it down to the air raids. He knew that the bombing had bad effects on some people. When this bloody lot was over he would sort it out, you see if he wouldn't. Sometimes, she was so quiet, she wouldn't utter a word and she seemed to have no energy. At these times she did nothing. Then she would gradually become talkative and more active. She would rush around like a whirlwind, cleaning everything in sight. He relied on her to pay the rent and the milkman and the Stores. She either spent the money or lost it. He never knew the truth. Luckily, his posting was in this country so he was able to take leave on a regular basis. He usually came home to mayhem. Either the place was rotten filthy or the money he had sent had all gone.

The biggest mystery of all was her ability to put pen to paper. She was a very good letter writer, with perfect spelling, whilst he himself could hardly form words. It was always a painful exercise for him.

He had scanned the latest one in disbelief. She had written to him to tell him that she was pregnant and had to go to Loughborough, Leicestershire, for safety. He was even more alarmed when he heard how unhappy she was in her lodgings. Her reluctant landlady vented her wrath out on the pregnant Lydia for the Government's audacity in forcing her to open her home to all and sundry. She forced her to walk the streets of Loughborough every day until the baby was born. She made it plain that she had no intentions of taking her back, either.

On July 30th 1942, Lydia gave birth to a boy. Her mother was at her side.

Together they returned to Abbey Wood, where Lydia would doggedly remain for the duration of the war. Harry hurried home on leave as soon as he could, only to learn that his mother-in-law had gone against his wishes and registered the baby as Bernard Lawrence Randall. And it happened again when I was born in on May 27th 1944 at the British Hospital for Mothers and Babies in Woolwich. He got there too late. So, I was named Joyce Margaret Randall. He made sure it didn't happen when Bobby was born.

At last, the hostilities were over. Harry relaxed. He remained in Somerset throughout his call up, carrying out local coastline duties, until he managed to wangle a transfer to the cookhouse. He had had an easy war, slipping off home as often as he could manage. Now, to his horror, at the last knockings, the balloon had gone up, for his regiment had received a sudden posting. They were to embark for Germany immediately. He was to be away until May 1946.

The question of Lydia's malady was in abeyance, for now. Inevitably, she became pregnant with Bobby on his return. He was born on the 8th May 1947.

Nothing had changed. In fact, things were worse. Somehow, she had to deal with three children as well. Unwillingly, Harry now had to admit that Lydia's behaviour was not the fault of the war. His anger and dismay turned to her family and her mother in particular. All this was their fault. Someone should have told him what was wrong. Now, he was stuck with her *and* three kids. There was nothing he could do; he just had to make the best of it.

The next day WAS different, though. It started out the same. I woke up steaming as usual. Dad was in the scullery where he always was. He stood as he always did with his trousers hung low on his hips, exposing the waist of his greying long johns. His braces hung in loose loops around each hip. The top half of his body was bare; it was insipidly pale, with scraggly patchy hair and pink pimples dotted all over it. A day never went by when he didn't stare into the cracked piece of mirror propped on the window ledge, lather his chin with soap and scrape an open razor across his face. Every now and then, he would plunge the razor into an enamel mug, filled with steaming hot water. When he had finished, he would carefully wipe it dry and put it away in a silver case, shutting the lid with a snap. All the time he would be talking to me, warning me to stay there, as the razor was dangerous. He kept this repartee up, until he had lifted the iron kettle off the gas stove and filled the chipped enamel bowl on the draining board with hot water.

I knew the routine by now and removed my wet nightdress so he could wash me first. He always did that. But he didn't turn to me at all. He ignored me completely. I stood there naked and stared at him in disbelief.

I poked my head around the door, expecting to see Bobby, up earlier than usual. He was a master at taking Dad's attention. However, there was no sign of *him*. Instead, I saw my mother. She was sitting, in her long nightdress, jammed between the cabinet and the table. Her eyes looked red and sore as if she had been crying. An ugly rash was all over her face, neck and arms. Seeing me, Mum dissolved into noisy tears. The high spots of colour on each cheek glistened wetly. I stared at her open-mouthed.

"Don't look at me love," she said.

"Hush, hush, now, "chided Dad. " We'll get it all sorted out, never fear."

"You had better see to Joycie, hadn't yer," she observed. "She'll catch her death standing there like that."

Dad passed a weary, indecisive hand over his forehead.

"Yes, yes," he conceded.

Uncertainly, he turned to me. I was a little piqued to find he didn't seem to pay me the usual attention. He gave me what he called 'a lick and a promise', which meant just rubbing the damp flannel over the worst bits, my lower half. All the time, he kept up a monologue. This seemed to be half thinking aloud and half talking to Mum and me. In a preoccupied fashion, he shooed me away, to get dressed.

I did my best. I sorted through the clothes hanging on the fireguard to find things that might be mine. I held up a vest, a pair of knickers and a small, liberty bodice that was definitely mine. Did I *need* the bodice, I wondered. Because of my chest, I knew that I had to wear it when it was cold. It didn't *seem* like winter. Usually, I would be shivering and flames would be licking at the grille of the range. Dad always saw to that, first thing in the morning. It wasn't alight, so it must be summer, I thought. Just to make sure, I grabbed the edge of the table, stood on tiptoe, and strained to see the sky out of the grimy window. You couldn't really see it, just the window of the house opposite. The sun glinted on the glass. Hooray! It *was* shining. I hated that bodice. It was itchy. I put it back furtively and slung a faded dress over my head.

Bernard appeared carrying a struggling Bobby in his arms. He dumped him unceremoniously on the floor. Pandemonium broke out as Bernard tried to restrict Bobby's attempts to reach Dad. Soon everyone was in that room. Dad slapped his hand in the air at Bernard. Bobby howled loudly for effect. Mum rushed in from the scullery. She was naked and sobbing wildly. In shock, we saw her whole body was red and blotchy. My agitated father ushered her back into the scullery. His loud whisper penetrated the thin wall.

"Stay out there. You're not decent woman. Can't show yourself like that in front of the children. Tch! Tch! Tch! What's the doctor going to say when he sees this lot? You're covered in it. Put your nightdress back on, eh."

We heard her voice rise.

"Doctor, doctor, I don't want no doctor. S'pose you're gonna call that Doctor 'olt. I don't need 'im coming here. Get me some more cream, man. It's only a rash. It'll go. I know it will."

She sobbed loudly, keeping up a tortured tirade, desperately trying to persuade him to try again to treat it himself, like he always did.

We heard him tell her with a deep sigh.

"It's no good, missus. My 'ands are tied, you've 'ad it far too long, now. It's got worse and worse. In any case, I told the doctor I'd let him know how it was."

She screamed out loudly.

"What! This is all you're doin' innit. I knew it. I knew you were up to something. You and that doctor."

We could hear Dad fruitlessly trying to calm her.

Bernard and I sat on a homemade woollen rug with Bobby in between us. We clung worriedly together.

As young as we were, we knew that things weren't good.

Dad hurried past us to the fireguard and selected a striped collarless shirt. He dressed quickly, fixing a white collar to the shirt with studs and sliding elasticated armbands over the long sleeves of his shirt. With a flick of his wrists, he lifted his braces back into place, until they made a perfect cross on his back. He grabbed a jacket from behind the door. Then he was gone.

We sat in silence for a few minutes. Then we all tiptoed out to the scullery.

We crowded around her. Weakly, she tried to make us leave her, to go back in the other room. We wouldn't go. I knelt on the floor and laid my head in her lap on her poor hands. So did Bernard. Bobby hugged her knees and laid his face against her nightdress. When she saw that we were staying and that we were going to hang on like limpets, she smiled weakly through her tears. Her head hung on her chest, she continued to cry softly and to rock backwards and forwards, but there was now a new wonder in her face. She knew then, that we all loved her utterly.

We heard the door open, all too soon.

Two sets of footsteps echoed across the floor and continued into the scullery. We scrambled up hastily and melted into the other room. The doctor wrinkled his nose at the poor scullery and followed us. He stood in the centre of the room importantly, stroking his chin and observing us through horn rimmed spectacles.

Dad followed, leading Mum.

The doctor spoke to Dad in low tones.

He told us to go and play in the bedroom.

Reluctantly, we obeyed, shooting worried glances at Mum.

But we didn't play.

We left the door open a crack so that we could see what was going on.

Then it all happened so quickly.

We heard a bell clanging down the street. There was a loud knocking on the door. Someone downstairs must have opened it. Two men in uniform came up the stairs two at a time. The door opened and Doctor Holt was ushering Mum forward. She was crying and screaming that she didn't need to go to hospital, that it was only a rash. Her only coat covered her long nightdress. I remember it being bright red, which stood out against her jet-black hair. The men dragged her none too gently down the stairs. The doctor and my father followed. We dashed into the front bedroom, to the bay window and saw an ambulance standing there. The street was filled with people. Tears rained down our faces as we watched the men push her into the ambulance. It chugged away up the road. The people melted away. Our mother was gone.

Chapter Four: The Plot

We heard our father's tread up the stairs. It seemed lighter, now, somehow. We could hear his chuckle from here. This seemed wrong; it was a kind of betrayal, in our eyes. We all stood mesmerised by the window, staring up the empty street as if we hoped she would materialize again, by magic, but in a normal guise.

Dad stood in the bedroom doorway.

We all stared at him as he tried to joke with us.

For us, what we had just seen was no laughing matter.

Guiltily, he reflected.

"I know. I know. I wish it didn't have to be like this, either. Come on. Come away from that winder. It won't do no good."

Reluctantly, we dragged ourselves away, knowing that as we did so we were breaking the last flimsy link we had with her.

We followed him down the stairs into the other room.

Bernard and I collapsed onto the mat before the fireguard. He twisted his forefinger in his hair in agitation. I slumped dispiritedly against him.

Dad sat down heavily at the table.

Bobby scampered across the floor and sat at his feet. He played with his shoelaces.

Dad patted him on the head and made soothing noises.

"Alright, boy, alright."

Bernard and I glared at them both.

Dad sighed loudly.

"There was nothing I could do, you know. She had to go to hospital. I 'ad no choice."

He swallowed hard and made vain attempts to placate us.

"I know what. Its Saturday tomorrer, isn't it. What do you say we go for a ride?"

Our expressions changed slightly, *now* we were a little interested. *Any* sort of outing was an adventure.

"A ride?" queried Bernard. "Where to?"

Dad's eyes opened wide as he emphasised his point, his Adam's apple bobbed up and down excitedly as he outlined his idea.

"We'll make some sandwiches. If I cut the bread first, Joycie can help spread marge on them, can't you."

I nodded in agreement. It wouldn't be the first time I've knelt up on the chair where my father sat now, wielded a knife in my little hands and spread jam on large slabs of bread for Bobby and me.

Dad continued, "We'll wrap them in greaseproof paper and we'll make a flask of tea for me and we'll make up some lemonade for you children. You can drink it out of the flask cups. We can take it in turns."

Three year old, Bobby hopped excitedly up and down.

"Go tram, eh."

Dad grinned.

"And a trolley bus, too. And I've got a secret!"

A broad smile spread across his face.

I began hopping up and down in excitement, too, now.

"What is it? What is it?" I cried.

Dad drew himself up to his full height and puffed himself out. He paused effectively until we all looked as if we would burst.

"We are going to Peter Pan's Pool!."

Now all gloom had disappeared. Fickle kids that we were, we had temporarily forgotten our mother's plight. We raced around the room in anticipation of the day out. Not even the extra bit of news that Dad had tacked on somehow that we would be visiting Auntie Nell, too, could dampen our spirits.

He held up his hand to gain our attention and calm us down.

"Whis-s-t!"

We stared at him questioningly.

He began slowly as he always did, usually needing to emphasize every point carefully.

"Well, we have all got ourselves a buckshee day off today. You and me both! It's too late for you to go to school now and I've got leave. If we are going out tomorrow, we 'ad better give this place a bit of a boogey out today. It looks as if it needs it! And you can all 'elp, can't you."

Bernard and I looked at Bobby, meaningfully. Dad caught our look.

"Yes, yes, 'e can help, too. There's little jobs'll suit him down to the ground!"

Immediately, Dad bent over the fireguard and unhooked the miniature brush belonging to the companion set. He handed it to Bobby. At once, he began sweeping the worn lino, in all directions!

Dad and I spent the rest of the day catching up on the washing and cleaning. I stood on an old wooden chair in the garden, and helped peg the washing on the line, chattering to him as I did so, whilst Bobby played at our feet.

Bernard went to the shops to do the errands. This was his usual chore.

There were two ways to reach the few shops. One was along the alley, which eventually broadened out into a square, with closed railway crossing gates blocking if off at one end and the other end running into Knee Hill.

Dad warned Bernard as usual, not to go off with Patrick Townsend & Co. and to keep off the railway lines. Still, he seemed to be gone ages. We seemed to be doing all the work.

On one side of the square, there was an oil shop, a butchers and the Co-op. Across the road was The Harrow public house. Narrow tramlines threaded through the cobbled road and continued onto the tarmac surface, curving around into McLeod Road and disappearing towards Plumstead Hill.

The trams were an endless source of fascination to Bernard and his cronies. Despite Dad's warnings, they always appeared like magic as soon as he had slammed the front door. They linked arms and marched along the alleyway together. It was also possible to reach the shops by going up Abbey Terrace and turning left into Abbey Wood Road. But it was much more exciting to go along the alley. And of course, the lure of the trams proved too much. They ran at fifteen-minute intervals, so there was never too long to wait. One soon rattled and wheezed along the track, holding up its metal arms to the thin wires strung between metal gantries, which stood at intervals like gaunt skeletons. White sparks showered down on the disembarking passengers, much to the boys' amusement. They watched the driver slide big wooden chocks under the front wheels, as if they had never seen it before, although they had watched it over and over again. They pestered the conductor for foreign coins and unwanted tickets. Eventually, they retreated, laughing when the crew told them to 'sling their 'ooks.'

Bernard suddenly remembered Dad's warning words and his outstanding list of errands, which I had written out. (At six, I could write faster and easier than Bernard or Dad could, and I possessed a natural ability to spell). Realising how long he had been gone, he hurried around the shops and got the shopping, hoping against hope that he wasn't in trouble again or that he hadn't done anything to cause the outing to be cancelled.

In fact, it didn't happen the next day, but it wasn't because of Bernard or even Mum. Either of them usually got the blame for everything that went wrong.

It was more to do with Auntie Elsie. She was ill, due to her diabetes. Seems, she had a funny turn and needed Dad, which meant we ended up at Knee Hill for the day, again.

It wasn't mentioned anymore for weeks.

Dad still had to go to work.

We became used to having to go to anyone that would have us before and after school. We rarely saw the inside of our own rooms, except at bed and breakfast time. Sometimes, we stayed with the only 'friend' of Mum's, I ever knew, Mrs Clare and her family. Often we had to split up. Bernard stayed with the Townsend's. Sometimes, I went next door to stay with my friend, Susan. Auntie Rose looked after Bobby. She didn't mind him as she had a thing about babies and small children.

The only place we never stayed where we would have ALL been welcome was Gran's.

And we all missed Mum.

I can't vouch for Bernard or Bob, but I know how I felt.

Apart from my usual cough, which caused me chest pains at times, I felt this deep, sickly ache, which seemed to stick like a rock in my bony chest. I was too young to know it was heartache.

Going to Peter Pan's Pool seemed like a distant, innocent dream.

Then Dad told us he had a week's holiday. He was going to take us on our long promised outing. We could all take a day off school and nursery.

The next day, we hurried at last, into the entrance of the small boating lake, stuck incongruously between Bromley and Catford, which was definitely nowhere near any other water, and couldn't be more inland if it tried!

We queued in the bright July sunshine for a rowing boat and looked longingly at the brightly painted pedaloes bobbing up and down on the water. It wasn't to be. Instead, we watched other children having fun in them and made do with Dad rowing clumsily around the lake, past the weeping willow tree, and bumping close to the little weir.

After that, Bernard, hair standing on end with excitement, begged Dad to let him have a go of the three wheeled bikes. Dad was reluctant. He turned his pockets out and checked his cash. Casually, he flipped the necessary coins to Bernard. He raced away, whilst we all sat at a picnic table and ate our doorstep sandwiches and drunk our lemonade. Then it was over. Dad told us it was time to go.

"I'm afraid so, Nell. She's as 'igh as a kite, again."

The small, rounded figure of Nell nodded her head and clucked her tongue in sympathy for her brother's plight.

In a soft voice, she said.

"Might be a blessing in disguise, you know, 'Arry."

I sat on the overstuffed sofa, hoping to be invisible. Since I was very quiet by nature, I was often overlooked, which suited me today.

Bobby was on the other end of the sofa, fast asleep.

Bernard was in the garden playing. He was mad about dogs. Auntie Nell had a very fat black and white bitch called Flossie. He seemed to have a way with them and boys he met, wherever he went.

Harry asked, puzzled.

"Whadja mean?"

Nell shot me a glance. I flapped my eyelids shut. Satisfied, that I was asleep, too, she continued.

"Perhaps she'll get put away, now. Probably a turn up for the book, her having a go in the 'ospital."

I opened my eyes wide in alarm!

Dad put a warning finger to his lips.

Nell shot me a sharp glance.

They both disappeared into the scullery.

Auntie Nell's own children, Sidney, Joan, Mary, John and Margaret were mostly grown up and married. The only one at home was Margaret. She was twelve and not very friendly. I hoped it would soon be time to go home.

Suddenly, I felt sick and I wanted my Mum, badly. I realised sadly, I missed her many faces, each with their own character. And I was worried now. I wondered what Auntie Nell meant by 'put away'.

I had this uncomfortable feeling it wasn't good.

Tea was though. Auntie Nell's food was lovely! Lots of little decorated cakes and shaped sandwiches. She had managed it despite the rationing, because she knew lots of tricks of the trade. Dad told us to tuck in to the cakes, which Auntie Nell had made for us, without using eggs. He told us to eat them quickly as they wouldn't keep. He needn't have worried. They disappeared without difficulty, for they were a delectable luxury for us. And they tasted fine!

If only we could spend the same amount of time in Peter Pan's Pool as we had spent here!

It seemed to be an excuse for Dad to spend the afternoon with his sister, 'chewing the fat', as he called it.

His parting shot was, "I'll see to it. Don't you worry!"

She smiled secretively.

I looked at Bernard. He raised his eyebrows in query. Bobby was all innocent smiles. I sighed with the heavy burden of my few crumbs of knowledge and was unable to shift the utter sense of foreboding, which sat in the pit of my stomach.

It seemed strange having Dad home from work, even for a few days. I wished we didn't have to go to school but he wouldn't hear of us not going. It seemed he had mysterious 'things to sort out'. He was always there to meet us, though, putting Mrs Clare temporarily out of a job. I know he hated having to ask ANYONE to help him. He used to say they only wanted to poke their noses in his business. I think Cissy Clare was genuine enough, though. Her life was hard as well. She lived three doors away with four children and a disabled husband. He didn't trust her because she was sympathetic to Mum, but he couldn't manage without her help. Auntie Elsie couldn't walk right up Knee Hill to Bostall Lane, which was where the school was.

And the only other alternative was to ask Gran!

One particular day has stuck in my mind all over the years. He was late. I stood alone in the playground. Mrs Clare had already been and gone. I refused to go with her because I was waiting for Dad. Bernard was due out, but he hadn't appeared.

My weak bladder control was always a problem for me. I had to go! I ran to the outside toilets and hurried inside. There was a man in there, standing up against the wall. He began to talk to me.

"Hello little girl. Where's your Mum?"

All the while, he was walking towards me. I stood frozen to the spot. I was afraid, but I didn't know why. He told me that he had come for me and that he had to take me home. I remember distinctly that he had a dirty mackintosh on and very dirty fingernails. He grabbed my arm tightly. Then I heard a voice, calling me. It was Dad. I snatched my arm away and ran sobbing into my father's arms. I couldn't tell him what had happened or explain why I had wet myself, when I had just come from the toilet! I had a lucky escape as it turned out because some weeks later, the same man took a little girl into Bostall Woods (which were at the back of the school) and assaulted her.

Cousin Peggy told me years later, that was the day Dad went to Woolwich to the Education Office.

Several weeks later, a letter in a buff envelope came in the post. It seemed to affect my Dad a lot. He sat and read it over and over again.

After this, he was often 'popping out to the phone box' around the corner. He would never tell us why. Mysteriously, he would say.

"That's for me to know and you to find out."

He was always dumping us whilst he went off somewhere.

Things just didn't seem the same anymore.

And Mum was fading from our memory. We hadn't seen her since she had gone to hospital. She was in an isolation ward and they didn't allow children to visit.

Bernard and I often talked whilst we lay in bed. He insisted he had heard Dad telling Mr Towner that Mum was now in Fulham Mental Hospital. We wondered what that meant, as we were just children, we had no idea.

Now it was the summer holidays and Bernard's eighth birthday on the 30th July. It passed unnoticed. That wouldn't have happened if Mum had been there. She set a lot of store by such things. But she wasn't.

The holidays soon passed and we were due to go back to school the following week. I was looking forward to it. I loved it. I only owned two books, despite the fact that I was a very good reader. I was hungry for more, always.

Dad took another day off and made one of his mysterious trips the next day.

On his return, we were surprised when Dad told us we had to get dressed in our best clothes as we were going to visit Auntie Nell, the next day. It was a weekday, which was strange. We usually went there Saturdays or Sundays. Normally, now, he would be saying we had to have a bath because we were going back to school soon. It was puzzling. He didn't normally make all this fuss over visiting Auntie Nell.

The next morning, we got ready. He lined up all our shoes and took out a divided wooden box out of the sideboard. This was a usual ritual. Using a well-worn brush and a tin of polish, he buffed all the shoes until they shone. Then he dressed Bobby in a red check shirt and grey trousers. He had parted his hair down the middle and slicked it down with Brylcream. Now it was my turn. He seemed his normal jovial self. His prime comment as he helped me dress to his satisfaction was the same as always.

"Turn around, Lady Jane."

Then he fixed a ribbon in my bobbed hair, tying it into a neat bow.

All the while, he chivvied Bernard impatiently to hurry up, that he was big enough to dress himself. Magically, he would transform himself into a neatly dressed man in a shirt and tie, neat pullover and tidy jacket.

When we got out in the street, we were surprised to see Auntie Elsie and Cousin Rose waiting for us. Dad explained that they were coming with us.

They chatted to us all the way to Waddon. We saw that Auntie Nell and grown up Cousin Joan were dressed in their coats. As soon as everyone was refreshed, we were outside in the street, again, although we had only just arrived. This was a puzzle.

The whole lot of us got on a bus, then. It drew up right beside a high red brick wall, which seemed to go on forever. We all crowded off the bus again. As we moved nearer, I saw a shiny brass plaque on the wall. I struggled to form the words in my head.

They read;

Sh-ir-ley Res-id-ent-ial Sc-h-ool for Ch-i-l-dr-en.

Chapter Five: Birch Cottage

I gaped in awe at the enormous iron gates and staggered against my grown up Cousin Joan. Impulsively she grabbed my hand. I buried my face in the protection of her clothes.

Meanwhile, a large metal plate stretching across the entrance, which seemed to wobble about like a jelly, took Bernard's attention. He jumped on it experimentally.

Dad muttered in disgust.

"Look at that little devil. Trust 'im to go jumping about on the weighbridge."

Big Joan and big Cousin Rose exchanged glances. Rose laughed good-naturedly, whilst pulling him off with a dimpled plump hand. (She always had a soft spot for Bernard).

"Leave the boy alone, 'Arry, he isn't doing any 'arm. I don't s'pose he's ever seen one before."

Dad shot Bernard a pained look before renewing his grip on Bobby's little hand.

He gazed about him anxiously. There was a little brick building on the right, which looked just like a miniature house. It had several steps leading up to a glass-panelled door. Dad looked uncertainly towards it. Auntie Elsie nudged him forward.

"Go on, 'Arry, I reckon you've gotta go in there."

Reluctantly Dad moved towards it, still clutching Bobby tightly.

Distinct shapes were visible behind the glass.   His hand fluttered hesitantly towards the doorknob. Before his hand landed, the door opened. A uniformed man stood on the threshold. He cleared his throat and settled horn-rimmed glasses more firmly on his nose. His gaze swept superciliously over the assembled group of people, who were now milling about uncertainly.

"Yes?" he inquired, looking as if he had a bad smell under his nose.

Dad swallowed and shot an anxious look at Bernard and me.

"Not out here," he muttered worriedly.

He disappeared inside the little house with Bobby. I renewed my grip of Cousin Joan's hand. Bernard stared open-mouthed all around him.

In not many moments, Dad emerged, red-faced and gulping. He spread his fingers wide and shrugged his shoulders dismissively.

"They won't let us take the children. Its no use, I've tried."

The man stood impassively with his arms folded.

"It's the rules," he stated baldly.

The family looked him over. Auntie Elsie stepped forward. She thrust her chin out belligerently and stabbed a forefinger in the air.

"We don't care about yore bloody rules, mate. 'Arry was promised that he could take the children in himself by the Welfare. It's bad enough it's gotta 'appen at all. Pore little sods got to be taken away from all they know."

She broke off guiltily, shooting a glance at all of us.

Dad groaned.

Quickly, I picked up the vibes that something unpleasant was about to happen.

I stared quickly from one to the other and burst into tears. I threw myself against my father's best trousers and beat my arms fruitlessly on the cloth.

"There," moaned Dad. "See wot you've done."

Bobby burst into tears, too. Bernard contented himself with aiming a savage blow at Dad's ankle. He held his head with both hands and rocked it from side to side.

"Wot 'ave I done," he moaned. "Jesus All Riley, wot 'ave I done."

He, too, burst into loud, harsh sobs.

Auntie Nell hurried over to him and slid her arm around him.

"Here, here," she remonstrated in her soft voice. "What else can you do Harry? You have to go to work. It's too much. We'll have a talk to them. Don't worry."

Cousin Rose sympathised.

"'Ere, don't take on so. Your Dad don't mean you no 'arm. 'E loves you, God help him. It's only for a while. It's just 'til your mother comes home from hospital."

Joan gave me a comforting squeeze. Rose gave Bernard a big wink. He winked back.

The man had been joined by his colleague by now. He was a different kettle of fish altogether.

"Let them, Bert," he urged. "What harm can it do?"

He shook his head.

"More than my jobs worth, Ted," he said.

Ted's face lit up.

"I've got an idea."

They all looked at him expectantly.

"You get off, Bert," he suggested. "I'm here, now."

Bert made a big play of looking at his wristwatch.

"Not due off yet, mate," he said.

"Go," suggested Ted.

He ushered everyone over to one side, so the gate wouldn't be blocked. Then he waited whilst Bert unhurriedly put his coat on and collected his things.

Bobby and I huddled against our Dad. He hugged us tightly, whilst linking arms with Auntie Nell. Bernard kicked a stone idly onto the road ahead. Cousin Rose smiled indulgently at him. Joan checked her watch again.

At last Bert left, walking purposefully through the gates.
Ted gathered us all around him.
"It's true what Bert said," he admitted. "It's against the rules. But in light of me being on the gate on my own and no Welfare Officer being present I am prepared to bend the rules. Just this once."
Dramatically he held up a hand.
He didn't need to for we were all ears and eyes.
"I can't let you all go. Dad can take his children. That's the best I can do."
We all stared at him.
Auntie Nell slid her arm from her brothers and drew herself up to her full height.
"I think we had better go along with that, Harry. Joan will have to go now, anyway. She has to pick up the baby from nursery. The rest of us will go back to my house. We'll wait there for you."
Everyone nodded in agreement.
One by one they kissed us goodbye whilst whispering utterances about being good. Then they walked through the iron gateway and disappeared from sight.
We were alone with our Dad.
Timidly, we began to walk down the long road before us. We all held hands, forming a line across the road. On one side there was an endless vista of browned grass. On the other, there were lots of little trees tangled together surrounded by a thick privet hedge. It looked scary and dark in there. I gave an involuntary shiver. Our feet quickened as a building with a steeply sloping roof came into view. It was almost hidden by trees. I thought of the wicked witch in Hansel and Gretel. Maybe this *was* the witch's house. It *was* all alone and was also surrounded by a thick privet hedge. I was sure I *even* saw a black cat sitting in a window. We passed it quickly and came to another area where a new pair of 'cottages' were being built. (This is always the way they were referred to, although to us wide eyed children of low means they looked more like palaces).
They looked uninhabited and were surrounded by flattened yellow earth with a few wispy strands of grass struggling to put in an appearance. Stark white concrete paths snaked around them. I saw Dad glance at them then shake his head. A fairly new roadway branched off to the right. We could see cottages in the distance.

Dad hesitated, glancing at the piece of paper in his hand.

"I don't think it's this one, luvvies," he said. "It must be the next road further down."

Now we were passing more cottages. I could see little children playing outside.

That cheered me up a little. We passed a tall house with a metal staircase at the front of it. The stairs led to a small wooden door. A large bizarrely shaped tree sat in the middle of a perfectly manicured lawn.

We had reached the other road. Our footsteps dragged. Not so our father's. He had quickened his. I don't think he wanted to prolong the agony any more.

Cottages appeared on our left. They were like fingers, built in twos and spaced apart with luxuriant bushes hugging their walls and dark grey bobbly concrete paths separating them from each other. Oak Cottage was halfway along. Grabbing Bernard by the scruff of the neck, Dad propelled the surprised boy forward up the path to a glass panelled door. Even I thought it was a bit unnecessary! Bernard struggled to get free, bursting into angry tears of frustration with the effort. He kicked out mutinously, landing a blow on Dad's shin.

He suddenly let him go.

"You little sod," he exclaimed. "They'll soon sort you out, you mark my words. You'll get what's coming to you, you see if you don't."

Bernard bristled.

"They won't you fat old pig. I won't go."

Dad cuffed him lightly around the head.

"We'll see about that," he said, nodding his head wisely.

He rapped on the door whilst Bernard stood and sniffed. Bobby and I clung closely together and backed away from the door.

It opened.

A large woman stood on the threshold.

"Hello there, "she said. "Can I help you?"

Dad stuttered.

"Why yes. I've brought, er, Bernard Randall. I, er, understand you're expecting him."

She stared at my father.

"I am Miss Ivan, the housemother of Oak Cottage. And yes I am expecting an arrival. I am a little surprised. The Children's Dept usually bring them."

"Ah," Dad cut in. "I wanted to bring them myself. It was all sorted out at Deptford."

She nodded without a hint of a smile.

"I see. Come along then, Bernard is it?"
She held out her hand.
Dad chipped in.
"See he behaves himself."
She sucked in a deep breath.
"We don't stand any nonsense, here."
Bernard twisted an agitated finger through his hair and shot us a panic-stricken look. Still he stepped forward and meekly took her hand. He disappeared into Oak Cottage. The door closed firmly behind them.
"Come on you two" Dad said, pushing us in front of him down the path, back to the road.
We soon reached another 'cottage'. This one was Laburnum. That was what it said on the nameplate. I spelt it out to myself whilst I stood there waiting for an answer to Dad's knock.

The door opened and a kindly looking lady stood there. The late afternoon sun glinted on her snowy white hair. She glanced down at Bobby and smiled.
"You must be Robert. We've been expecting you."
Dad nodded.
"We usually call him Bobby. He's the baby of the family."
"Esh," lisped Bobby, warming to this friendly woman.
She beamed.
"Well you *have* come to the right place. This *is* the babies cottage."
"Ah," nodded Dad.
She gestured with a brown forearm.
"Come along in. All of you."
We all stepped over the threshold into a dark green passageway which smelt of polish.
She turned to me.
"You must be Bobby's sister."
I nodded shyly.
"Well you happened to come at teatime. I think Bobby should join the others for his tea, don't you?"

We all followed her to another room where small tables were placed. Various babies and young children were sitting and eating. She helped Bobby into a curved chair. He looked around at me worriedly. Then, a plate of sandwiches was put in front of him. He began to tuck in. A sense of panic was rising inside me. Obviously, the invitation didn't include me. Something was amiss. I had assumed that we were going to be together. I tugged Dad's arm. He was intent on watching Bobby tackling a large piece of cake with great gusto. He always *did* love his food. He batted me away absent-mindedly. I bit my lip as tears threatened to bubble to the surface.

The snowy-haired lady motioned to us to leave the room.
Reluctantly Dad tore himself away and made a great play of tiptoeing out of the room. I followed him worriedly. I turned to the lady.
"I want to stay with Bobby," I pouted.
She smiled.
"I am afraid you can't my dear. As I have said this is the babies' cottage. It is for children up to the age of five."
She crouched down earnestly to my height.
"Look," she said. "My name is Miss Mandy. I am the housemother, here at Laburnum. You can come and see Bobby, whenever you want."
She turned to my father.
"Where is she being placed?" she asked.
He pursed his lips.
"Birch Cottage."
Miss Mandy pulled a face.
"Oh," was all she said.
Just then, Bobby had realised we were missing. He ran to join us.
"Blast," muttered Miss Mandy.
Bobby ran to me and clung onto my dress. We both burst into tears.
"Oh dear, dear me," exclaimed Miss Mandy. "This won't do."
An assistant ran out with a toy fire engine and gave it to him, trying to pacify him. He yelled loudly and threw the toy at the wall. A large chunk of plaster dislodged and landed on the floor.
"Go," said Miss Mandy grimly. "Now!"
Dad hustled me out of the door.
Bobby's loud screams followed us all along the road.
I clung to Dad anxiously.

He held tightly to my hand and steered me past the cottages we had seen in the distance earlier. I thought wildly that we were going home. We were walking past them all. My Dad had changed his mind! I was staying with him! Then he stopped on the new bone white path. Was he just having a look at it? I didn't mind, just as long as he held my hand past those horrible dark trees. He *was* looking around it. We walked around the front. I mouthed the words on the nameplate.
Birch Cottage.
Before my father could knock, the door opened. A sharp faced woman stood there. I stared up at her in awe. Her dark hair was in tightly

waved ridges. A high starched collar sat around her lined neck and was fastened by a single pearl button. She pressed thin lips together and glared at us both grimly.

"You're late," she said.

Dad flustered, trying his best to explain. He stammered futilely.

"Er...I 'ad to get the other two settled, first. Bernard, why 'e always gives me trouble. An' as for poor little Bobby... right upset 'e was .... We could 'ear 'im crying all the way up the road."

She pressed her lips together in stern disapproval and waved a veined hand dismissively.

"Never mind about that! Because you are late, your daughter has missed her tea. She should have been here half an hour ago."

"Oh dear oh dear," murmured Dad. "I'm sorry I'm sure. Surely she can be found some food. She can't go without, can she?"

He stepped forward and made as if to enter the house.

She blocked his way.

"I'll take over from here," she said. "Your job is done. Pass her over."

Dad staggered back onto the concrete pathway. He held onto me.

Reproachfully, he stated, "My Joycie is a special case. She needs special care."

The look of disapproval was back. She retorted.

"There are no special cases here. Everyone is treated the same."

Dad shrugged his shoulders unhappily.

I could feel tears again pricking my eyelids. And I felt fear filling my body.

Dad tried again.

"As long as you can assure me that she can see her brothers now and again."

She drew herself up.

"I sincerely hope that your daughter's behaviour will warrant her seeing her brothers."

Dad bristled indignantly.

"My Joycie is a good girl. She needs to see Bobby. Miss Mandy has said she can see him whenever she wants."

Miss Harmon stretched out her hand to grab me. Taken aback, my Dad let go suddenly. She yanked me up the step.

"*I*, Miss Harmon will say when she can see her brother, not Miss Mandy."

She addressed me.

"Say goodbye to your father."

Dad protested.

"At least let me kiss her goodbye."

Miss Harmon held my shoulder in a vice like grip.

"Be quick."

My Dad bent forward and clumsily hugged me. He planted a wet kiss on my lips. I wanted to wipe it off but I didn't. I stood in this woman's grip.

She released me and shoved me inside. The door slammed in my Dad's face.

I was alone with Miss Harmon. I was at her mercy.

Chapter Six: The Shock

Harry trod heavily up the worn stairs and wearily entered the living room. He looked around and saw remnants of his children's presence. There was a sock of Bobby's and three little metal dinky cars lined up at the edge of the rug. Harry felt sharp pricks behind his eyelids. He tutted softly when he saw his daughter's little plastic matchbox doll on the floor. She played with it continually, making little outfits for it out of tiny scraps of cloth. He stepped over it carefully. There were also paper aeroplanes dotted about the room. He knew these belonged to Bernard. Despite the gathering gloom he made no attempt to light the gas mantle on the wall. He sat down and stared into space.

How had it come to this, he wondered?

Everything had occurred since that buff envelope had arrived.

He had read it over and over again in order to make proper sense of it. Now, he stared at it once more.

London County Council
Education Officer's Department

District Organiser of Children's Care.

Telephone Woolwich 0135
2/7/50

Dear Mr Randall
With reference to your visit to this office yesterday I have since been in touch with the Children's Department at 34, Watson Street, Deptford and understand that if you wish accommodation to be found for the children you must go there yourself and make an application.
If you think your wife is going to stay much longer in hospital and you are not able to make really satisfactory arrangements to have the children cared for during the holidays, I should strongly advise you to do this. Please would you let me know sometime next week, what you finally do.

Mr Randall
6,Abbey Terrace   Yours Truly
S. E. 2   Ann Walsh

He had *tried* contacting this Children's Department by phone, time and time again, hurrying around to the telephone box near the Co-op. He knew he should go there, but he wanted to get the lie of the land first, just to see what's what. It was no use. He spoke to someone different every time and they all said he needed to go there in person. That it couldn't be discussed over the phone. And they kept him hanging on. Twice his money had run out.

He had a few days leave from work next week. That's when he would brave it. Yes, time was getting on. Soon be the school holidays.

Harry pushed open the heavy door and stepped inside the cool interior which was painted predominantly green. He walked carefully down the long, quiet passageway until he reached a small glass window set in the wall. A small plaque read 'Inquiries'. Timorously he stood before it, trying to establish some sort of eye contact with a young lady who sat at a small switchboard. She looked very busy, flicking switches up and down and winding a small handle furiously. At last she was free. She had seen him. With a flick she opened the window and demanded haughtily,

"Yes?"

"Er," he stuttered.

His mouth was as dry as a bone. He licked his lips nervously.

"Er, I need to see someone. It's regarding my children. Well it's like."

He broke off in embarrassment.

In a bored tone she said.

"You need to see the duty officer."

She waved to a point behind him.

"Take a seat," she invited.

He stumbled over to the row of wooden chairs he hadn't noticed and sat down.

Doors kept opening and shutting and men and women walked smartly along the corridor, disappearing into other rooms. Sometimes they smiled encouragingly at him. Some of them didn't. *They* just looked down at him as if he was a bad smell. At last a woman stood before him.

"Hallo," she began. "I'm Miss Jones, the duty officer for today. If you would like to come this way...."

She pulled open a door and waited for Harry to follow her. She stepped around a large desk and sat down, gesturing to him to do the same.

"Now," she began cheerfully. "What can I do for you?"

"Why," said Harry, "I was told to come here by the Education Office."

He paused and fished in his pocket for the letter. Opening it carefully, he handed it across the desk. She scanned the letter quickly.

"I see," she said. "I am going to need some more information from you."

"Ah," acknowledged Harry.

She continued.

"I need to know about your children."

Harry swallowed.

"Why I've got Bernard, he's the eldest, Joycie who's six, and the baby, Bobby who has just had his third birthday."

Miss Jones nodded, scribbling quickly on a pad in front of her.

"Now, we need to know what hospital your wife is in and how serious her illness is."

"Well," began Harry dubiously. "It started out she was in the Miller hospital, up the road."

"Yes, yes, I know of the Miller," cut in Miss Jones. "And is she not there, now?"

"Why no, she isn't. As a matter-of-fact, she 'ates 'ospitals. She begged me not to send her, but what could I do?" Harry spread his hands dramatically. "She 'ad this rash all over her."

"Yes, yes," continued Miss Jones impatiently.

"Well it started her off. Always does. Then she was as 'igh as a kite. 'Aving a turn, like. They couldn't put up with it. The doctors and nurses. They 'ad to do *something*."

Miss Jones waited.

Harry went on.

"Why, she's been moved to a mental hospital. She's gone to Fulham this time."

"I see," acknowledged Miss Jones. "Are you saying that your wife has an *ongoing* problem? That this is common! Has she been in a mental hospital before?"

Harry pursed his lips.

"I'm not sure. It would have been before we got married, understand."

"Oh dear! Are your children at risk?"

"Why yes," admitted Harry. "She doesn't do anything for 'em. I do it all. It's a bit much. I've got to go to work."

"But is she likely to harm them?" she asked.

"It's highly possible. Who knows what she'll do! I never know what she is gonna do next," finished Harry.

Miss Jones enquired.

"Do you know if she's been certified?"

Harry shook his head from side to side.

"No, she hasn't. She's under observation."

"That will be a problem," she told him. "She will have to be if we are going to find your children accommodation. I'm sorry there is nothing we can do unless she is."

A disappointed Harry stood up.

"So that's it, is it?"

"I am afraid so," said Miss Jones. "I advise you to go and have a word with the doctors at the hospital, and possibly your G.P."

Dr. Holt stared at Harry over his glasses.

"What we have to consider is what would be the best course of action."

Harry nodded.

Dr. Holt continued.

"Might be best if we can get her nearer. I can have a word with Dr. Cameron."

"Nearer?" queried Harry.

"Yes," the doctor said. "We'll see if we can get her transferred to Bexley. Then we can get the ball rolling. Be better for you anyway."

Harry smiled gratefully.

Many weeks later, he sat in Dr. Cameron's office. The white-haired doctor sat opposite him shuffling papers around on the desk.

"I need your signature here, here and here. That will certify your wife, Lydia Randall as insane."

Harry ducked his head sideways.

"Is it that simple?" he asked.

"Not quite," smiled Dr. Cameron. "It has been counter-signed by two other doctors and a welfare officer."

He had parked the children at Elsie's yet again. He knew the older two were suspicious. They wanted to know *why* he kept going off. He lifted up the fountain pen with a sigh. Again he was signing papers.

It was true it was his original intention to only let them go for the school holidays. Things had snowballed out of his control. Now September was dawning. September 1950.

And here he was signing the necessary papers which would take his children away from him. That it had come to this. He had begged the woman to let him take them himself. That was all he could do to ease their pain.

Below is a section of the Children's Act in existence at that time.

An Act to make further provision for the care or welfare, up to the age of eighteen and, in certain cases, for further periods of boys and girls when they are without parents or have been lost or abandoned by, or are living away from, their parents, or when their parents are unfit or unable to take care of them and in certain other circumstances; to amend the Children and young Persons Act 1933, the Children and Young Persons (Scotland) Act 1937, the Guardianship of Infants Act, 1925 and certain other enactments relating to children; and for purposes connected with the matters aforesaid.

(30TH June 1948)

1 (1) Where it appears to a local authority with respect to a child in their area appearing to be under the age of seventeen.

(a) that he has neither parent or guardian or has been and remains abandoned by his parents or guardian or is lost ; or

(b) that his parents or guardian are, for the time being or permanently, prevented by reason of mental or bodily disease or infirmity or other incapacity or any other circumstance from providing for his proper accommodation, maintenance and upbringing; in either case, that the intervention of the local authority under this section is necessary in the interests of the welfare of the child.

I opened my eyes sleepily and a little crossly. A hand clamped tightly around my upper arm and yanked me cleanly out of bed. I hit the wooden floor with a thud.

"Get up," she hissed at me in a low whisper.

Hurriedly, I blinked sleep from my eyes and stumbled to my feet. She pushed me viciously in the direction of the door. I shuffled along the passage towards the bathroom, very aware that my nightdress was wet. Bony hands yanked it over my head and threw it to the floor. She grabbed my hair in a bunch. I winced as pain filled my scalp. I felt a sickening crunch as she cracked my head on the clean white tiles. I cowered in fear as she raised a hair brush high in the air and rained blows upon my naked body. She lifted her shoe and kicked me toward the cubicle. I scurried across the floor like a crab.

"Get on there" she hissed. "That's the proper place. And don't you move until I say so."

I sat there for ages and ages but she didn't come back. Eventually I crept back to my dormitory. My mattress was on the floor beside the bed, without any sheets on it. All that was on it was a red rubber mattress protector. Somehow I had to struggle to put it back on the bed. I didn't succeed. I didn't even know where I could get another nightdress from. I lay naked on the mattress on the floor and slept fitfully. I awoke with a start in the morning when she was standing over me with a bamboo cane. The three other little girls in the room sniggered. She rained blows down on my body and whirled around to catch the culprits. One by one they held out their hands, sobs catching in their throats as she belted blows upon them. There was no more sniggering.

When I had washed and dressed another surprise awaited me. I was told to report to the locker room instead of the dining room. Hurrying down the polished passage to the locker room, I saw Miss Harmon standing on a long strip of coconut matting, in front of tall lockers, where we kept our coats and shoes. She still had the cane in her hands.

I flinched nervously.

She grinned evilly and pointed the cane to a pile of sheets lying on the tiled floor.

"These have got to be washed, miss. Your father says you are a special case. Well, I am going to give you special treatment. Every time you are wet you will have to wash the sheets, before breakfast."

With that she turned on her heel and strode out of the door.

Tears bubbled up behind my lids.

I picked up the sheets and struggled over to a row of hand wash basins which were sandwiched between a toilet and a cupboard.

My mouth was dry and parched. I was looking forward to a mug of milk that I would get at breakfast.

At last, with the help of the grim-faced daily worker who let me know that she would get into trouble if Miss Harmon knew she had helped me, I was done. The sheets were folded up and pressed down in a large laundry basket. I ran down the corridor to the dining room, dying for my breakfast. I noticed with horror, everyone was leaving the tables. I went to my place.

Miss Harmon sat at one table, eating a slice of toast. She laid it down carefully on her plate and addressed me.

"And just what do you think you are doing?"

I mumbled.

"My...b. b.. breakfast."

She sneered.

"You are too late. Breakfast is over. Go to school."

I slunk out, my belly rumbling and my throat contracting.

Lydia sat in the armchair next to the bed and muttered to herself. She was dressed in just a robe which was open down the back. This is what she had been told to put on. She hadn't had any breakfast and she had to take even more pills than usual. They gave them to her, standing over her until she had swallowed them. Oh she hated this place. It really frightened her. She would think about the children and try not to think of *him*. She felt the anger rising inside of her in spite of everything. *He* had done this to her. Calling the doctor like that when all she had was a rash. She had tried hard to get back there...to go home...make things the same as they were. It was impossible. Her anger was vented by loud rage. She knew it was wrong to keep going on and on and on. She just couldn't help it. It rose up inside her and spilled out in a torrent which became worse whenever *he* was near her. He brought her things. Clean clothes one day. A bunch of grapes the next. He didn't bring her what she needed the most. Her children. She was desperate to see them. They all said they couldn't come. That was a big disappointment to her. It was hard for her to cry. Years of putting up with many indignities had taught her not to. She felt a hard knot in her chest whenever she thought of them. Sadness washed over her. Suddenly she didn't care what they did to her.

A plump nurse helped her to her feet.

"Put your slippers on," she said cheerily.

"Why?" asked Lydia dully, trying to shake off the fuzz inside her head. "Wh...ere am I go...ing?"

"You'll see," said the nurse, holding her firmly by the elbow.

She grabbed futilely at the gown as she fought to preserve her dignity.

The nurse smiled

"Never mind about that."

She pushed her into a room.

Lydia looked wildly around.

White-coated Dr. Cameron and his assistant, a junior doctor stood by a long couch. The nurse encouraged Lydia forward. Her feet were rooted to the spot. She had a bad feeling about this. The nurse shoved her until she was next to the couch. The junior doctor grabbed her feet whilst the nurse grabbed her arms. They swung her onto the couch, despite her weak protests. They manoeuvred her into a satisfactory position. Swiftly, they grabbed large canvas straps and buckled them around her ankles, her waist and her chest. Her arms were pinned to her side.

Dr. Cameron bent over her.

"Now, don't worry," he soothed as he smoothed paste on her temples.

"What.... are.... you doing?" she squeezed out. "What's... that... stuff?"

"You just relax," he smiled, clamping pads on each temple from which two large wires ran to a machine next to the couch. He turned to his colleagues and nodded in satisfaction.

"She's ready."

The nurse shoved a hard block into her mouth.

"Bite on it," she ordered.

In panic, Lydia tried to throw herself back and forth. The straps held her fast. Dr Cameron fiddled with the buttons on the machine. Lydia felt a huge spasm fill her body and jerk it about violently. Her last thought of her children choked in her mouth as Dr. Cameron flipped the switch again and again. Each time her body thrashed about violently. Strangely enough she could hear voices.............coming and going. In and out of her mind. She tried to talk. To tell them she didn't want this.......................... She couldn't, she gave in. Once more he flicked the switch. This time, mercifully everything went black.

The trainee doctor was visibly shocked.

"Is that usual when Electric Convulsion Treatment is applied?" he asked.

Dr. Cameron stared at Lydia then turned to his colleagues.

"It's interesting," he said. "You can never tell, they are all different."

Chapter Seven: The Letters

Harry shivered slightly in the cold, dank February air as he stepped off the trolleybus. He dreaded these visits. She always got upset. Went on and on about the children, especially Joycie. And she went on and on about coming home, too.

Harry walked past the grim buildings that rose out of the gloom. Occasionally he heard an unearthly cry or saw a face at one of the windows. It didn't bother him. He knew they were locked up. Harry yanked open a door and stepped into a long corridor, which smelt of stale cabbage. He came to a set of stairs. He glanced at the figures G4 painted on the wall, coupled with a faded arrow pointing upwards. Harry gripped the metal rail and climbed the cheerless stairs to the corridor above. He stepped forward to the barred door and rang the bell. A blue uniformed nurse let him in.

"She's in the sitting room, waiting for you," she said. "She's been worrying herself sick that you weren't coming."

Harry shook his head and weaved his way through dining room tables and chairs to the sitting room beyond. She sat in a winged chair and stared out of the window. Her head snapped around when she heard him approach.

"Oh there you are. I thought you weren't coming," she reproached.

"I always do, don't I?"

"How's Joycie?" she asked, then added, "an' Bernard and Bobby of course."

Guardedly, Harry answered.

"Joycie's alright, so are the boys."

Artfully, he changed the subject and held out the bag.

"I've brought you some clean clothes. Look. Here's your flowered dress. You like that one don't you?"

She shot him a look.

"I don't want you bringing me clothes. I want to come home. I'm alright now. The doctor's coming, later........................"

Her bright blue eyes held a look of pleading.

"Ask him," she begged. "Ask him if I can come home at the weekend." Harry waved his hands at her agitatedly.

"Shush, now missus," he implored her. "Be quiet or everyone will hear."

"I don't care," she answered obstinately. "I don't care who knows it. I've told them all that I want to come home. I'll be alright. I'll take my pills. I miss the children. I've been here long enough........................"

Dr. Cameron fiddled with a paper weight and turned disappointed eyes on Harry.

"Well, Mr. Randall. If there is nothing I can do or say to dissuade you then you leave me no choice. I'll have to discharge her into your care, if that is what you want."

He opened a file on the desk in front of him and said regretfully.

"It's a pity because I really think the Electrical Convulsion Treatment *was* working."

"It *is* what I want," insisted Harry. "We'll never get offered a house with her stuck in here and my children gone. My brother and his children got a place. They've been gone some time. Downstairs is empty."

Dr. Cameron sighed and shook his head.

"I'll sign the papers," he agreed, but added as a last afterthought. "I just hope you don't regret it."

Dressed in my school clothes, I hung around outside the cottage and waited. I knew I had to go to school but I wasn't making any effort. I usually went with Victoria who shared my dormitory. She was six, nearly seven too. And she was in my class. I wanted her to wait as well. But she wouldn't. She was frightened of being late. I was sorry for her. I knew it was hard. She hated fish and just couldn't eat it. The very sight of it made her retch. We had it for tea, two days ago. And of course she hadn't been able to force it down. Every mealtime it was brought out for her to eat. Nothing else, just the fish. Just taking a mouthful made her physically sick and of course she never made it to the toilet! Out would come the hated bamboo cane or the hairbrush.

Sure enough a tousled haired boy appeared from the next cottage. Bernard! I wanted my brother. I rushed up to him. He grinned in delight.

"Ello Joycie, what you doing waiting 'ere?"

"Waiting for you."

"Oh! oh! What's *she* done now?" demanded Bernard.

I slipped my hand in his and looked up at him.

"I'm thirsty."

"Haven't you had your breakfast?"

Sorrowfully, I shook my head from side to side.

"I am not allowed anything to drink at mealtimes any more."

"What?" shouted Bernard. "She can't do that."

He started to make for the front door of Birch Cottage.

"I'll give 'er what for."

I dragged him away.

"No don't. Please don't. You'll get into trouble with Miss Ivan."

"Pooh! I don't care," he declared.

He squeezed my hand.

"Don't you worry. We'll get you a drink. There's a water fountain in the junior playground. And I'll bring you round some extra milk at playtime."

Lydia climbed the old familiar stairs after Harry. She felt excitement rise inside her. She had waited so long. .Oh she knew they would be at school, yet. Still, she could go to meet them. She entered the living room. It was strangely bare. There were no signs of children there. No little toys. No items of clothing hanging on the fireguard. Fear clutched at her heart and rose to her throat.

She said out aloud.

"I think..I think.. I'll walk up to the school later. After we've been to pick up Bobby from the nursery, that is."

Panic filled Harry's face. He bit his lip worriedly.

"I think we need a cup of tea," he said. "Sit yourself down by the fire and make yourself comfy. I'll put the kettle on."

Lydia watched the hands on the clock on the mantelpiece. They didn't seem to be moving.

"Come on, man," she said. "Can't we go to the school, now?"

Harry sat in his usual place at the table. He cleared his throat in readiness.

"It's no use, missus," he said. "They're not at school or nursery. They've gone I'm afraid."

Lydia stared at him incredulously.

"Gone?" she squawked.

Harry swallowed awkwardly.

"I just couldn't do it missus."

She looked at him in abject horror. Her hand flew to her mouth.

"Couldn't do what?" she croaked.

"I couldn't go to work and look after them. It was hard. Then there were the school holidays............," he finished lamely.

A heavy silence hung between them as Lydia took this in.

It was true. All this time she had waited. And it was all for nothing.

She made as if she was going to get up from the chair but flopped back down again helplessly. Her head buzzed and sang. She heard her own ragged voice asking from far away.

"Where are they? Where are my children?"

Harry covered his face with his hands.

"I 'ad no choice in the matter. Things got taken out of my 'ands."

She forced herself to concentrate on his muttered words.

He spoke guiltily, through his fingers.

"They're in a children's home, that's where they are."
She sucked in a long painful breath.
"Oh my gawd. You've 'ad them put away. Not just me. You've done it to them, too."
Her eyes filled with hopeless tears.
"I'm sorry," Harry said. "I was wrong. I know that now."
She lifted her tearstained face.
"What are we gonna do?" she asked pitifully.
He gulped.
"I am going to *try* and undo what's been done," he assured her.
She stared hard at him.
"Well you better 'ad then, 'adn't you. Cos I want them back."

I was happy at school that day. We had learned to write letters. And the teacher, Miss Swann had taken us outside the gates to post them. Below is a sample of a typical letter I wrote to my parents.

Joyce Randall
Birch Cottage
Shirley Residential School

18th June 1951

Dear Mum and Dad,
Thank you for my birthday card. I don't like Birch Cottage. I want to come home.

Yours Faithfully
Joyce

I walked home from school on a cloud. I had had a good day. I had seen Bobby. He was in the nursery playground. I was even allowed to go in and play with him for a while. Birch Cottage drew into view. Victoria and I clutched each others hands tightly. We were only allowed in the back door, which opened straight into the locker room. We went in reluctantly. Eight other little girls followed us in dribs and drabs. Miss Harmon stood in the doorway, hairbrush in her hand.
"No talking," she demanded. "Put your coats away in your lockers."
She stood and watched us and then pointed to the long, thin coconut matting.
Her voice grated on.

"I want to see you all sitting, cross legged on the mat. There you must stay until teatime or else."

To demonstrate her point, she waved the hairbrush in the air. It caught on her almost invisible hairnet which held the rigid waves of her hairstyle in place. Someone sniggered, whilst she untangled it.

"Who was that?" she demanded.

No-one owned up.

"Right," she demanded. "I can see I'll have to make an example of one of you."

She dragged me to my feet.

"Get to bed," she hissed.

"Yes, miss," I whispered tearfully, knowing it wasn't me.

She shoved me towards the stairs and turned to the nine other little girls.

"I don't want to hear a word out of you or see *any* of you move off of that mat until you are told."

With that she turned on her heel and left the room.

Lydia sat at the table, twisting the pen in her fingers.

"Do you think I should write a letter to Joycie? It might cheer her up a bit."

Harry sat opposite her, sighing gently.

"I don't care what you do Missus," he said. "Yes, write to Joycie. And you can write the other letter if you want. You're much better at the letter writing than me. Do it if you want to."

She flipped the writing pad open, picked up the fountain pen. She wrote.

> Mrs L Randall
> 6 Abbey Terrace
> Abbey Wood
> S.E.2
> 11ᵗʰ October.

Dear Joyce

I hope this letter finds you well and happy. It was nice to get letters from you every week. I am going to try to reply to every one. You will soon be coming home. I am going to write a letter asking for you to come back where you belong. Hoping to see you soon. Give my love to Bernard and Bobby.

> Your loving mother.
> Lydia

Satisfied, she tore it out, folded it in half and put it in an envelope. Then she took a deep breath and picked up the pen again.

Mrs L Randall
6 Abbey Terrace
Abbey Wood
S.E.2

11th October

Dear Madam

I am writing to know if it will be possible for me to have children home for good on Friday 19 October. Hoping to meet with your approval.

I am Yours Sincerely
Mr. H. J. Randall

Miss Harmon sat at her desk in her study, examined the post she had just opened. She picked up Lydia's letter disdainfully. With great satisfaction she tore it into tiny pieces, which she threw in a waste paper basket at her side.

Miss Champion read quickly in disbelief. She turned to her colleague, Miss Lewis.

"Just look at this," she said, waving the letter in the air.

Miss Lewis took the letter from her and scanned its brief contents.

"Well it's obvious who wrote it, isn't it."

"Yes," Miss Champion spat out. "Well we'll see about that. We'll put this on the agenda for the next meeting. In the meantime we will do nothing."

Miss Champion shivered in the cold November air in the corridor. The heating was broken, again. Normally, in her position she could have cried off coming in but there was a meeting today which was extremely important.

"And now," began Miss Champion. "Can we examine this situation we have with the Randall family?"

"Yes," agreed a grey-haired man, with a pile of books on the table in front of him. He shook his head.

"I am afraid our situation isn't good. We really don't have any basis for keeping these children in care, unless we can prove Mrs Randall is a danger."

"There must be something we can do. What about The Children's Act?"

"We have to prove that her disability is permanent. And as you know Mr. Randall discharged his wife."

"Oh dear," mouthed Miss Champion. "Well, I shall see what I can do first. I'll get in touch with the Medical Superintendent at Bexley Hospital. In the meantime, I think we can all fob Mr Randall off, if we try hard enough."

She gathered up her papers and left the room, stopping at the first door and entering the typing pool.

"Ah, Jean," she smiled. "Will you take a letter? It is urgent. I need it done today."

"Yes, Miss Champion," murmured the typist demurely. "Right away."

She fed a clean sheet of paper into her typewriter and began.

C06/GMA

34 Watson Street
Deptford
S.E.8

The Medical Superintendent
Bexley Mental Hospital
Bexley, Kent.   Tideway 4275
13th November, 51
Dear Sir,

Mrs Lydia Randall

I understand that the above named woman was a certified patient in your hospital and was removed from the hospital by Mr. Randall, against advice, on 17.02.51. Mrs Randall does however continue to have treatment and is visited by Mrs Branch, the Psychiatric Social Worker. There are three children of this couple in the care of the Council, and in view of the mother's mental condition consideration is being given to the Council assuming parental rights under Section 2 (1)(b) of the Children's Act 1948. It is necessary, however, to satisfy this section of the Act insofar "that a parent or guardian suffers from some permanent disability rendering the said person incapable of caring for the child...........

I should, therefore, be obliged if you would inform me whether, in your opinion, Mrs. Randall's disability can be regarded as permanent within the meaning of this sub-section of the Act. I think it would also be helpful if

you would give your permission for Mrs. Branch who
visited the home quite recently, to let me have a report
at the same time.

Yours Faithfully

D. F C

Area Children's Officer 6
5th December

The phone trilled out loudly. Miss Champion leaned forward and picked it up.

"Hallo," she said.

A voice at the other end replied.

"It's Dr. Neville here. Your letter has been passed on to me. I apologise for not getting in touch sooner. I have been run off my feet. I am afraid the Medical Superintendent Dr. Cameron, who was really in charge of this case died suddenly last month. What I can tell you is I am unable to make out a report as in my opinion, as a manic depressive, Mrs. Randall can really only be admitted on a voluntary basis. She is not likely to physically harm anyone."

"Oh, I see," said Miss Champion, through stiff lips.

Chapter Eight: The Surprise

It was Saturday. I hated them, because there was no school and we were all at the mercy of Miss Harmon. We didn't have long to wonder what new cruelty she could think up. Today was Saturday and we were stuck here

I didn't pay much attention when she threw us all outside, as soon as breakfast was over, even though it was a cold February day. She didn't give us time to put coats on and it was freezing. The scrubby ground surrounding the cottage was where we played. It hadn't been seeded and large clumps of long grass grew intermingled with spiny thistles and dandelions. Today they were rimed with frost and the ground was hard. Despite a weak watery sun there were still icy patches on the concrete path. We huddled together by the wall of the house. She banged on the window and indicated to us to go away. I was cold, but I was also worried. I had been invited by Miss Mandy to go to tea with Bobby. And there was another thing on my mind. Sunday was a visiting day. And as usual Mum and Dad were coming. At least Miss Harmon told me that much, although she had turned it into a threat at the same time. She said she would stop me from seeing them if I wet the bed tonight. She used this threat whenever we were going home for the weekend, too. Although I knew I shouldn't, I worried myself until I was physically sick. I didn't want to get in her bad books or else all would be lost. It was a favourite sport of hers to stop me from seeing Bobby. And I didn't want to disappoint my Mum. Her face was a picture that was hard to forget.

Then, to all our horrors, she called us in. We never knew what this meant. It didn't feel like lunch-time. We all wondered what we had done. To our amazement we were to be allowed in the playroom. Apparently Mr. Instrell, the Superintendent was paying an impromptu visit to each cottage, sometime during the day. We tiptoed into the hallowed playroom, which most of us had never seen the inside of. We listened with dizzy heads and rapidly thawing fingers which gave us pain. There was to be no messy games played. All we could do was to sit on a chair and read a book. No one was to go to the white painted lockers, which were in a stack. I remembered I had a doll and a teddy when I came here. Was that where they were?

I glanced at the closing door and wondered if I dared take a peek. There was nothing to tell which one belonged to which girl. I sat on my chair pondering this thought when the door opened. Miss Harmon entered with a man.

She snapped.

"Say good afternoon to Mr. Ilford."

We spoke in unison in a loud whisper.

"Good afternoon, Mr Ilford."

Miss Harmon snapped again.

"Get up all of you. Where are your manners?"

Guiltily we scrambled off the chairs. She poked the nearest girl with a bony finger.

"This is Susan, her mother is in hospital. Her stay is temporary."

She did the rounds of each girl until she got to me.

A sickly smile coated her thin lips.

"This is Joyce. Her mother is mentally ill. That's why she's here. She's long term. There will be no chance of her ever going home."

With that they swept out, leaving me in tears.

Hastily, I escaped from Miss Harmon's clutches. I almost ran to Laburnum cottage. It was a bright, sunny day and Bobby's birthday. His was just several weeks before mine. My excitement grew for Miss Mandy and her helpers were lovely. They were nothing like Miss Harmon.

Bobby was sure to have a birthday cake, unlike me.

It was even better than that. We were having tea outside! There were little tables and chairs arranged on the grass. Bang in the middle was an iced sponge cake decorated with hundreds and thousands and five candles. And I could see Bernard, too! I rushed over to them both after saying a quick hallo to a beaming Mrs Moody.

Bernard twisted his hair excitedly.

"Guess what, Joycie?" he burst out. "I'm moving in here, with Bobby."

My excitement bubble burst.

"What about me?" I sulked. "It's not fair."

Miss Mandy appeared as if by magic. She put an arm casually around my shoulder and hugged me to her quickly, before releasing me.

"If it was possible we would have you, too," she said regretfully. "These cottages are not mixed. This one used to be just for children under five. That's changed, as well. From now on, we are going to take all boys up to fifteen, especially brothers. If it changes again I'll let you know."

I smiled sheepishly, ashamed of my outburst. Comfortingly she patted me on my head.

"You go off and play, now. Make the most of the time you have got."

I took Bobby's hand possessively. This cottage had nice lush grass all around it and it seemed to stretch for miles. We wandered over it until we reached a tall hedge. Bobby pointed a sandal at a brown object on the grass.

"What's that?" he asked.

I frowned.

"I'm not sure?"

Bobby said sensibly.

"I know, let's ask Miss Mandy."

"Yes, yes," I replied. "We'll pull it up and take it to her."

So, we tugged at it very gingerly and carried it back to where Mrs Moody sat.

She examined our find.

"Well, well. It is a mushroom. I think we should cook it for tea, then we can all have a taste of it."

So, a group of happy children sat at the low table and sampled the first sliver of mushroom they had ever eaten in their lives. They also had a slice of birthday cake each, which to most was a new experience.

All too soon it was time to return to Birch Cottage and Miss Harmon.

Bernard and I helped Dad carry cups and saucers and paper cups full of weak orange over to a wobbly trestle table, where Mum stood waiting for us, with Bobby. There were green canvas chairs to sit on. Dad set the cups down carefully and indicated to Mum to be seated. Bobby sat next to her. She cast me longing glances so I chose the chair on the end nearest her. She beamed with satisfaction.

Dad said, "We were hoping to take you out today. So we could have a look at Shirley Hills, maybe." He sighed. "They wouldn't allow it on a Saturday visit. Instead of which we have got to sit 'ere in this hall and while away an hour or so. Still, we've got some things for you. Get that bag up Bernard, will you."

My brother did as he was told and lifted a canvas bag onto the table.

Dad had his hand on his tobacco tin.

"You do the honours, missus," he said. "Get the stuff out for 'em. Give it to 'em."

"Alright," Mum agreed amicably, handing out comics and sweets to each of us.

She was very quiet and glanced from one to the other of us as if she couldn't get enough of us in the allotted time.

We were more interested in our treasures.

There were also cheap little toys. I squealed with delight to see a tiny baby doll complete with cotton shawl. Bernard had a ball game and Bobby had some puzzles.

"Well now," Dad said in satisfaction at seeing our pleasure. "That's all right, then."

His face then took on a more sober look.

"I have got something to tell you all."

We looked at him in alarm. He glanced around him to the other trestle tables in the large, cavernous room. There was no-one within earshot.

"For a start off," he began, "we've got new neighbours downstairs."

We looked up with interest. Those empty rooms had been useful to play in when we were there.

"Yes, they've got a baby, too."

Dad sighed.

"Trouble is they've bought the house. Me and your Mum are what they call sitting tenants, now. And they've taken our front bedroom. Things'll be a bit tight. We'll just have to manage at the weekends. You must keep quiet about it though. Wouldn't do for anyone to get wind of it. They might stop you from coming home altogether. We just hope that we'll get a house, soon."

He paused for a few seconds until this information was absorbed.

Then he continued, lowering his voice.

"Course, I 'ave got something else to say. I've got a surprise!"

We all looked interested. We loved surprises.

He wagged a finger.

"Not so fast," he admonished us. "Be patient. When do you break up from school?"

We all burst out, "July 18th, of course."

Dad removed a small book from his inside pocket. He opened it and stared at its pages.

"Now, let me see. Yes. That's two weeks time. Good. I'll ask for you to come home for a few days. I'll get some leave. To tell you the truth, I've bought something. It's for all of us. You'll see………………."

True to his word Dad *did* arrange for us to go out, but it turned into just a day, not the three or four days he promised. Of course we had no idea of what was involved every time he wanted to have us out or wanted us to go home. He would usually phone first hoping that it would do. The conversation always finished with him having to confirm it by letter. This would be written by Mum, supposedly in Dad's name. Sometimes the letters would get muddled.

6, Abbey Terrace
Abbey Wood
S.E.2
14. 07.1952

Dear Madam

Will you please forward pass for Sunday July 20th From 10am till 6pm

.

I am yours Faithfully
Mr. H. Randall

Remarkably this time he had a fast reply.

```
CH/ACO/6/V3
34, Watson Street
Deptford
SE8

16th July,    52

Mr H Randall
6, Abbey Terrace
Abbey Wood
SE2                         Tideway 4275

Dear Sir

With reference to your letter of the 14th July, I wish to
inform you that permission has been granted for you to
have your children out for the day from 10am to 6pm on
Sunday the 20th July, 1952.

Yours Faithfully

Area Children's Officer
```

We all noticed that he was alone. And that he wore a haversack and carried a bulging bag.

We probably all wondered without putting it into actual words, why Mum wasn't there. Was it because of her 'sickness', which we could never talk about? Or was it some other reason? Dad didn't explain.

He did say, "Chop, chop. Come on, lets be 'aving you," as he hurried us up the drive to catch the trolley bus.

We soon changed buses for another one and another one until we were climbing on a green one. These were always known as country buses. So were we going to the country? We still didn't know where we were heading. We appreciated the doorstep sandwiches Dad had made though, and the bottle of warm orange juice which he produced from his bag. We had arrived at Gravesend bus depot. Dad withdrew a watch from his breast pocket and checked the time. He nodded happily.

"We'll just be in time for the Meopham bus," he said. "Come along. Let's get there. We can't afford to miss the bus. They only run once an hour."

Dutifully, we trotted behind him. Across the road from the bus depot, past the railway station, across the road and we made it before the bus arrived. It trundled into view, a cream and green affair. It was different to the London buses and even the Greenline bus which had started its journey in London. The bus conductor playfully tweaked Bobby's nose and gave him a few spare tickets. The bus whirled along, soon leaving the town of Gravesend behind and heading out into the country.

All Dad would do is wink and say.

"You'll see."

Bernard and I smirked at each other. Bobby sat on Dad's lap and played with his tickets.

The conductor called out.

"Culverstone."

"Aha," beamed Dad. "Here we are."

Mystified we hopped off the bus. All we could see was a few houses and a field opposite.

"This way," commanded Dad. "Follow me."

He led us to a side road which said Whitepost Lane. We noticed that there was a small school and a row of bungalows on either side of the road. One of these was actually a shop. A faded sign said Carters Post Office and General Store. We trooped after Dad up the flagstone path into the cool interior of the shop. Our eyes were wide as we saw all the goods on display covering every surface, piled high to the ceiling.

At the back of the shop was a metal grille. This was the post office. A rosy cheeked lady appeared from behind it.

"Can I help you?" she inquired of Dad.

He wore a jovial look on his face.

"Why, that you can," he said.

He made a few purchases which included some sweets and pies for our dinner.

After they had been packed away, he inquired about paraffin.

"No, no," she said. "You need to go to Cooksie's just around the corner. He's got the hardware store. He does paraffin and he'll get you anything you want."

"Ah," said Dad.

He led the way out of the shop and backtracked down the road and around the corner. Sure enough there was another shop. This too was like an Aladdin's cave. There were all manner of things hanging from the ceiling and from a long brown counter. Beyond the interior of the shop a yard containing all sorts of wood stacked high could be seen through an archway. Dad dug his wallet out again. This time he bought a metal can. The man behind the counter took it and ambled through the archway. Fascinated we all followed him and watched him squirting a pink liquid directly into it.

"Right, young fellow me lad," Dad said to Bernard. "Do you think you can manage one bag?"

Soon all the baggage had been redistributed amongst us, with Dad still wearing the haversack and carrying the paraffin can. He hustled us all back down the road, past Carter's store, until we came to the end of the bungalows. A gap appeared in the thick hedge. To our amazement he wanted us to walk through here onto a muddy path. We followed him a little uncertainly. On either side there was nothing but trees. The sky darkened.

"We 'ad better get a move on," he warned. "I don't like the look of those clouds."

Soon we came to another much wider path, liberally covered with cinders. He told us that this was Rhododendron Avenue. The land on either side of the path was divided into sections. There were low buildings in each section with wooden paling fences. Dad stopped in front of a narrow path running up a high hillside. To our amazement he wanted us to go up there. We just followed him until we reached the top, where it flattened out.

"Aha," he said. "Here we are."

All we could see was undergrowth and trees. He smiled and beckoned for us to follow him through a narrow pathway in the tangled brambles. With trepidation we did. He led us to a clearing where there was a tent strung between the trees. Just then it began to rain. He hustled us all inside it.

"Never mind," he said, swinging the haversack off his back. "I wanted to talk to you all anyway."

We looked at him expectantly. He didn't answer straight away as he was concentrating on what he was doing. Diving into the bag, he withdrew a primus stove, a bottle of water, a tiny kettle and a small tin of sugar. He filled up the primus stove with paraffin and lit it.

"I am afraid you'll 'ave to rough it. We'll 'ave a bite to eat in a mo'. Then when this rain stops I want you all to do something for me."

He had our full attention.

"I want you to look for markers with me. We've got to find them so I know where to put a fence. I've bought this piece of land. I am going to build a chalet on it. And it will be ours. Then let anyone try to take it away from us."

Chapter Nine: The Move and the Meeting

Mr. Arkwright beckoned to me with a crooked finger. I hurried over to him, climbed eagerly on the little chair and whispered the answer in his ear. He patted me on the head.

"You're a clever little girl," he told me.

I sailed home from school on a cloud. My new teacher thought I was clever. He had given me a new self esteem I didn't have.

Miss Harmon constantly knocked me down. She had taken the doll with the cotton shawl. I never saw it again.

> 6 Abbey Terrace
> Abbey Wood
> S.E.2

> 26/7/52

OH/AC06/WJC

Dear Madam

In reply to your letter received Sat 25 July for permission for Summer leave for my children.

My brother has a piece of ground in Meopham and has made arrangements for me to use it, the ground is private and its attached to a farm of which address I forward on immediately. I would like to have the children from Fri 1st Aug not later than 7.30 hoping this arrangement won't inconvenience you

> Yours Faithfully
> Mr. H. J. Randall

PS. I will give you a ring not later than Tuesday 29th.

Children's office notes: Man phoned. They will be living in a bungalow.

I have no idea who penned this letter. It is not Mum's handwriting. It certainly wasn't Dad's. It's possible it may have been a work colleague.

We spent a lovely fortnight there. On this occasion, Dad successfully managed to dupe the Children's Office. We stayed at Uncle Jack's place. He had a big chalet he had built with his own hands. It was at the end of Whitepost Lane, along Beechwood Drive and then down Ridge Lane, which was an unmade road like Rhododendron Avenue. We had a great time, despite the conditions. There was only a chemical toilet and no running water. There was a standpipe in the lane. But, in order to use it you had to have a key, which had to be paid for. Luckily, Uncle Jack had one. He was my Dad's older brother and as mean as they come. I have no doubt that my father paid a heavy price for being allowed to use the land. His brother's so called 'farm'.

It *did* give him the opportunity he sought. He needed time to erect his own chalet. He had his children, he had two whole weeks and he had help from Uncle Jack, who had since bought another plot of land in Whitepost Lane and was in the process of having a brick bungalow built on it. Mum enjoyed our company, too. She was distraught when we had to return.

Every time she went to Woolwich she paid a visit to the Housing Office, supported by her loyal mother. Always she met with excuses. These usually took the form of being too far down the housing list, which meant they didn't have enough points. She even tried to use us as leverage, pointing out to them that she needed a house in order to have her children home. By October she was deeply depressed and desperate.

She put pen to paper, with Dad's approval.

> *6 Abbey Terrace*
> *Abbey Wood*
> *S.E.2*

> *9.10. 1952*

Dear Madam
*   I am writing to know if it will be possible for me to have my children's discharge to come home for good as I keep having letters from Joyce to say could she come home for good as she is fretting to come home also Bernard and Bobby as they have been away from me 2 years. Will you kindly see into the matter for me.*

> *Yours Truly*
> *Mr. Mrs Randall.*

Her letter was ignored.

June 1953

It was Coronation Week. We were having a party at school. It was said that everyone would get a present. Victoria was waiting for me. I was trying to hurry up. Nothing had changed for me. I still had sheets to wash, and I still hadn't had any breakfast. I couldn't get to the sinks, as the daily help Mrs. Aaron had lots of stuff soaking in them. She was as sour-faced as Miss Harmon. I did try to ask her in a loud whisper if I could use the sinks. Her lips had twisted in a grim smile as she retorted.

"You can see I'm using 'em can't you. No, you'll have to wait until I'm finished."

Victoria's face lit up.

"I know," she suggested. "Let's put them in your locker. You can wash them when we come home tonight."

So, she helped me to stuff them into the tall locker, once I'd removed my shoes. Victoria was really hurrying me up today. I still had to put my shoes on. We had to wear proper lace-up shoes for school. I shoved my feet into them and hurried out of the door after Vivian. I tried stopping and stooping to do them up, but it didn't do any good for she grabbed my hand.

She panted, "Because of you we're going to be late. The least you can do is hurry up."

I wailed, "My shoes aren't done up. The laces are undone."

As I spoke the words I tripped. The first bit that hit the tarmac was my lips, followed by the rest of my body. It was my face that suffered the most.

Victoria disappeared.

I burst into helpless tears as blood poured from my mouth. Luckily I was nearly at school. I continued to my class. Mr Arkwright sat at his desk. The whole class had a party air. All the tables had been arranged in a semi-circle and in the middle was a photograph of Princess Elizabeth. This made me even more upset. I burst into fresh tears.

Mr Arkwright got up.

"What has happened here?" he asked in wonder.

"I fell over," I grizzled.

"Dear me," he said. "I think you'll have to go to sickbay. You're bleeding badly."

He examined me.

"And you've got a badly grazed knee."

I nodded and pointed at my shoe laces.

"My l-l-laces are undone."

"What a silly goose you are," he exclaimed, bending down and tying them for me.

He patted me on the head.

"Off you go to sickbay, then."

I never did get to the party. And worse was yet to come.

Once the sickbay was satisfied that I wasn't any longer at death's door I was sent back to Birch Cottage. Miss Harmon was waiting for me. She pointed angrily to the pile of dirty sheets she had pulled out of the locker. She didn't inquire why I had iodine all over my face or why I had a bandage on my leg. Grabbing me by the scruff of the neck she shoved me upstairs.

"Get those clothes off, you dirty hussy," she hissed.

I noticed that in her hand she held the dreaded hairbrush.

She rained blows on my naked body with the edge of it, even catching my sore mouth and deliberately attacking my bad leg.

"Get to bed," she ground out. "I don't want to see or hear anything more from you."

Unable to see through my tears, I stumbled into my bed, dreading the night ahead. I wanted so much to go home. I had asked and asked and asked. But it was no good. I had reached rock bottom. I was nine years old and I just wanted to curl up and die.

7th July 1953

Miss Armitage gazed around the sparse room dispassionately. Lydia Randall stood awkwardly, twisting her hands together anxiously.

She said without any guile.

"I am sorry it's taken so long to get in touch with you."

"S'alright," Lydia mumbled self consciously.

"I am afraid I need to carry out an inspection. It's important for the Children's Department to check these things out. Your children have become used to a good standard of living. We have to make sure these things can be maintained."

She crossed the room to the scullery. Smiling thinly, to reassure Lydia she poked her head around the doorway and withdrew immediately.

Apologetically, she said, "I'll need to see the bedrooms."

"Oh," muttered Lydia. "Well we've only got one, now. It was them."

"Them," echoed Miss Armitage, not understanding.

"Yes," said Lydia. "The people downstairs. They've bought the house and they've taken the front bedroom."

"Oh, I see," said Miss Armitage.

"I'll show you," offered Lydia anxiously.

They left the room and climbed the three little steps to the bedrooms. The first door they came to was ajar. Miss Armitage soon saw that it was impossible to shut the door for there was a double bed, and three single beds crammed into the room where before there had only been three single beds.

Miss Armitage followed Lydia back to the living room.

As gently as she could she told her.

"I am afraid that the children sharing your room is most unsuitable. We would be unable to sanction the children coming home for good. And I am also afraid that I would not be able to make a report to say favourably that the children could even come home for the weekend."

A very disappointed Lydia burst out.

"But, it's Joycie. She's upset. She's not happy. I get letters from 'er every week saying she wants to come 'ome. Besides, I want all my children 'ere with me."

Miss Armitage soothed.

"I'm sorry. In view of the lack of suitable accommodation there is nothing we can do is there."

"No," agreed Lydia in a subdued voice.

11th July 1953

Harry sat down and waited.

Soon, Miss Armitage poked her head around the door.

Adopting a jolly voice she said.

"Ah there you are, Mr. Randall."

"Yes?" agreed Harry in a puzzled voice.

"There's nothing to worry about," reassured Miss Armitage.

Harry pulled a face.

"It's easy for *you* to say."

"What do you mean?" puzzled Miss Armitage.

"Why," Harry began. "Due to the visit she had last week she's 'aving one of her turns again. I can't get a word in edgeways. Oh and she is saying now she doesn't care about having the children home for some time. That's what she's saying."

"Well," enthused Miss Armitage, "that is all to the good and brings me to the next point we wish to discuss with you."

"Yes," asked Harry a little suspiciously.

Miss Armitage smiled widely, cocking her head on one side.

"Mr Randall, I'd like to discuss your daughter."

"Joycie?" queried Harry.

"Yes," agreed Miss Armitage. "We are aware that she isn't happy in her present cottage. We want you to consider allowing us to board her out in a foster home."

"Well, I don't know," blustered Harry.

"She's a bright girl who deserves a better future," insisted Miss Armitage, in a soft, but persuasive tone.

"What do you mean?" Harry asked.

"Fostered with a view to adoption is what we are considering."

Harry licked his lips nervously.

"That's a bit drastic," he said quietly.

Miss Armitage examined her fingernails minutely.

Finally she said. "Just when are you going to be able to provide Joyce with a home?"

"Well..well.. I just don't know," stammered Harry.

Miss Armitage smiled in triumph. She laid a small form which she produced from a thick brown file on the desk. Purposely she removed the cap from a fountain pen and handed it to Harry.

"I think it is in your daughter's best interest to sign the form, don't you?"

Meekly, Harry took the pen and scrawled his name.

28th August 1953

Miss Blanche (who was the latest in a long line of Welfare Officers to visit the Randalls' house) made sure she had clarified the situation regarding the fostering and my eventual adoption. Lydia accepted it very well on the surface. Even when she was told that a Mrs Haywood of 109, Boxley Road, Maidstone was going to be my foster parent. Harry showed her out.

Lydia was waiting for him on his return.

She exploded, in fury.

"What do you think? You can give my children away? Well I won't have it, do you hear me. You 'ad better undo what you've done. I want 'er 'ome 'ere, not being given away to some other woman."

Harry held up his hands for silence, gulping guiltily.

"It wasn't what I wanted at all, woman. They talk you into these things. You know what they are like."

"And what about her brothers, man. She'll never see them again. You know how much she loves them, especially Bobby."

Harry covered his face with his hands.

"What are we going to do?" he mumbled incoherently.

Lydia stabbed a forefinger in the air in his direction.

"*You* 'ad better tell them. Before they give 'er away. You phone them up."

On the 18th September, The Children's Office received a letter.

A.V.WHITE. A.I.M.T.A. F.1. hsc
HOUSING DEPARTMENT
TOWN HALL
WOOLWICH, S.E.18

Please quote ref: 5.1/3/45/1957
TELEPHONE WOOLWICH 1181
17th September, 1953

Dear Sir,

Re: H.J.Randall-6, Abbey Terrace, Abbey Wood, S.E.2

The children of the above-named housing applicant are at present under your care, and Mrs Randall is pressing for alternative accommodation so that the children can come home once more.
Before the application is considered, I would be grateful if you could let me know the exact position regarding this family, so that I can inform my Committee.

Yours Faithfully

A.V. White

Director of Housing

The London County Council
Children's Care Committee,
34, Watson Street   Received 18th September.
Deptford
S.E.8

The reply was to shape all our lives, especially mine.

I had been summoned to Miss Harmon's study. I was very scared. I tried hard to think what I could have done wrong. Anymore than usual that was.
Timidly I knocked at the door.
A voice called out. "Come in."
Trying hard to disguise my trembling, I turned the knob and walked in.
Miss Harmon sat at her desk. I could see a paper bag on the floor at her feet. It contained toys. They were things I had never seen since I had entered this house.
They were mine.

Her lips curved into a semblance of a smile.

"So you are leaving us."

I looked shocked for it was news to me.

She went on.

"Welfare Officer Miss Simone is picking you up any minute. Do you know where you are going? Are you going home?"

I shook my head and mumbled.

"I don't know."

To my amazement she launched into a speech, in which she said she hoped my stay had been a happy one!

A knock on the front door saved me from any reply..........................

Confidential
GMA 5th October 1953

Dear Sir

Re: H.J. Randall, 6 Abbey Terrace,

Abbey Wood, S.E.2

I thank you for your letter of 17th September and would inform you that I could not recommend the discharge of these children to the care of their mother, although I have no power to withhold them should the parents be given more accommodation and they insist on their discharge. These three children came into care in September, 1950 by reason of the mother's admission to a mental hospital as a certified patient. Five months later her husband took her out against medical advice. She was later re-admitted to another mental hospital, but was not then considered certifiable, and although in need of treatment refused to remain as a voluntary patient. The hospital authorities do not consider that she is fit to look after her children, and from our observation of Mrs. Randall and the state of her home, I must endorse the hospitals view.

We are holding these children now only on the ground of lack of accommodation. If this is given to the parents the mother will have the children home, and in view of Mrs. Randalls medical state she may do harm to them.

The Director of Housing   Yours Faithfully
Housing Department
Town Hall, Woolwich,
S.E.18   Area Children's Officer

A lady was there, waiting for me. I could see a car. She helped me into it. Bernard was sitting in the front. He smirked at me knowingly. Bobby was in the back. I sat next to him. Soon the car pulled away.

Miss Simone made conversation with us as she drove out of Croydon. She pointed the little black car in the direction of Sidcup.

She told us, "We all think at the Children's Department that you are a very close family and that you will be better off together."

We shot a happy look at each other.

She continued.

"You are going to a place *now* called The Hollies. It is in Sidcup. You will be together, here, in the same cottage. It is called Rowan and the housemother is Miss Lang. You will like her, she is very nice."

She turned the car through large green metal gates and drove it around a circular road past large areas of grass and trees. I noticed some big boys on a path, throwing stones at each other. I bit my lip anxiously, for I feared they would get into trouble. But no-one appeared to shout at them.

The car pulled up outside a house with a glass door. I noticed there was also a monkey puzzle tree, here, in the middle of a fine lawn. As we stepped out of the car I saw a little brass plaque on the wall. It read Rowan Cottage. We all followed Miss Simone. Her knock on the door was answered by a large lady in a flowered pinny with a scarf tied around her head.

"Ello ducks," she said, smiling at us all. "Come along in. I'll go and fetch Miss Lang."

We shuffled obediently through the doorway and onto a large coconut mat.

The lady winked at us and ambled away, her swollen feet in battered house slippers, slapping rhythmically on the tiled floor.

Miss Simone smiled at us encouragingly.

"That's Mrs Sphantum, she's the daily help."

We stared open mouthed at the room on our right. It was a playroom. And the untidiest I had ever seen. Music blared from an old wireless precariously balanced on a window ledge. There were children of all shapes and sizes throwing books and toys about.

I noticed one boy in particular. He had jet black hair and a sulky expression on his face. I sucked in my breath and stared at him as he threw a book across the room. He poked his tongue out at me. Shocked, I turned away.

A small, stout woman appeared. I could tell she was different from the daily help. She had an air of authority and wore a uniform. I shuddered slightly, dreading what might be to come.

She pushed past us.

"Excuse me," she said.

She stood with her hands on her hips at the entrance to the playroom and shouted at the top of her voice. For good measure she stamped her foot as well.

"Just what is going on here? Someone turn that blasted wireless off."

The boy with the black hair made a face at her.

She advanced swiftly across the room towards him. He backed away slightly.

I couldn't help noticing that he was nearly as tall as her. I covered my mouth with my hand. She poked him hard in the chest. Defiantly, he stood with his hands tucked in the pockets of his short grey trousers. He stared her out. She turned away first. He smirked at her receding back. The other children in the room sniggered.

She turned back and shot at him.

"Eric Shurmer. You are the ringleader. You can stay and get this mess cleared up."

She stared around the room angrily.

"The rest of you can get washed for lunch. Now!"

The room emptied swiftly. Children pushed past us. We stood pressed close to Miss Simone, feeling in the way. Out of the corner of my eye I watched Eric throwing stuff into lockers which were the worst for wear. Most of the doors were hanging off and stuff bulged out of the interiors. Miraculously soon the floor was empty of toys. He stamped out of the playroom. Again he poked his tongue out at me, before running down the corridor.

Miss Lang turned to Miss Simone.

"Ah! The Randall children, we've been expecting them."

The Welfare Officer smiled and handed her a sheath of papers. They both vanished into another room with a large table in it. Miss Lang pointedly shut the door. After what seemed an age they reappeared. Miss Simone said goodbye to us. Her parting shot to me was.

"I am sure you will be happier here."

I looked at her doubtfully and held tightly to Bobby's hand.

Miss Lang smiled.

"You are just in time for lunch. Come along I will show you the washroom. Then you can take your place in the dining room."

Shakily we followed her.

A new era had begun.

I thought fleetingly about the boy I had just met.

Privately, I thought he was horrible. But I couldn't help wondering why he was here.

PART TWO: THE LITTLE ONEN

Chapter Ten: The Birth

Henry and Ivy Shurmer lived at 17, Marsden Place, Southwark with their two sons, ten year old George and eight year old Ged.

Henry was a hard man who believed in his role at the head of the family. His wife Ivy stayed home to look after the house. She also obeyed her husband in every way. It would have been unthinkable for her to express an opinion of her own. George and Ged obeyed their father and mother, too. They knew their place.

There was no doubt that he had a deep regard for his first born son, who was a bright boy, much older than his years. Henry knew that he could rely on George to help his mother when she needed it. He didn't feel the same way about Ged, however. He was a much slower, dreamy boy, who clung to his mother's apron strings. He was as opposite to George as he could be. Henry dealt with him with impatience and derision, which usually sent him flying to his mother's side. She loved her two sons with a deep passion. She was proud of George who was the brightest boy in his class. It was to him she turned when Henry was missing. Ged was her bespectacled 'baby' whom she needed to nurture constantly. It was she who persuaded the popular George to include Ged in his games and sports that he liked to take part in. Reluctantly, he did.

Henry was not best pleased when he learned that his wife Ivy was pregnant after a gap of eight years. It wasn't by accident that there had not been any further pregnancies. It had been by his design.

He was a printer by trade. This was a fact of which he was proud. Unlike his neighbours who could hardly boast a trade between them. He worked on a three shift system in peacetime. Now, in wartime, he was part of the Home Guard, too, so even his evenings were taken up.

Henry was a good looking man with a bit of an eye for the ladies. He had strong opinions about the war. It was his belief that, at thirty-seven years, he was too old to be called up. He also believed, in line with every other Londoner that the 'phoney' war would continue. He and the rest of London had received a severe shock the night before when the whole of East and South East London had been blitzed. It had sent Ivy and the boys scurrying down the shelter in the next street. She did swear that she wouldn't go down there again, though. She said it was filthy. The acrid smell of burning had lingered on.

Neither of them believed that it would happen again tonight.

Henry also believed that Ivy was too old to give birth again at age thirty four. It was a worry to her, too, to have to start over again. She nursed a secret thought that it might be a girl. There was a time when she had craved another baby, if she could only choose the sex. But Henry was unwilling, saying they didn't need anymore. He earned good money in the print and he didn't see the need to throw it away, rearing more children. No, things were all right as they were. The boys were growing up. It meant he, Henry got plenty of attention, which was the way he liked it.

Ivy eased her swollen body down into the chair. She tried her hardest to ignore the throbbing ache in the small of her back.

1st October 1940.

"I must 'ave been overdoing it. I'll be ...alright," she gasped, as a sharp pain rippled across her belly. A little voice inside her head warned her that this could be the start of it. Could be she was going into labour? She brushed it away, knowing that the baby wasn't due yet. Worriedly, she stared at the violet night sky through the scullery window, listening hard for the sound she dreaded, along with her neighbours.

Sharp stabbing pains assaulted her body again, coupled with the distant drone of an airplane.

"Oh oh," she moaned.

George and Ged rushed into the scullery.

"What's up, Mum?" asked Ged. "Is there another air raid?"

George rushed to the back door, yanked it open and stood in the small backyard. With an air of importance and more than a little excitement, he studied the night sky.

He shut the door with a bang.

"I can 'ear planes. They're coming," he announced.

Just then, as if to back him up, the loud wail of sirens penetrated the walls and echoed all around them

Ivy groaned, half in pain and half in the realization of their situation. George rushed over to her.

"S'alright, Mum, we can go to the shelter, like we did last night."

"We can't," she stated. "The baby's comin' an' I need you 'ere with me."

He said in a state of panic.

"We 'ave to. We can't stay 'ere. Dad did say in case of an air raid we 'ave to go to the shelter, didn't 'e."

A hysterical sob escaped unwittingly from Ivy's lips, followed by a frightened squeal from Ged.

Ivy ground out through clenched teeth.

"Oh Ged be quiet! I wish 'e was here to tell us what to do, but he isn't. 'E would know what's best...I can't move far now this lot's started."

George flew to her side.

"Oh Mum."

She stretched out an imploring hand.

"*You* can 'elp, though son."

George's eyes lit up.

"What can I do?"

"You can go and fetch the midwife."

George paled.

"You want me to go out in that?"

Ivy nodded her head.

"You know where it is. 80, Amelia Street."

George stood stock still for a moment.

"Pl..e..a..se," implored Ivy.

Ged tugged on her dress.

"Can I go?" he asked.

George balled his fist and struck him on his thin, weedy arm.

"No, you idiot. You gotta look after Mum."

With a wry look on his young face George thrust his arms into a threadbare mackintosh and snatched up a square box threaded with string. He slung the gas mask over his shoulder. The door banged. Then he was gone.

Ivy gestured to Ged to help her.

"I want to get out of this chair, lovey," she said.

The little boy strained and pulled at her swollen body.

Slowly she raised herself up to a standing position.

She took halting steps to the enamel sink. Thankfully, she gripped the cold edge. Her dark curly hair clung damply to her forehead, and rivulets of salty sweat ran down her pain-wracked face. She attempted to flash a reassuring smile at Ged, who looked at her fearfully.

"What shall I do?" he asked.

She gasped out.

"For now, just keep me company."

They both shuddered as a loud crump shook the house.

"Aw Gawd," she whispered.

George gazed around in awe. The streets looked like another world at night, especially during an air raid. He stared wonderingly at the sky above him. It had a deep orange hue but was speckled with the bulbous shapes of barrage balloons and black criss-cross cables which hung suspended in the air. All the buildings on either side of the road cast long yellow shadows on the ground. It was almost as bright as day. The constant noise was deafening. There were sharp human cries, the persistent clanging of fire engine bells, a staccato rata-tat-tat of anti aircraft guns firing long streams of tracers into the stained sky and there was the monotonous drone of unseen aircraft high up in the clouds.

George was caught off guard by a loud whooshing sound and an icy blast of air which catapulted him along Marsland Road into Manor Place. He struggled fitfully against the draught, maintaining his balance with difficulty. Breathing hard he dived in a shop doorway, leaning back thankfully on the wooden shuttering. He stared hollowly across the road, craning his neck to see what had happened. There was a raw acrid smell. A deathly hush fell sharply, making George suck in his breath. He still couldn't see anything. Terrible thoughts welled to the surface of his reluctant mind. All his consciousness was willing him to go back. But he knew he couldn't. He rubbed his knuckles vehemently in his watering eyes. *It was the baby!* He *had* to go on. George gathered his courage and decided to make a break from his cover. He waited until the next sweep of searchlights lit up the ground momentarily and broke into a trot, ignoring the thumping of his heart and the tightness of his chest. He ran past the public baths into Penton Place, his chest shuddering violently. It wasn't far now. He was nearly there.

Ivy now lay on the floor, on her best eiderdown. Ged had done his best to help. It didn't matter that he had brought the wrong one. She watched helplessly as a pool of water spread right over it. She fell backwards against the gold quilted fabric, gasping in pain as a tight spasm rippled across her body and seared into her aching spine. She lay helplessly, waiting for it to pass. Her hands plucked uselessly at the quilt which was tangled in a jumble under her body. She wiped the back of her hand against her sweat soaked brow and stared blearily up at her eight year old son, who hovered above her in terrified silence. Just then her body tensed convulsively. She braced herself for a new onslaught, blinking rapidly to shatter the thick tears gathering unwittingly in her eyes. She fought to control the irresistible urge to open her mouth wide and scream loudly with sheer abandonment. Despite herself her throat spewed forth a harsh gurgle which grew.

The eight year old boy backed away in fright. He clapped his hands over his ears and ran in panic from the room. Ivy saw his flight with despair. She held out an imploring hand and broke down into harsh lonely sobs. Her fingers desperately clawed the air, searching for something solid to hold onto. They found nothing. A disembodied voice screamed out helplessly.

George ran down the length of Amelia Street, not stopping until he reached the green door. He crashed loudly on it with his balled fists. The sound echoed deeply inside the house. No one answered his frantic knocks. He gazed around in panic, but the street was deserted. There was nothing for it. He had to get home as soon as possible. Quickly he retraced his steps, hurrying into Manor Place. His mouth fell open when he saw a wide expanse of water gushing all along it, eventually winding out of sight into Walworth Road.

Ged sat huddled on the front step, his knees drawn up to his chin, his face buried between them. His shoulders heaved uncontrollably. He was oblivious to the scene above or the scream of raining bombs, which fell from the yellow sky. All he could hear were the terrifying screams and moans which poured from inside the house. He didn't like them one bit! And he wanted them to stop! Right now!

Ivy raised herself onto her elbows. All her inbred instincts to be modest had flown away. Something *was* happening! Gingerly she probed the painful area between her thighs with her fingers.
"It's the head. It's the head," she muttered to herself.
A large excruciatingly painful ripple began again, flowing tightly down to her hips. It was worse than ever before. Unable to help herself she disappeared inside it.
"A.r.r.gh! Mummy, Mummy, Mummy, please help me. I don't even *want* this baby. Please God make it go away," she sobbed, tears raining down her cheeks.
She struggled to surface and take control, scrabbling for patches of eiderdown to grasp.
"Mm...mm..mm..mm," she moaned.
She gasped as a small bloody form slithered onto the stained eiderdown.
"Thank God that's out," she cried.
The room swirled dizzily around her. Her eyes fluttered and closed. Her hands relaxed their grip, flexed and were still. The baby lay motionless on the floor.

Reg straightened his tin helmet, fixing the woven strap more firmly. He slid his armband to show the lettering ARP clearly. He continued his last round of the night, turning into Marsland Road, with a sigh of relief. He checked carefully to make sure everyone had their blackouts in place. He rounded a bend in the road and saw to his amazement a child crouched on the step of No 17.

"Hallo. Hallo. What have we got here, then?" he asked kindly, noting the distressed state of the boy.

Ged lifted up a tear stained face.

"It's me Mum. She's 'aving a baby in there. An' I think she's dyin. An' George' 'as gone and left us. An' me Dad's not here, eivver."

Reg shook his head in disbelief. With difficulty he crouched down to Ged's level.

"Come on young fella, sitting 'ere isn't helping any."

He dragged him to his feet.

"Don't you take on so. I'm sure it won't be as bad as you think. Women have little 'uns every day and they mostly seem to manage. Why my missus had seven, just popped them out like peas, she did. I think our best bet is to go an' see what's what, don't you sonny?"

Ged drew back in alarm.

"No. No. I want to wait for George."

"I think your Mum'll be best pleased to see *you*. She won't be expecting an old codger like me. Now I don't know who this George is but since he isn't here I think we had best go inside, don't you."

Ged burst out.

"'e's me bruvver. 'e's gone to fetch the midwife."

Reg paled.

"Are you sayin' he went out in this?"

Ged nodded.

"It's the baby. It was comin' and me Mum didn't know what to do."

Reg offered up a silent prayer for an unknown child caught up in the horror of war, then turned his attention to the job in hand.

George sat down on the pavement and removed his plimsolls. He tied the black laces together and slung them around his neck. Gingerly he stepped into the broken water main, sucking in his breath at the coldness of the water. He didn't care. He needed to get home. Going across it was the only way.

Reg hurried into the scullery and surveyed the scene, concern flooding into his face. Ged sped over to his mother's prone form, falling to his knees beside her.

"She's dead. She's dead. Me Mum's dead, aint she?"

His gaze turned to the mauve object between her legs.

"Is that the baby? Ugh! Why is it a funny colour? Is that blood on it? Why 'as it got blood on it?"

Reg twitched the bloody nightdress over Ivy's knees, whilst examining the baby. It twitched slightly.

"Aha," announced Reg. "The little un's alive."

He turned to Ged.

"Don't you worry about your Mum. Look she's coming to. See..."

Ivy's eyes fluttered.

"There, see," he demonstrated to Ged. "Now all we need is that brother of yours to show up."

Reg severed the cord and rubbed the baby vigorously, He was rewarded with a cry. He helped Ivy to her feet and sat her in her chair, handing her the baby wrapped in a towel. Half an hour later the door opened and a barefoot George walked in.

"Hello son," said Ivy weakly. "Meet your brother, Eric."

Chapter Eleven: Penryn

Henry was very angry. He had just heard that Ivy and the baby and the two boys were being evacuated almost immediately.

George and Ged had been evacuated once before, when the war began. Along with hundreds and hundreds of other children had drifted back home when the predicted war on London just didn't seem to happen. They were prepared. All strategic points had been sandbagged. Older men and young singles had been engaged to serve in the Home Guard. They spent their evenings guarding the capital against nothing. Too many mothers couldn't stand being without their children. A lot of them weren't happy in their evacuation billets. So they came home.

Now, it was really happening.

Henry tried everything to talk Ivy into staying. It was not in her nature to go against him usually. But she was frightened of the Blitz. There had been bombing every night. She had lay in bed in hospital with baby, Eric, at her side, worrying about her boys. No, this time she didn't agree with him. The government were pushing for mothers and children to leave.

Henry blamed the baby. As far as he was concerned it was his fault. He wouldn't even look at him.

Next day, as soon as she was sent home from hospital, Ivy prepared for evacuation. She had no clue where they were going. They weren't given any information about their destination. She was told to take food and drink as the journey could be long. Even she didn't dream how long, for her furthest trip in her entire life was Southend.

She and her family joined hundreds of others at the railway station. Many more would travel on coaches or in lorries. The majority of evacuees were unaccompanied children, who had labels pinned to their lapels and carried an incongruous assortment of bags, haversacks or suitcases. But there were also women like Ivy with young babies or expectant mothers.

She boarded the train with trepidation.

The two boys, however, saw it as an adventure. They were especially pleased when they and all the other children were given a bag of goodies by a posh lady. Their time was spent running up and down the corridors and sticking their heads out of the carriage windows. They withdrew their heads, laughing gleefully, when clouds of billowing smoke from the engine blew in their faces.

The train chugged on and on. The two boys sat quietly now, bored with the morning's escapades. They, too, longed for the journey to be over. At last, Ivy decided it was lunchtime. She handed out squashed packets of sandwiches and lukewarm lemonade. She was having a terrible time with baby Eric. He had been fractious since the train left The Elephant and Castle. She had fed him lukewarm milk and changed his nappy with great difficulty. Nothing could soothe him, not even when another young mother offered to help. She had commented on his compact size, which was unlike her own large baby. Huffily, Ivy had told her that he was born a little early and he wasn't feeding very well. Ivy's new found friend had told her that she should nourish him herself. That, in her opinion, was the trouble, babies needed to be close to their mothers. Ivy shuddered in revulsion. She told her friend it was not for her.

After many, many hours, the train stopped. Eager hands rubbed the misted up glass. They stared in wonder at the small sign that read 'PENRYN'. This meant nothing to the weary travellers. They would soon find out that they were in the county of Cornwall.

Reluctantly, they fell off the train that had become like a second home. They had eaten, drunk, played and sang on it. Now they were loath to leave its protective shell. Fearfully, they milled about in a bewildered fashion, pushing towards the station entrance, spilling into the tiny waiting room.

A gormless looking porter took great delight in pushing them out into the yard beyond. They stood and shivered in their thin London clothes.

"'Ere," said Ivy indignantly, hoisting the baby higher in her arms. "No need to shove."

"Yeah," agreed her new found friend, Peg. "We ain't animals, you know."

The porter grinned sheepishly at them.

"Cummice my flowers. Canee maids gwap queckly."

"What's 'e on about," laughed Peg. "Can't understand a word 'e's sayin'."

"God knows," remarked Ivy. "It's like 'e's speakin' a foreign langwidge."

Together they inched their way into the dark yard. Ivy made sure the boys were by her side. In the darkness, they could just make out a woman with a clipboard dressed in an expensive dark coat which virtually reached the floor. Only a small white circle of a face was visible as a dark fur hat covered her hair.

"Welcome," she voiced cheerily. "I am Miss Jessie Dunn, your billeting officer."

She extended a coated arm and a gloved hand and smiled sweetly. The two women shuffled forward with their babies and baggage, the boys trailed behind.

"Yes, that right get in line," Jessie encouraged. "You will get chosen quicker."

"Chosen," muttered a furious Peg. "What do they think we are? Bloody cattle?"

"Sssshhhh!" remonstrated Ivy in embarrassment. "She'll 'ear you."

"Don't care," muttered Peg mutinously.

Ivy put her hand to her mouth in consternation.

"All I'm hoping," she said worriedly, "is that we can stay together."

As she spoke a kindly looking man wandered along the line and stopped before them. He looked searchingly at Ivy and the boys. Smiling, he addressed her.

"I think I can take these young men, mother."

"No!" countered Ivy indignantly. "I want us all to stay together."

The man looked over his shoulder at a young lady.

"Wendy," he called. "I need your help, here."

She was talking to Peg and looking interestedly at her fat, butterball baby.

Reluctantly, she broke away and joined the man.

He said to Ivy.

"This is my daughter, Wendy. I think you and your baby might be what she is looking for. I and my wife will take the two boys. Sorry, it's the best we can do."

"Well...." considered Ivy. "I don't know."

Wendy smiled at her winningly and bent over baby Eric enthusiastically.

"Oh what a dear," she cooed.

Despite her reluctance, Ivy was swayed.

Wendy touched her arm.

"It won't be so bad, you'll see. I live in a lovely place right at the top of the hill. And we'll see lots of mother and father and your sons."

"Hmmm," murmured Annie.

Wendy smiled broadly.

"Come on," she persuaded. "Let's get out of the cold."

Ivy sighed.

"Oh alright then. We'll give it a try."

Before parting, Ivy and her sons had eaten a much-needed hot meal together at the Bennett's house. She was in a better frame of mood, now. It seems she and her family were lucky in being chosen by the Bennets. Graham was a local businessman and owned a lot of property in the town of Penryn and surrounding villages.

A weary mother and baby followed Wendy to the front door of a squat looking bungalow. Ivy had mixed feelings. She missed the boys already. She knew George would settle down, but she was worried about Ged. And she missed her husband and her home. She was proud of her little house and sad to leave it. What sort of state it would end up in just didn't bear thinking about. That's if it survived. Now, she had to share another woman's home. And for how long? She didn't know. After a perfunctory inspection around the bungalow, which Wendy insisted on, she begged to be able to retire for the night. She was very grateful when Wendy insisted that she could leave the baby to her, declaring herself *desperate* to be occupied.

Next morning, Ivy cradled baby Eric in her arms and stared at the photographs which sat on the sideboard. There were several of a baby and one of an airman and more of Wendy and a young man.
She came up behind Ivy.
Sadly, she said.
"That was my baby, Ellie. She only lived for six weeks. And of course that's my husband, Roy."
She hesitated before continuing.
"They say his plane went down over France. I haven't heard anything. I don't know if he is alive or dead."
Ivy recoiled in horror.
"I really am sorry. I wasn't being nosey."
"It's alright, really."
Ivy soon settled down at the bungalow, marvelling at the new fangled washing machine, with the ringer sitting on top of it, unlike her old gas copper and her separate mangle which had to be dragged out of the shed every time it was used.
Wendy was very good with baby Eric. She seemed to be able to charm the little boy. Ivy soon left her to cope with him. In return she did what she did best. She cleaned the bungalow from end to end. And looked forward to their many visits to see George and Ged at the Bennett's big house.
Life in the big house was fine! The boys enjoyed it immensely. Even school was a lark! They went in the afternoons, whilst the local children went in the mornings. Their own teacher had stayed in Truro with another trainload of children. A lot of the little Londoners found it all too easy to run rings around the Cornish teacher. George and Ged were well behaved, due to their nature, but there were a lot that weren't. Before school Graham Bennett did his best to amuse them. He helped them make a soapbox with old pram wheels and odd pieces of wood. They had great fun hurtling down the steep incline of West Street, continuing into Lower Market Street, careering crazily along the

high pavement and around the clock tower, finishing up right at the bottom in Quay Street, only just avoiding ending up in the river Fal.

Ivy held the thin piece of paper in her hand and read the words again. Henry was coming to Cornwall on a visit. Strangely, she had mixed feelings about this.

There was a time when her whole world revolved around him. Everything she did was for him or because of him. Now, she wasn't so sure. She had become used to managing her own affairs, with Wendy's help of course. With her head whirling around trying to accept this latest piece of news, Ivy made tentative arrangements for him to stay on his arrival.

Eric was now five months old.

"I'm going to get off to the railway station, then," Ivy stated.

Wendy looked up from the depths of the armchair, her arms full of a doting baby boy.

"Mmmm," she said absentmindedly. "Yuce get off."

She broke into a chuckle at the baby's antics.

Ivy shook her head and reflected that at least the baby had love from somewhere. As she walked from Western Place on her way to the station she realised that she didn't feel anything for him. All there was inside her chest was a cold hard lump and a curious anger. But she didn't know why. She adored her other two sons. It was a mystery. And it wasn't one she was proud of.

Her mind slewed quickly back to the present when she noticed a large crowd of people gathered in Station Road. She hurried over to them.

"What's up?" she asked a large woman, who stood moist eyed, clutching a handkerchief.

The woman answered in a loud stage whisper.

"There's been a bomb. The railway lines been bombed. They say a train has been hit. My 'ubben was on thet London train. Coming home on leave, 'e was."

"What?" cried Ivy. "'as the London train been 'it?"

The woman dabbed at her eyes.

"They don't know. No-one knows nothing."

Ivy made a move to push through the crowd. The woman grabbed her arm.

"Stay here," she advised. "It won't do any good."

So, Ivy stayed put and waited patiently.

Eventually her vigil at the station was rewarded by the haggard appearance of Henry. She rushed forward, overjoyed by his unharmed presence. He pushed her away.

"Give me a break, woman," he begged. "It's been an 'orrible journey, the train in front of us got bombed. So we were stuck. They've bin all night clearing it."

Hesitantly, Ivy ventured.

"Yes, we heard about the bomb. I've been waiting for ages."

She giggled hysterically.

"I nearly gave up."

He shot her a derisory look and changed the subject.

"Where are they then?"

She looked angrily at him, wounded by his cold treatment of her. Waspishly, she said.

"You know where they are. They are staying with the Bennett's."

He rounded on her.

"What, still?"

She shrugged her shoulders.

"I can't do anything about it, can I?"

"Well I bloody well can. Oh yes, we'll see about that," he retorted.

Henry still had no time for baby Eric. He tried to persuade Ivy to get Wendy to adopt him. Ivy refused. Henry wasn't unashamed of his actions. He said they made a lovely pair in his opinion.

Trying desperately to ingratiate herself Ivy offered to return home. To her surprise Henry was adamant that they should all remain where it was safe.

He was determined to sort out one thing, though, before he left. Whilst he was visiting the boys, he had a quiet word with Graham Bennett. Triumphantly, to Ivy's amazement, Henry produced a set of keys. They were for a cottage, right in the middle of Penryn. It was in fact just past the clock tower, through an archway, into an alley. Ivy was thrilled to have one of the cottages which lined both sides of the walkway, for her and her family.

She could have her boys back at last.

Chapter Twelve: The Betrayal

Ivy was pleased with her two up and two down accommodation and was delighted to meet her new neighbour, Honor.

She was a great character who had lived in Penryn all her life. She made and distributed potions to all the locals. They often came to her rather than visit the doctor. Her speech was a broad rich Cornish dialect. And of course she knew everyone that was anyone. She soon introduced Ivy to all the local shopkeepers. She learned under Honor's guidance whom to deal with. And who not to.

Thanks to Honor, Ivy rarely had to join a queue. For everyone else rationing had begun in earnest. By 1941 clothing could only be bought with coupons. The war looked like dragging on for some time. The shock of what was happening had begun to bite hard with the English people. It was a fact that two thirds of normal everyday items of food were usually imported. Luxury items had completely disappeared. However, for Ivy, staple food still seemed plentiful, if you knew where to get it. And clothing wasn't an issue, for Honor had an answer to that, too. To Ivy's horror she introduced her to the second hand clothes market. She was powerless to protest. She just declared darkly that she would make sure they were good and properly washed, first. It was all she could do with two growing boys and a baby to clothe. They also made regular trips to The Women's Institute to exchange or purchase children's clothes.

So, she should have been contented.

There was one flaw on the horizon.

Eric.

Now she was lumbered with him. And he was teething and crawling.

Wendy had soon found another Mum and baby to take in.

However, Honor had a soft spot for Eric. She called him the little Onen. In old Cornish this meant roughly The One Who Stands Alone. Honor swiftly saw that there was a problem with Ivy and the baby. She did what she could to take him off Ivy's hands as much as possible. When she could she slipped him a potion to make him grow, for in her opinion he was much too slight to be coming up to nine months old.

George and Ged were more than a little disgruntled. They didn't like having to move to Park Cottages. They had begged to be allowed to keep the soapbox. It had been exciting living with the Bennett's and they couldn't bear to lose it. They were also sorry to leave Annie Bennett. She was soft and indulgent. Annie had always wanted more children but it hadn't happened. The two Shurmer boys were better than she could have hoped for. She had heard all the stories about the little Londoners from very poor homes with barely a rag to their names, possessing the manners of guttersnipes and using language that would have made her shudder. Annie Bennett admired Ivy. She had done a good job of bringing up her boys, for they were nothing like that. And she had heard from her daughter, Wendy what a brilliant housewife Ivy was in every way. She said the bungalow shone like a new pin. Wendy soon learned to leave the cooking to her. She was extremely thrifty and could make food stretch a long way. So they were sorry to lose their billeting allocation, but happy to gain them as tenants. Graham Bennett knew the cottage and its furniture would be well looked after.

As for George and Ged, it wasn't that they didn't love their mother. They did. They adored her as much as she loved them. No, she knew them only too well. She knew their weaknesses as well as their strengths.

Still, it was great seeing more of their baby brother, even if he did wake up during the night and disturb them. However they both had a sense of foreboding that they would have a much bigger part to play other than dangling a second-hand toy in front of him to make him smile and laugh.

They were right.

"Aw Mum," protested George. "We can't take him with us. He can't play in our games. He can't even walk yet."

Ivy stood her ground, an impassive expression on her face.

"Oh yes you can. It won't be long before he's walking anyway. Not the way he was walking around the furniture this morning."

"Well he isn't walking yet," insisted George.

"I can't 'elp that," said Ivy. "I can't 'ave 'im under my feet today. I've got to give this place a good clean."

Determinedly she wheeled a large cumbersome black pram into view.

"Ere. Put him in there. Take him down to the Quay to watch the boats. He likes that."

George sighed.

"Oh alright."

He shot a meaningful glance at Ged, who stood shuffling his feet non-committally. George glared at him furiously.

He just never ever backed him up.

Ivy smiled happily at her eldest son.

"He's just been changed, so he'll be alright."

With stiff shoulders and a face like thunder, George plonked Eric in the pram and shoved it out of the door. Ged followed sheepishly.

The two boys parked the cumbersome pram outside a shop in Lower Market Street. George squeezed into the soapbox.

Excitedly, he threw over his shoulder to Ged.

"Yeah! It'll be great. Give 'im 'ere, quick."

Ged struggled with the pram straps that held his little brother in. He lifted the struggling baby and passed him to George.

He squeezed him between his knees, clamping a leg either side of him.

"Right 'o we're ready. Off we go," George commanded.

Ged hung onto the back and scooted his foot along the ground, before jumping up on the back ledge when the soapbox, gathered speed down the steep hill.

George pulled hard on the string 'handle' and the two front wheels twisted and turned. Baby Eric chuckled happily as they careered downwards.

Honor was out and about. She had heard that Spillers the grocer's had a delivery and she was determined to be there first. She glanced up Quay Street. Her eyes widened in horror.

Honor bustled up the road to meet George and Ged. They were crouched over the front of the soapbox examining one of the front wheels. Despite her diminutive size, she pounced on them.

"Look 'ere my flowers, thass a real baabee you gawt there. Lil cheeld aren't ebben a toy."

"S'alright Honor," insisted George. "He loved it. Didn't he."

Ged nodded.

"Yeah."

Honor's face remained unconvinced.

George shrugged his shoulders noncommittally.

"And it don't matter now, anyway."

"How's thet?" she queried.

"Front wheel's buckled. Gotta go back and get his pram."

"Thass good," she approved before heading up the hill.

"Come on Ged," encouraged George, with an air of frustration.

He wheeled the big black pram along the alley and began to bump in down a flight of stairs that were cut steeply into the hillside.

"Well, 'elp me, then," he burst out.

Ged whined in a low voice.

"I'm s sc..scared, George. What if we fall?"

The older boys face grew red with fury.

"What, you wanna end up in a fight, do yer?"

Ged grasped the bone handle of the pram and helped his brother manoeuvre it down to the tufty grass below. He shivered despite the balmy September air. His eyes blinked hard behind his thick glasses.

"They wouldn't really fight us would they?"

George nodded grimly.

"I reckon they would. They don't like us London kids, do they?"

A crestfallen Ged agreed.

Grimly, George stated.

"So there's nothing we can do is there. We have to climb the bridge, and cross the railway lines and climb down the other side, too. And we have to do it today. They will be there waiting for us. If we don't turn up they'll be after us."

Ged observed gloomily.

"And they're all bigger than us."

The country boys were better nourished, therefore larger and well covered. By comparison the London children were skinny and undersized. Even so, George knew they could usually hold their own in a fight as they were streetwise and wiry.

The two boys continued their progress down the long flight of stairs in silence.

Baby Eric was oblivious to his brothers' moods. He chuckled with glee at the bumpy ride. His face was smeared with jam. The remains of the bread he had been chewing was scattered in the pram. A large bottle with a rubber teat constantly dripped milk on the sheet and cellular blanket which was meant to be tucked around him. Instead it was scrunched up in a heap.

They blew out their cheeks in relief as they, at last, reached the bottom of the steep incline.

Their eyes were instantly drawn to the object of their fears.

Stretching across the sky and dividing it in two was a tall viaduct. Its many arches stepped across the countryside like giant legs. Occasionally a train would trundle across it, sounding a haunting whistle as it did so.

They could also see faint figures of local boys gathered at its base.

Ged sniffed.

He nodded at the pram.

"And what about 'im."

George stared hard at his little brother.

"We'll 'ave to leave 'im at the bottom."

Ged looked at him doubtfully.

"What's Mum gonna say."

George breathed hard.

"She won't know."

He shot a sharp look at Ged.

"Well she won't if you don't tell her. You won't will you. Promise."

Ged held up his palm solemnly.

"I swear."

They wheeled the pram to where the knot of boys stood and noticed there was one girl. She stared them out. They looked away.

A tall dour looking boy said mockingly.

"Ee came then."

George stepped forward and said airily.

"Course."

Ged stayed nervously by the pram.

George spat on both hands. He began to search for footholds in the very old uneven brickwork. Quickly, he progressed up the span. Soon he had reached the top. He yelled down.

"Come on Ged, its easy."

A loud roaring noise filled the sky. George ducked automatically as he saw a plane wheeling towards him. Then there was another. He dropped to the floor and lay face down on the railway track, his heart thumping so loudly he was sure *everyone* could hear it.

Down below, the local children ran away across the hill, making for the town.

Ged stood helplessly by the pram. Baby Eric's face creased at the loud noise; he burst into tears. Frantically, Ged rocked the pram back and forth.

He saw the planes dip their wings and fly over the town. A loud explosion filled the air. They roared away into the distance and soon faded from sight.

There was no sign of George.

Ged, too, began to blub loudly.

George got to his feet. He felt his body. It was still there. He wrinkled his nose at the acrid smell that hung in the air. Quickly he shinned down the span and joined Ged by the pram.

To his dismay he saw Ged and Eric's distress.

"What's up?" he demanded. "They've gone now."

Ged sniffed.

"I was scared. I thought you were dead."

George leaned over and rubbed Eric's back like he'd seen his Mum do many times.

It seemed to work to his relief.

He stated.

"I fink that was a bomb, they were Huns, I saw all the markings right close. I even saw the pilot in the first plane."

"Wow," breathed Ged.

Simultaneously they came to the same conclusion. They stared at each other.

"Mum," mouthed George.

Ged nodded urgently.

"Let's hurry up."

They began the descent to the bottom of the town. Soon they reached Quay Street where pandemonium had broken out.

Two parachute mines had been dropped. One had destroyed six houses and damaged many more. There were five people seriously injured and sixteen people with slight cuts and abrasions. The other mine had not exploded and was caught in the church spire.

The street was impassable. There was no access to Lower Market Street or Park cottages. Everyone was being taken to rest centres.

Ivy was frantic with worry. Luckily, Park Cottages were unharmed. She consulted her friend Honor. Impatiently they waited for the debris to be cleared. Over Penryn there was an air of disbelief and utter outrage. The bombers had committed a cardinal sin. The unthinkable had happened. Even here!

Ivy had no way of knowing whether her children were alive or dead. With Honor, she witnessed the sight of the unexploded mine hanging from the church spire at close hand. Honor said it was a pity the boys missed the sight of that. The two women were only too glad that the Navy were taking care of it. There were sailors swarming everywhere.

At last they were able to search for the boys and baby.

They were safe in a rest centre. Ivy was over the moon to see them. She was even pleased to see Eric alive and well.

Four months later Ivy opened the door to a loud, insistent knocking. A telegram boy stood there holding out a flimsy piece of paper.

"Mrs Ivy Shurmer?" he asked.

She agreed that she was.

"'Ere you are," he said. "Ee need tee know if there is any answer."

Ivy had an inbred fear of telegrams. Everyone knew they were bad news.

With trembling fingers she slit it open.

She read................

```
MRS.IVY SHURMER
2 PARK COTTAGES
PENRYN
CORNWALL
```

MUM PASSED AWAY STOP FUNERAL NEXT WEEK STOP HOPE YOU
CAN COME

DORIS

Quietly she told the telegram boy.

"There's no answer."

"Thass et mawther," he said cheerily. He threw his leg over the crossbar of his pushbike and rode away, whistling tunelessly.

Ivy's hand went to her throat then to her mouth. She couldn't think. It slowly dawned on her that she had no choice. She *had* to go home. Her Mum. Dead! And she didn't know anything about it. She had been stuck down here while her Mum was ill and even dying. No wonder she hadn't had a reply to her last letter.

She went next door to break the news to Honor.

Ivy and the two boys and the now fifteen month old baby climbed aboard a train two days later. They weren't excited as they had been on the journey there. They sat glumly staring out of the window and watching the countryside disappear and turn back into smoky war torn London. Many hours later they arrived at Elephant and Castle station.

Ivy lifted the crotchety, tired baby up into her arms.

"Get the bags, both of you, will you," she pleaded. "It's as much as I can do to carry 'im."

George shared the bags between them. A sulky Ged eventually picked up his ones. With trepidation they entered the familiar streets. They stared in amazement at the changes that had taken place since they had seen them last.

All around them the jagged remains of buildings leant drunkenly in the bitter January air. Angry fingers of splintered wood pointed accusations at the arcing lights, which sprinkled spasmodically into the surroundings, only to fade and die immediately. Large bulbous shapes of barrage balloons cast ghostly shadows all around.

Ged whispered dejectedly.

"I 'ate this place. It..s..dirty. I wish we was back in Cornwall."

His thoughts spoken aloud echoed what Ivy and George were thinking. They all felt like fish out of water. It was as if they didn't belong any more.

Ivy remarked with a feigned lightness.

"I 'ope our house is still standing at any rate."

As they turned the corner into Marsland Road, George remarked in a low voice.

"There it is."

They stopped several yards from number seventeen and stared at the familiar flaking paint and darkened windows with apprehension.

Ged spoke first.

"It don't look like anyone's in."

Ivy countered.

"Silly. Your Dad is the only one who might be."

She took a determined step forward. George followed her lead, dumping his bags with a relieved sigh. Ivy put the baby down on the step and fished in her bag for a key she hadn't used in a long time. She turned it in the lock and pushed open the door.

"Hallo," she called out uncertainly. "We're home."

She stepped into the passageway. The boys and baby crowded in after her.

A distant tinny voice, music and canned laughter came from behind the nearest door. Henry was in. Excitedly, she entered the living room. Henry sat on her couch in his best clothes, his hair slicked with Brylcreem.

Next to him was a young woman dressed in a severely cut green dress with accentuated shoulder pads. Her long auburn hair was fashioned in whorls above each ear. He had an arm tightly around her shoulder. They sat with their legs pressed together and gazed dreamily into each others' eyes.

Chapter Thirteen: The Brat

The two boys hovered uncertainly in the doorway. Ged backed away and sat on the stairs. He hugged little Eric to him. George stayed put, clinging to the door jamb.

Ivy took an involuntary step backwards.

"What the 'ell?" she burst out.

Hastily, Henry withdrew his arm. The woman jumped up guiltily and stood awkwardly in the middle of the room. Her fingers flew protectively to her neck. A string of bright green beads encircled her snowy white skin.

From the depths of the couch, Henry demanded.

"What are you doing here?"

Ivy stared at him.

"Didn't you get my letter?"

He rolled his head from side to side.

"No, I bloody didn't."

Ivy explained tearfully.

"Well I wrote you. It's me Mum. She's died. I've come back for the funeral."

Henry casually unfolded his legs and stood up.

"Well, well," he murmured. "So the old girl's pegged it 'as she?"

Ivy answered in a low voice.

"She 'as. I 'ad a telegram from Doris a few days ago."

Henry tossed his head in derision.

"Trust that interfering bitch."

Ivy countered.

"She just thought she was letting me know about me Mum. I'll bet she 'asn't got no clue that you're carrying on behind my back with this......floosy."

She flung her arm out dramatically.

Henry bristled. He laid a protective arm around the shoulders of the red-haired woman.

"No need for insults, Ivy. It ain't like that any'ow. Me and Sybil, we're in love. We've fallen head over heels."

He pulled the woman close to him before addressing Ivy arrogantly.

"Just ask her, go on."

She nodded briefly before looking away.

Belligerently, Ivy planted her hands on her hips.

"Oh, in love are you? You've got some nerve Henry Shurmer. And what about me? And what about your kids? They ain't far away. And they ain't silly."

To demonstrate her point she pulled George further into the room. She called for Ged to come to her. Reluctantly he did, towing Eric.

Henry glared meanly at the baby.

Ivy saw his look.

"You boys go upstairs, and take Eric with you."

George cast a miserable look at his father and one long look of hatred towards the young woman before disappearing through the door, pushing a tearful Ged and Eric before him.

Henry rounded on her.

"There's no need to send them away. I'm the one that's going."

Ivy's face fell at these words.

She asked in a frightened voice.

"Where are you going? You're not leaving are you? You belong here. This is your 'ome."

Henry sneered mockingly.

"Well I don't want to be here, right. I want to be with Sybil."

Ivy stepped forward in desperation.

"Have you thought this through, 'Enry. She's just a slip of a girl. Where you gonna go? Going to live with her folks are you?"

Henry swallowed a little uncertainly for he hadn't considered all his options too carefully.

In a measured voice he said.

"We'll get by. Me an' Sybil. We'll think of something."

Triumphantly, Ivy pressed her point home further.

"You'll 'ave to go an' live in some room somewhere. Is that what you want? To live in just an attic room at the top of an 'ouse with no runnin' water and a bit of a cooker on the landing?"

Henry removed his arm from Sybil's shoulder.

Ivy forced herself to look at her rival. Reluctantly, she took in her neatly coiffured hairstyle and her stylish dress, down to the expensive and impossible to obtain nylon stockings adorning her legs. She raised her eyes to the woman's soft, white neck. There encircling the soft expanse of flesh was *her* jewellery. *Her* necklace Henry had given her last birthday. She drew in her breath sharply and burst out.

"Well I'll be."

Henry leered at her.

Indignantly she ground out.

"That's *my* necklace, I believe."

Henry smirked.

"Blame me if you want to. I bought it. You didn't need it. I thought it matched the colour of her eyes."

Ivy swiped at Henry miserably. Her hand missed and landed in thin air.

Apologetically Sybil removed the necklace.

Henry grabbed her arm. He spoke to Ivy.

"We're off then."

Sybil handed the beads to Ivy.

In frustration she dashed them to the ground. Green beads burst everywhere.

The front door banged. They were gone, leaving Ivy alone.

A plumpish woman with a smart navy coat and a small circular hat with a large blue feather stood on the step of Number 17. Repeatedly, she banged on the peeling door. Doris knew there must be someone in. Hadn't she got Ivy's letter. They were all coming back home, including Eric, the baby. She had only seen him briefly, before he was evacuated along with the rest of the family. Well she wouldn't give up. She would carry on banging until someone answered. Doris was keen to pass on all the information she had about their Mum's sudden illness and resulting death. Ivy also needed to know what arrangements had been made for the coming funeral. Her persistence finally paid off.

The door opened a crack. It was the tear-stained face of George. Doris pushed open the door and stepped determinedly inside.

"'Ello Georgie, what's going on? I've been crashin' on the door for ages."

He didn't answer.

"Don't speak to your Auntie Doris, then. Where's your Mum?" she asked, without drawing breath.

Ged appeared on the stairway. His face was tear-stained, too.

"She's in the scullery," he volunteered.

Doris thought, surely these kids hadn't been crying for their Grandma. They couldn't have seen her for ages. It hadn't been exactly a close relationship. Henry had seen to that. He didn't tolerate any interference from anyone. Doris and Ivy always met in secret, whilst he was at work. She knew it was the same for Mum. As a result she saw little of her two grandsons of this union. She had confided to Doris that it hurt her feelings, but at least they weren't the only ones. She had other grandchildren from her other children's marriages.

Doris was a bit disturbed by the general appearance of the place. This was confirmed when she entered the scullery. Piles of dirty washing up were piled on the wooden draining board. The lino floor was dirty and stained. Little Eric sat under the table. His clothes and his face were very filthy. And a rich aroma arose from his direction.

She didn't know the situation with Ivy and Eric, but she was still appalled.

Her sister was houseproud to a fault, usually. And she knew that in the past her children were well turned out, thanks to Henry's good job as a printer. It wouldn't have made any difference what she thought of Eric. She would have still seen to it that he was properly dressed.

Her sister sat disconsolately at the wooden table that was pushed against one wall. Doris was shocked to see her puffing hard on a cigarette. There was an overflowing ashtray in front of her.

"'Ello, our Ivy," she said disapprovingly. "When did you take up smoking?"

Ivy started.

"Oh, it's you, Doris!"

She drew up a chair and sat down heavily.

Grimly, she said, "Well you 'ad better tell all."

Ivy relayed to her all that had happened, including Henry walking out and leaving her and the boys in the lurch.

Doris vowed to stay and help her to get the place cleaned up. In return she told Ivy all that had occurred whilst she had been gone. She made a promise to her sister that, after the funeral, she would find Henry, even if she had to go to his work. She, Doris would sort him out. She would have a talk with him.

A week later the front door opened and Henry walked in.

Ivy sat in her usual place, at the table in the scullery.

Henry sought her out.

Before she could utter a word, he held his hand up.

"Keep your 'air on," he warned. "I'm not stoppin', I'm just 'ere to collect a few things."

Huffily, Ivy said.

"Suit yourself. You must like slummin' it amongst all the rubbish."

Henry demanded tetchily.

"What do you mean by that. 'Ow do you know I ain't found me and Sybil a nice little place?"

Ivy tossed her head in the air.

"Good places cost money. You 'ave never been good at 'anging onto it. Which reminds me."

Henry snapped.

"What! What do you want, now?"

Ivy gave him a sickly grin.

"Your kids won't keep themselves. Nor will the rent pay itself. And I need money for the gas. You haven't forgotten have you that you will still 'ave to keep us as well as keepin' 'er?"

Henry wagged his head from side to side sadly.

"Never thought I'd live to see the day."

Self consciously Ivy mumbled, "What now?! Aren't I supposed to say anything about anything, then?"

Henry pursed his lips thoughtfully.

"Didn't think *you'd* get nasty, though."

The tears that had been threatening to fall since Henry's arrival overflowed and coursed down Ivy's cheeks.

"That's not fair," she sobbed. "Me an' the kids 'ave got to eat."

Henry grabbed Ivy's hands impulsively and squeezed them hard.

"Look," he said pensively. "I never meant to hurt you, Ivy. It just 'appened. I'd give *anything* to have spared you the sight of me and 'er together."

Hope suddenly soared in Ivy's battered heart.

Was that the smallest of chinks that had appeared in Henry's armour?

Losing all control and throwing caution to the wind, she begged him.

"Stay! Please don't go."

He withdrew his hands sharply.

"I never said nuffin about that."

Just then, a white faced George stalked into the kitchen. Ged and baby Eric followed.

"'Ello boys," began an unsure Henry.

George refused to acknowledge him. Plainly, he saw the pain in his father's eyes. But he didn't care. In horror, he witnessed Ged whisper a greeting. He vowed to get him when they were alone.

Eric toddled over to Henry. He stepped aside thrusting the baby away from him. Ged just caught the little boy before he fell.

Pleadingly, Henry turned to George.

"Won't you talk to me son? I'm still your Dad."

George turned away.

Henry burst out angrily.

"It isn't fair. It's not all me you know. She has been up to 'er tricks as well."

A shocked Ivy countered.

"What are you saying, 'Enry?"

He pointed an accusing finger at Eric.

"Well I know for a fact that little bastard isn't mine."

Ivy staggered to her feet.

"You're off your trolley, you are."

He sneered at her.

"Oh yeah! You've been carrying on with that fair-haired copper. The one who behaves like a smart Alec. I've been told he used to come here, when I was at work."

She choked.

"You're bloody jokin'. What, Jim? He just used to call in with messages from my mother. It was because you wouldn't allow her in the house. She was frightened to come even in the daytime. All I did was to make him a cup of tea, now and then."

Henry pointed out peevishly, "Well it's more than you do for me."

She raised a shoulder in derision.

"An' why should I. Why should I wait on an' 'usband that doesn't want to be one anymore?"

Henry smirked.

"I will say that for you. You do make a good cup of tea. There ain't no-one who can make it better."

Ivy conceded.

"I will make you a cup of tea. But we have to talk seriously. We can't go on like this. Have you seen what its doing to the boys?"

A sober Henry stared after the disappearing backs of his sons. He was visibly upset at the effect on George. Since he was a small baby they had enjoyed a good rapport. He nodded curtly and sat down in his usual place at the table without thinking.

"Alright, then. I agree."

Henry and Ivy sat and supped tea in a charged silence.

She said softly.

"Well what are we going to do?"

"Search me."

Ivy prodded away.

"We can't just leave things up in the air can we? We have to sort something out."

Henry stared at his outstretched fingers.

"I know. It's Sybil. She'll be 'urt. I don't think I can bear to do that."

Hope soared again in Ivy's heart. She thought for the first time that she may just have a slim chance of winning this battle.

Knowingly, she pressed home a point.

"The boys 'ave been right upset. I can't believe the way George 'as been."

Henry held up a hand.

"I get the point."

"What are you saying' 'Enry?"

He stared at her stonily.

"Alright. I will come back to you."

Ivy smiled for the first time since they had returned to London.

Then she frowned.

"Just a minute."

"Yeah, what?"

"I just 'ope you are gonna see sense an' stop seein' that Sybil. I wouldn't feel right if you carried on with 'er."

"Is that a fact? Since when did you lay down the law to me?"

"I can talk to George for you."

"Alright. An' while we're on about conditions. I 'ave a few of my own I'd like to air."

A worried Ivy asked.

"Oh and what are they?"

Carefully, Henry placed his empty cup on the saucer. He wagged a forefinger at Ivy.

"I'm being serious 'ere."

She nodded quickly in agreement, whilst fear lurked in her eyes.

He doodled on the tabletop, before speaking.

"I'll only come back if you get rid of the little brat."

Chapter Fourteen: Sheepleas

Ivy had to face up to her dilemma. She had a choice to make. Did she lose the husband she still loved in spite of everything? He was the father of her children and the breadwinner of the family. Or did she choose a child she doesn't really feel any affinity for? And if she chose that child, what will they live on? She had a real fear of losing all that she had.

And of course things were changing, too. It *was* the custom for women to give up work as soon as they married. Then it was thought that looking after a house was a full time job. Lots of single women had joined the forces and lots more had started working in armaments factories or joining the Land Army at the outbreak of war. It was now 1942 and there didn't seem to be any foreseeable end to it. It dragged on and on. Married women all over the country were taking up jobs, too. There was no option. The Government was strict on this issue. Everyone must do their bit. Only the women with young under school age children and the very old were exonerated. This was causing Ivy a lot of frustration, too. She was keen to join them. But she couldn't because of Eric.

Henry had kept to his word. He had refused to come home until Eric was gone.

He had told her that he had finished with Sybil. She was supposed to have left the printers they both worked for and gone into the MOD deep in the countryside. Henry was living in one room. He came to visit Ivy and the boys every weekend. He refused to acknowledge Eric's very existence, leaving the room where the toddler was, causing the baby bewilderment and shock.

Ivy was excited. She had secured a job as a fitter's mate working on Victoria Station. It seemed that her mind was made up.

However, getting rid of a child was a tall order. All Ivy and her sister could conjure up was a temporary solution. It would placate Henry so he would come back home. It was the first step. She would take everything else as it came.

With determination and ready excuses she set out with Eric. She headed for the evacuation office which is housed in a tall grey building, next to the Town Hall.

Ged had pleaded to be able to go with her. She refused. Taking two school age boys would be asking for trouble. She didn't want any complications or queries as to why they weren't being evacuated as well.

Ivy pushed open a glass door and entered a room with a row of desks. Men in suits and women in tweed skirts sat behind them. Nervously, Ivy humped the baby in her arms whilst she dithered about not knowing which desk to go to. She tried to weigh up who would be the most sympathetic to her cause. Before she could decide, a stern looking grey-haired lady at the nearest desk to the door looked over her horn rimmed spectacles at her.

She waved an arm.

"Please take a seat."

Gladly Ivy slid down onto a chair. Eric slithered from her grasp. He trotted happily around the room, touching everything he could reach. It was especially exciting as he wasn't being told off as usual. He grabbed a coloured leaflet in his tiny fist and proceeded to screw it up, throw it on the floor and stamp on it with great glee.

Unhappy Ivy had more important things to think about than rebuking her son in her usual strict fashion.

The woman behind the desk watched Eric's antics with disapproval.

Coldly, she turned her attention to Ivy.

"What can I do for you?"

"Er," began Ivy with embarrassment. "I wonder if we could 'ave a word."

"I'm listening," continued the lady. "That's what I am here for."

She waited politely.

Ivy stared at the nameplate at the edge of the desk. It read 'Miss Almond'.

She swallowed and collected herself.

"I'd like to 'ave Eric 'ere evacuated."

She nodded her head with satisfaction. There. It was out. It wasn't so hard.

Miss Almond stared at her.

"I see," she said. "I will need some details."

Ivy stared at her blankly.

"Details," she mumbled in fear.

Miss Almond held a fountain pen above a pad.

She prompted.

"How old is he?"

Ivy cast her eyes downwards and muttered.

"Fifteen months old."

Miss Almond doodled on the pad in front of her.

"I see. What are you asking? Do you want him to be sent away alone."

Ivy mumbled somewhat incoherently.

"Yes. Yes. I wanted him to be safe from the bombs. I wanted him away until the war is over."

Miss Almond stared at her gravely.

"Children of his age are usually accompanied by their mothers. It is rare for a child with two parents to be evacuated alone."

Ashamedly Ivy bleated.

"I can't go. I've got two other boys an' a husband to see to. An' I've just got meself a job, doing war work."

Miss Almond leaned forward.

"What about the two boys? If you all went you could be together."

Ivy's agitation was beginning to show.

"Leave the boys out of this," she cried. "They've been away twice now. They won't go again."

Miss Almond held up a hand.

"Alright. Alright. Please calm down. And let's see what we can work out."

After what seemed like hours to Ivy it was decided that baby Eric was to go to a little place near Guildford, called Tilford.

There was a boarding school here which had been adapted to take all ages of children, with a nursery section for the very young. It was the property of Surrey County Council and in peacetime was used for problem children. Now, in wartime it was being used, with Surrey's consent, by London County Council to evacuate their needy children.

Ivy had to accept that she was responsible for seeing that Eric got to the boarding school. She would have to take him herself by train. Miss Almond and the other people in the evacuation office have assured her that there was no other transport available. And there was no person free. If she wanted him boarded she must make the effort to see he got there. And it was her responsibility to see him settled in. She realised that this was her punishment for abandoning her son. Her life was gathering speed for disaster. Somehow she had to stop it. She felt that this was the only way to shock all their lives back to some normality.

It was going to happen within a week. She had decided that she would take the boys with her. They would all have a ride out to Guildford.

Ivy sat quietly with her thoughts. The train jerked to a halt once again. Everyone on it wondered what was wrong. It was the umpteenth time it had stopped that day. Ivy told herself that if it got bombed and she got killed that it would be no more than she deserved. She could no longer help herself. All that mattered to her was getting her husband back. It was something to look forward to when they eventually returned home. She would go around to his digs and tell him that Eric had gone. And then he would come home. In the meantime she had to face what was in front of her. She and only she were to blame for sending away her baby boy.

George and Ged did their best to keep little Eric entertained and out of their Mum's hair. They knew she was having a bad time.

The train pulled into Guildford station, two hours late.

The weary family got off the train, laden with bags containing Eric's clothes.

George grabbed Eric's reins and held him fast. He held a brown paper carrier bag in the other hand. He made sure Ged had one too. Only Ivy was free of any baggage except a large handbag she took everywhere.

Ivy passed the back of her hand across her forehead.

"We've got to get a bus now," she said.

"Where from?" asked Ged worriedly. "It just looks like country."

Ivy rummaged in her bag.

"It's alright. I've got instructions here."

She produced a sheet of paper on which there was copious writing.

"Come on, this way," she said.

Several hours later, they all stood on a country track which wound into the distance. The bus conductor had insisted that this was the right direction.

Ivy stared down its length dubiously.

Large overhanging trees on either side of the lane stretched their branches forward until they met in the middle and grew together. Tangled bushes and brambles scrambled along either side of a muddy track from which brown clumps of grass were struggling to survive.

Ivy stared at it in dismay.

"Surely we 'aven't got to walk in that, 'ave we?" she asked.

"Look," said Ged, "there's a sign over there under the brambles."

George, still hanging onto Eric, went to investigate.

"Sheepleas Lane," he said.

Ivy remarked.

"Hah! It's a wonder they've left that there. Most of them are covered up in London. Suppose it doesn't matter out here in the sticks."

George asked.

"Is it right, Mum?"

"It *is*, worst luck. On my bit of paper it should be down there."

"Mum," said George seriously. " I'll have to carry Eric. It's too muddy to put him down."

"Dear oh dear! Can you manage?"

George nodded, "Well I can if he takes my bag."

"What?" Ged shouted. "I've already got one. It's not fair."

"Please," pleaded Ivy.

Sulkily, he took it.

They trudged through the mud the best way they could. They were ill equipped both for the weather and the country. It was still January. Ivy had her best coat on which was thin and she wore her court shoes which were covered in mud now. The two boys only wore plimsolls and faded mackintoshes which were meant to keep out the rain. They were not thick enough to keep in the warmth.

Eventually, the miserable trio came to large gates across what appeared to be an open field. A wooden notice told them that they had come to Sheepleas Boarding School.

Ivy looked in horror.

All she could see in the distance were wooden huts, but that was at the end of a long muddy path.

"In God's name, what is this place?" she moaned.

"We had better go in hadn't we," said Ged.

"Let's do something, quick," retorted George. "Me arms are breaking."

He hoisted the baby higher up his body, settling him on one hip as he had seen his mother do many times. They made their way down another muddy path. Behind the huts a large house had appeared.

"Oh this is more like it," breathed Ivy.

Together they went up a wide staircase. Ivy rang the bell.

A young woman appeared almost instantly.

"Hello, there," she said.

Ivy apologetically explained the situation to her.

She smiled knowingly.

"We have a few young children here. So Eric will have company. If you come inside and wait in the warm I will fetch Miss Coates, the headmistress."

Thankfully they crowded into a large foyer. George was at last able to put Eric down.

The young woman disappeared down a corridor, turned the bend and was soon out of sight. After what seemed an age a tall fair-haired lady approached them.

She went over to Ivy and introduced herself.

"I am Miss Coates. I believe we are expecting you."

Ivy warmed to her kind tones.

Miss Coates gathered Eric into her arms. He cried and fought to get down. Her mouth curved into a slight smile.

"He'll be alright. Just give him a little time."

In her firm grip, he soon relaxed. She nodded.

"I said he'd be fine."

She moved off down the corridor and motioned to them all to follow her. They entered a light room with six cots in. Another young woman was standing by an empty cot.

Miss Coates smiled sunnily.

"This is to be Eric's."

She placed him in it. His face crumpled. He began to cry again.

The young woman stepped forward and took the clothes. Miss Coates indicated that they should leave the room. She strode easily down the corridor. They followed her. Eric's yells echoed loudly after them. Ged covered his face with his hands. George wiped away a sudden tear. Ivy stared stonily ahead.

Henry returned home, on his own terms.

However, in February, he was horrified to find he was being called up. This was despite having served his country in the Home Guard, He was to serve in The Royal Pioneer Corps and would be immediately sent away to Wales to train in telecommunications. He would eventually be sent to Normandy, where he would remain for the duration of the war.

Ged and George did their level best for their brother's welfare. They continually asked their mother why they couldn't have Eric home again, now. They were very well aware that their father was the fly in the ointment.

Ivy used two arguments against the idea.

Number one was that she was afraid that Henry would get leave from Wales. According to his letters he was expecting a weekend pass any day now.

Number two was that she wouldn't be able to continue with her job, if she had Eric to look after. She told them that now that their father was in the Army they needed every penny they could get as all they were living on was his much reduced wages. She also pointed out that she had to wait for him to send them every week. With the war, the post was patchy if it arrived at all.

When all other avenues failed the two boys had asked if they could go back to Sheepleas to see him. The nine and eleven year old boys had been standing there when Miss Coates had told Ivy that she could visit once a month. Again Ivy pleaded tiredness, lack of money and any other excuse she could think up on the spur of the moment to evade facing the issue of seeing her third son.

Soon, Eric even faded from George and Ged's memory.

Chapter Fifteen: A New Beginning?

Eric remained in the big house until he was three.

The regime here was fairly easy going whilst observing the disciplines of the day. All the children in Sheepleas House were babies. All of them with the exception of Eric were orphans of the war. They had all lost their mothers in bombing raids. Their fathers were away fighting. Some of these would never return leaving the children true orphans. They would eventually end up in residential children's homes of whichever borough they belonged to when the war ended. Eric was a special case. It was most unusual for a mother to leave a child under five. Most of the small staff assumed that his mother would miss him and come to collect him. They expected her any day. It was a great surprise to them that she didn't even come to visit him, or write him letters or send him birthday cards. It was as if he had completely faded from her memory and no longer existed.

Whilst on the surface he sported an easygoing personality which won him favours with all the other boys and girls, underneath there was a deep unhappiness and longing, which was certainly beyond *his* understanding. This wasn't unusual under the circumstances. All the children were afflicted because they had known little except pain. It should have been different for Eric. But it wasn't. There was a shadow at the back of his eyes which no pampering could erase.

And it wasn't without trying. Because of his good looks, he quickly became a favourite of the young women helpers who came in from the village. They vied with each other to look after him. It wasn't difficult to spoil him. It pleased them to dress him nicely when it was his turn to have his photograph taken. They were quite sure his mother would want a copy of it. In due course one would be sent to her. For some very odd reason and despite all that occurred in the future, she would keep this photo amongst her belongings. For this and his original birth certificate were found in her effects after her death. It was the only photo of his baby days. There *was* only one other photo of Eric as a child in existence and it *wasn't* complimentary. He wasn't aware of any of this of course at the time. The absence of his family in his life meant little to him. He was too young to remember their existence. And at the moment he had had plenty of willing substitutes to take their place and shower him with love.

Then in October, 1943 it all changed.

He was no longer the pampered darling of the nursery, which had been added to Sheepleas because of the need of the many orphaned babies that required placing away from the war. His belongings were gathered and placed in a cardboard box with his name on it. And he was taken to meet the stern new head, Miss Carstairs, of Sheepleas Boarding School proper. She looked at him over her pince-nez and read him the riot act about good behaviour.

He was amazed to find he would be sleeping in a wooden hut with a mixture of other boys. Some were *much* bigger. This frightened him at first. Until he realised he could use his natural charm to make his mark.

It was the usual practice for an older boy to sleep in the small room at the end of each hut. These were boys who had left the boarding school at the age of fourteen to seek work. Welfare Officers often played a hand in securing the boys such employment. They were known as shepherds. It was their job to look after all the younger boys. Of course such a position often went to their heads. It was irresistible to them to wield their influence, especially out of sight of a master or mistress.

In Eric's hut there was a boy called Robert Darcy. Woe betide anyone who talked after they should have been asleep. He would patrol the centre of the room swishing a bamboo cane back and forth. Every now and then he would bring it down on a bed with a thump. If the poor unsuspecting boy in the bed *was* asleep, he woke up very suddenly wondering where he was or what he had done wrong.

There were of course, girls, too. But they had their own huts. And they had their own older girls exerting their power on them. Sometimes, there were clashes between the huts. And sometimes, there were romances.

Many times a younger boy or girl stumbled on two such beings entwined together outside the shower block, as if their life depended on it. Of course it was highly frowned on by the staff that slept in the big house. Any shepherd or shepherdess that stepped out of line was sent away. Very often the problem was much worse than that. These girls had grown up deprived of one of the essential substances they needed, love. They and the shepherds were considered to be adult, taking part in an adult world. But they were all every bit as mixed up as their charges.

And it was worse than that.

Canadian soldiers were stationed all over Surrey. They had been there since early on in the war. The soldiers didn't take this lying down. They were far from home in the beauteous green countryside. It could have been worse. There were lots of much more horrible places to be stationed, such as some of the awful places our own countrymen were sent to, all across Europe, Africa and later on in the Far East. But still they moaned. They hated the phoney war which they thought brought them all here unnecessarily for it seemed that they weren't needed after all. They also hated the weather and the food. But one thing they did not hate was the compliant girls. The ones from Sheepleas were especially rapt. They were searching for something and someone. The soldiers weren't to know how young and vulnerable they were. Of course any contact with the soldiers in their smart uniforms was forbidden. That didn't make any difference. The girls who had set their sights on a particular young soldier became adept at inventing excuses for taking trips into the village.

The soldier's superior officers knew full well how bored their troops were. Often dances were arranged in village halls. The shepherdesses could only rant and rave and fume that they couldn't go, too. But the inevitable always happened. A girl would find a way of slipping out. Later she would pay the price when she would realise that the worst had happened. She would then be sent away to a mother and baby home. There would always be others willing to take her place.

Eric settled into the ways of Sheepleas. The next two years passed quickly. Soon it was May 1945. At long last the war was over.

And the baby had become a little boy. He was not a large child for four and a half. This was due partly to a war time diet and partly to inherited genes. The war wasn't over for him. The routine he was used to would continue.

Miss Soames flapped her arms in frustration.

"Eric, come along don't dawdle. What are you doing?"

The little boy smiled up at his favourite teacher from his crouched position on the floor of Hut 7.

"Just doing me sandals up, Miss."

She watched the little boy struggle to thread the brown leather straps through the silver buckles.

There was a look of utter determination in his eyes.

Gently, she said.

"Here let me do it this time."

He shook his head obstinately.

"I can do it," he insisted. Triumphantly, he glanced up at her as he finished the task.

She shook her head in mild despair.

"Everyone's waiting Eric. Don't you want to go to see the soldiers and go to the party afterwards?"

He nodded quickly. He had been waiting for nothing else. Most of his spare time was spent hanging around down by the front gate in the hope of the Canadian soldiers passing, especially if they were exercising in their jeeps and tanks. Mostly it was a vain hope. Now they were all coming to Tilford.

There was going to be a special celebration to mark the end of the war. It was happening all over the country. Every street everywhere would have a party. Here it would be in Tilford, on the perfectly triangular village green, which was well shaded by a huge oak tree. Some of the old locals were dubious. How would it fare with all manner of soldiers and children tramping all over it, never mind their adult minders? It was the place where in better times cricket was played all summer long. It was tended lovingly by old Tom Barnes. But, they were shouted down by the women of the village as being spoilsports. So the show was going on. And it was being staged by the Canadians. Soon they would be leaving for home. This was their last gesture for the people that had put up with them for the last six years. They didn't realise how much their presence would be missed.

The crowd of boys and girls gathered at the gate. Eric hurried to join them.

The adult at the front clapped her hands authoritatively. The children instantly formed a long line, two abreast. Eric linked hands with William next to him who was around the same age.

The long crocodile of children began the walk to the village.

As they approached Tilford they saw with amazement the tanks trundling around and around the road. There were stalls set up on the green, with games that could be played for prizes. One was throwing the wellington. Another was guessing the number of pennies in a jar. There were more. And over by the river there was a rope swing hanging from the oak tree. And there was a large marquee with lots of small tables and chairs. It was in here where the party would be held.

Eric and the other children returned to Sheepleas clutching a paper bag with gifts in it.

Eric had a scant memory of this day, especially the part where he is put on a tank. It would be many years later before he could place this memory where it belonged.

July 1946

Miss Carstairs sat at her desk lost in thought. The door opened and Eric walked in. She frowned slightly for it was the custom for anyone to knock before they entered her room. However, she decided to overlook it on this occasion.

She stared at the grave little face in front of her and a rush of pity filled her heart. It was hard to know where to begin.

She smiled a watery smile and patted a small chair beside her.

"Sit here, Eric if you will."

He stared at her in surprise. Everyone found her frightening. She could shout loudly. And he knew only too well that she had a cane. He didn't know what to make of this person who was trying her best to be nice. It wasn't something he was used to. Gingerly he sat on the seat right next to her. She bent over him so he could almost smell her breath.

She began, "I expect you know that William is leaving soon."

The little boy nodded.

She continued, "And lots of other children?"

He nodded again.

She went on.

"Sheepleas is closing down."

He bit his lip. There was talk of nothing else. He was too little to understand it all. No one had said anything to him however. He had wondered why?

Miss Carstairs sighed.

"These huts need razing to the ground. They are past their best."

The little boy looked at her blankly.

She picked up his hand. He flinched slightly and tried to withdraw it. Her grip tightened.

"Now, now," she said gently. "There is nothing to worry about. You and I just need to have a talk."

He nodded his head slightly.

She opened her mouth to speak, staring kindly down at him over her pince nez.

"I know this is hard for you. I know you are only five and a half, but I hope that as you are a bright little boy that you will understand."

He stared at her gravely.

"You are going to move. Everyone has to. Even me. But it is different for you. Unlike William, you have a Mummy and Daddy. And you have two big brothers and one small brother. So you are going home."

His face split into a bewildered smile.

He didn't know what any of that meant. All his memories were here. And his friends and his teachers were here, too. He had no memory of ever living anywhere else.

Miss Carstairs helped him off the chair. She gave him a little shove towards the door.

"Run along now, Eric," she said. "Go and find your friends. We'll talk again later when the arrangements have been made."

Obediently the little boy opened the door and walked dazedly into the brilliant July sunshine. He blinked hard at the brightness and walked slowly to his hut which had red robins painted on the door. He made his way to his bed. Savagely he kicked off his sandals and climbed onto it. Grabbing a battered teddy bear he hugged it to him.

His mind fought to take in all that had been said to him. He knew that in his story book the little boy had a Mummy and Daddy. But that was a story. He didn't understand about brothers, either. He supposed they were like his friends here. Miss Carstairs had told him that this place called 'home' was in London.

She had explained that it was another place like Tilford, but much bigger.

It was all too much for him. For the moment he didn't want to think of Mummy, Daddy and his brothers or this mysterious place called home. He closed his eyes, curled up into a ball and squeezed his teddy tight.

Chapter Sixteen: The Nightwatchman

Two big boys stood in the foyer in the big house. They gazed self consciously around them, remembering the last time they stood here over four years ago.

They had both grown up a lot since then. George was now nearly sixteen and Ged was fourteen. The older boy was angry and dismayed that he had been put in the position of fetching his little brother, despite having Ged along as moral support. Of course George remembered him. They both did. But he had faded from their minds because they were not allowed to talk about him at home.

And George had other interests now. He was an apprentice printer at the newspaper where his father was a foreman. He had started out as an apprentice printer, too. Upstairs, there were several pretty young girls working in the offices.

So, the last thing on George's mind was his little brother.

He had tried to protest about being lumbered to collect him, but he was silenced by his father's wrath. It had been difficult enough getting used to him being there after a four year absence. They had both forgotten what an authoritative figure he was. So it was useless to argue.

Eric walked beside Miss Soames, trying hard to push the bewildered thoughts in his tangled mind away. They climbed the steps together. She smiled encouragingly down at him and opened the door.

He saw two men standing there looking at him.

Through a mist he heard Miss Soames say.

"This is your brother, George and your brother Gerald."

The smaller one of the two piped up.

"They call me Ged, Miss."

He looked at them in surprise. He had been told they were coming to collect him.

But he thought they would be boys.

George crouched down to Eric's level and held out his hand.

"Hallo Eric," he said.

Ged followed suit.

The little boy held back. He looked to Miss Soames for direction.

She smiled.

"Go on," she said. "It is alright."

He didn't see the tears gathering in her eyes.

Eric looked into the eyes of his brothers. An inkling of a smile broke across his face. George and Ged grinned in return. Excitedly, he took their proffered hands and rung them up and down.

Miss Carstairs appeared from nowhere.

She made signs to Miss Soames that she expected her to leave the foyer. Sadly, she whispered goodbye to her little charge. She hurried off down the corridor wiping her eyes.

Miss Carstairs stepped forward.

"Ah there you are boys. Getting acquainted?"

The big boys nodded.

She walked to the big door. She swung it open to reveal a cloudless blue sky.

"Well you have a nice day for it."

The two big boys gathered themselves for they realised that this was a dismissal.

"Come on, Eric," said George. "Let's go home."

Together they travelled from Tilford back to Southwark.

The little boy peeped out of the window. All he had been used to had disappeared. In its place was a bewilderment of buildings all squashed together. He wondered at all that he saw, wrinkling his nose at the unfamiliar smells. He stared wide eyed at the big trams and the red buses winding their way along tarmacked roads.

At last they pulled into Elephant and Castle station.

Eric wrinkled his nose in disgust at the piles of rubbish in the crowded streets.

He had been told that it was only a short walk to their house which was now in Crampton Street. The shadows were lengthening as the day drew towards evening.

Soon he would be meeting his mother, whom he had no memory of and hadn't seen since he was a baby. He would also be meeting his little brother, Malcolm, who was two years old and apparently the apple of his mother's eye. And he would be meeting his father.

Poor innocent Eric had no idea what world he was walking into. Nothing could have prepared him for what was to come.

All three of them reached a green painted door. George put his hand through the letter box and fished around. He withdrew a large key attached to a length of string. Ged drew in a deep breath and cast apprehensive looks at his little brother. It was now or never. He exhaled as George fitted the key in the lock. The door opened and they walked in.

George led the way down a short corridor into the scullery.

He noticed Henry was in the living room.

Ged and Eric followed him.

A small woman stood by the large iron gas cooker, stirring something in a pot. A toddler sat on the floor at her feet playing with various toy cars.

She ignored Eric and addressed George.

"You're here at last then."

He sighed.

"Yes. It took ages."

"Yeah," agreed Ged. "Changing 'ere and changing there."

She smiled indulgently and asked him.

"What's that you've got there, son?"

Ged said matter of factly.

"It's Eric's clothes of course, Mum."

"Oh," she said turning back to her pot. "At least we won't have to fork out for *them*."

George shrugged his shoulders and left the room.

Ged placed the paper bag on a table covered with oilcloth.

Then he, too, turned on his heel and disappeared into the corridor.

Eric gazed after them both in panic. He stood where he had been left, not knowing what to do or what to say to anyone.

Still, this woman who was supposed to be his mother, too, didn't speak to him.

He had been told her actual name was Ivy. This was confusing. If he did speak to her what did he call her?

The toddler got up and held out a car for his inspection.

She spoke to him instead.

"Leave him alone Malcolm. You come over 'ere with me."

Eric felt tears prick at his eyelids. It was all too much. He rubbed his eye with a knuckle. A rush of homesickness and longing for green fields, Miss Soames and his friend William flooded through him.

A man appeared in the doorway. Without being told he realised that this was his father. According to George and Ged, *his* name was Henry.

He stood and stared before he addressed the frightened little boy in harsh tones.

"Oh you're 'ere are you?"

Eric nodded miserably.

Only then did Ivy turn her head to scrutinize the new arrival.

She spoke to Henry.

"Best if he 'as an early night, don't you think?"

Henry nodded.

"I'll get Ged to see to it. I think George has gone out."

"What?" exploded Ivy. "He's gone out without his dinner."

"Never mind, I'll eat 'is share," grinned Henry.

He left the scullery and yelled from the bottom of the stairs.

"Ged. Get down here, now."

There was a loud thumping noise followed by the physical presence of Ged.

He had taken the stairs two at a time. Nobody disobeyed their father. His word was law.

"Ye.s..s Dad?" he inquired tremulously.

Henry pushed Eric forward.

"'Ere do yer Mum a favour and put 'im to bed."

Ged inquired.

"Where. In the little room?"

Impatiently Henry waved an arm.

"Of course, in the little room?"

Ged looked puzzled.

"I thought Malcolm was having that bed when he's bigger."

A look shot between Ivy and Henry.

She said bitterly.

"Well he can't now can 'e."

Ged tittered nervously.

Swiftly, he took Eric's hand and led him down the corridor. Together they went up the stairs to a tiny room with one small window. It was bare except for a narrow bed. There was just enough space to stand beside it. Dust motes danced in the setting sun that streamed through the open window. Noises from the street filled the air. With fumbling fingers the little boy undressed down to his pants and vest. Ged shot him an apologetic look as he helped him climb into the hard bed. He melted away leaving Eric alone. Stiffly he lay still, listening to the sounds of eating coming from below. His stomach growled from hunger. He screwed his eyes tightly shut and prayed for sleep to come.

Maybe tomorrow would be a better day.

But it wasn't.

It was worse. And it deteriorated every day after that.

It became plain that his parents didn't like him. And didn't want him. Whilst it was obvious that at least his mother loved Malcolm, George and Ged fiercely. She made it plain that she had no interest in Eric. He was blamed for literally everything. He had many good hidings for very little. It wasn't unusual for him to bear the scars for many weeks. When mealtimes came around she fed him begrudgingly. She complained bitterly to everyone else without speaking directly to him that *now* she had another mouth to feed and clothe.

Eric's only solace was his relationship with his little brother.
He didn't see much of him during the week because he was in full time nursery. At weekends he would take Malcolm in his pushchair to explore all around the Walworth Road. George would occasionally give Eric a few coppers when he got paid his apprentice's wages. They would make for the corner shop to buy broken biscuits.
He was drawn to the animals that lived in the garden. He was fascinated to find chickens running about freely in the small back yard. There were also big furry rabbits in cages. And a family dog. She was a mongrel of uncertain lineage with a very friendly disposition.
They were the only comfort he had.
That and school.

In later years Eric would not be able to recall the fact that his own family had owned animals, especially a dog. It is thought that he was so traumatised by his treatment that his mind had blotted out all his memories with the exception of a few slivers. In fact it would be his older brothers who would later fill in the gaps.

He looked forward to going to school. He was a bright little boy who loved learning. He was especially good at numbers. And his teacher was kind to him. She knew something was wrong. It was obvious this boy was desperately unhappy. His clothing had at first appeared to be of a good quality. But that had changed. They had deteriorated becoming ragged and threadbare, exposing areas of flesh that were obviously bruised. And his hair was long and unkempt.
Some of the mothers who met their charges gossiped gladly. Ivy had a reputation for being a bit of a tartar. Everyone locally was unhappy about the obvious mistreatment of Eric. They knew it was going on. It was said that he was often locked in the cellar without food. No one ever came to meet him, despite his tender years. The teacher took her fears to the headmaster. He dismissed them telling her that they couldn't interfere, for they didn't have any proof. It was his belief that this boy disliked school which was why he appeared unhappy. She tried to tell him otherwise. Her hands were tied. There was nothing she could do to help him. It was with a heavy heart that she watched him walk slowly across the playground, under the arch which said INFANTS and into the street beyond. Then, London would swallow him up. She would shrug her shoulders and go home.

Things were to get worse for Eric when his mother decided that it was time for her to go back to work again. She had no worries about

Malcolm. He was in nursery. There was no concern for Eric. Even Ged had begun to work, now.

After school, the little boy banged fruitlessly on the door. He tried hard to find the key hanging on a piece of string. It was no longer there. Eventually he gave up. There was no-one home. Tearfully he ran across the road to the coal yard. It was winter by now and getting dark early. He took refuge in the night watchman's hut. It was early and the man didn't start work until six. He was kindly and took pity on the distressed boy. When the local bobby did his rounds he told Eric to hide at the back of the hut. When he had gone they sat before a blazing hot brazier warming their hands. They sipped tea from mugs and chewed on a thick cheese sandwich. He stayed with the night watchman until he began to fall asleep. Then the kind-hearted man sent him home. This became a regular occurrence, going on for over a year. So did the good hiding he received from his father when he got home. The little boy went to bed covered in welts from his belt. Nothing would stop him from going to see his friend. He was one of the few that showed him any kindness.

Then one night it changed. The hut was empty. There was no sign of his friend. Unbeknown to Eric he had been taken ill and suffered a massive heart attack. He had died instantly.

Soon, a new man would take his place. He was nothing like Eric's friend. He handed the boy over to the bobby on the beat straight away. He took him to Carter Street police station. There he would have to remain there until he was collected.

Eric has a vivid memory of being with the night watchman and of holding someone's hand although he does not know whose it is. It must be assumed that it was George's for he was always sent to collect him. Henry and Ivy would never go themselves.

Chapter Seventeen: Meeting Peggy

Eric was now seven.

Life had deteriorated further. Now he could no longer go to the coal yard. The last time he was there he was chased away. He wondered where he could go today.

Every day he would dawdle slowly from his school in Iliffe Street, as if he was reluctant to leave it. Always he would go home first. It was just a few steps around the corner. He would live in hope that this day it would be different. She would be there. Today she would smile at *him* not Malcolm. Maybe she would throw her arms around him and tell him she loved *him*. He hoped that she wouldn't slap him around the head and bare legs again with a wet dishcloth. That hurt. He could still feel the sting. Afterwards there would be red marks all over his calves. He would trace them with a fascinated finger. But what he hated most of all was being ignored. Tears pricked at his eyes. It was as if he wasn't there. He had tried everything to get her attention. Most of them were naughty. Anger flared up inside him. He didn't care. All he wanted was to be treated like the others. She couldn't do enough for all of them. And she waited hand and foot on *him,* his father. Anger flared inside him again. He hated him. And his fists which pounded his thin body all over. He never hit him on his head, though, like she did. But he would tell him every time that they didn't want him, there. That they were going to get rid of him and have him 'put away' again. He didn't know what that meant, just that it sounded horrible. So it was something he feared.

He banged on the door. The knock echoed through the terraced house. A clock chimed loudly inside. The lace curtain twitched next door. A pitying face stared back at him. The window slid up. The lady next door poked her head out.

"She's not 'ere, luvvy. She's at work that's where she is. Don't you worry your 'ead. Something going to be done. Mark my words."

The window slid shut.

Furiously he banged again. He kicked the door hard with his right foot. Still there was no answer. Hot scalding tears poured down his cheeks as he ran away in the direction of Walworth Road.

He was hungry. Last night he had been sent to bed without any tea. George had scoured the streets looking for him, praying that he could find him before their father got home. But he didn't. So he had beaten him as usual. Nowadays the little boy didn't react. He had become used to it. Sucking in his breath he willed himself not to cry. This made his father mad. Next time he would hit him harder.

Breakfast was non-existent because there was no bread left for him. She had hurried him out of the door without even a drink of water. He saw her give the last piece of bread to four year old Malcolm, spread liberally with margarine and jam. And she had made him tea with the last of the milk. It was often like that. If there was none left, Eric went without.

Whenever he had a chance he got a drink of water from the fountain in the playground. The last time seemed ages ago.

His pockets were empty. He had no money. Still it wouldn't do any harm to look would it? He pushed open the door of the grocer's shop he was walking past.

The bell on the door tinkled tinnily. There were several women at the counter. They were gossiping loudly and paying for the goods they had selected. The shopkeeper chatted whilst keeping one eye on Eric. This shop had been his for a long time and he had seen it all. By now he had developed a nose for potential shoplifters.

Eric's heart thudded loudly in his chest as he contemplated what he was about to do.

The shopkeeper's voice boomed out.

"What do you want boy?"

Eric licked his lips, asking lamely.

"Er 'ave you got any broken biscuits?"

He shook his head.

"No son," he said.

Defeated, Eric slunk back to the street, his stomach grumbling and his task uncompleted. It was his shame that he couldn't even lift a packet of biscuits.

He wandered the streets aimlessly until it grew dark. The longer he wandered the more scared he became of going home.

This was how it was every school day.

In desperation, he headed for the new three storey block of flats which were just opposite his house. It was one of the places where all the children played, much to the annoyance of the people living there. There was a very convenient space under the stairs. The children used to bring cardboard and old curtains to make a den with. When the boys played there it was their headquarters to fight the Germans with. The girls used it as their house.

Even today the space under the concrete stairs was occupied.

A young woman stood there in the shadows.

She stepped forward angrily, tossing her rippling hair over her shoulders.

"What do you want?" she demanded.

Eric hung his head and mumbled.

"Nuffin."

Her chest rose and fell rapidly, her low cut blouse revealing soft, swelling breasts.

"Well that's alright then."

She patted her hair and ran her hands over her low cut blouse, making sure it was tucked well into the tight, black skirt; she was wearing, which revealed every contour of her body.

"This is my patch, see."

Dejected, Eric shuffled away.

She called after him.

"Ere, it's alright. I didn't mean it. You can stay if you want to. Come back."

Wearily the little boy stumbled over to her. He couldn't help staring at her for he had never seen anyone look like her. Impulsively, she hugged him and planted a kiss on his cheek, leaving a bright red lipstick mark on his face.

She suggested in a friendly fashion.

"'Ere I bet you're 'ungry."

He nodded.

She shrugged.

"It's early yet. No tricks about. How would you like some chips?"

"Yes, miss" he whispered.

Airily, she said, "Don't they teach you kids to say please, now?"

"Sorry," he mumbled, fearful that she would withdraw her offer.

She ruffled his hair with one hand.

"You stay 'ere. Your Auntie Peggy'll sort you out. I'll be back in a trice."

Her high heels tapped loudly on the stone floor. She vanished through the glass door. Eric crouched down under the stairs.

She appeared much later arm in arm with a man and clutching a bag of chips.

Eric was fast asleep on the floor.

She laughed.

"Oh bugger," she said.

This became a regular occurrence. Eric would watch Peggy plying her craft until he fell asleep.

If he wasn't home by nine o'clock George and Ged were always sent to find him. It was Ivy and Henry's dread that the police would get to him first. They had been warned before that the Welfare would have to be involved if Eric was found in the streets again. Their eternal fear was to suffer shame and lose face.

Usually he was found by the two brothers before the police got involved.

One night that changed. The police were having a monthly purge on prostitutes and the places they frequented. The flats were checked because of the complaints that had been received from the residents. They didn't find Peggy but they did find Eric curled up on the floor. Gently, the policeman woke the boy up. He was taken to the police station again. This time a Welfare Officer from the Children's Office was called. When she arrived she spoke gently to Eric, questioning him about his home life. When she had finished she led him from the police station to her little black car. Eric would spend the rest of the night and the following weeks in a safe place.

May 21st 1948

Eric was seated on a chair. Miss Abraham, the Welfare Officer sat next to him. There were tables directly in front of them. Miss Abraham placed a stack of papers on them and spread them out in a fan. Eric swung a trembling leg to and fro. She placed comforting hands on his and smiled encouragingly at him. His leg gradually stilled.

A boyish curiosity led him to twist his head around to look behind him. There were rows and rows of chairs. Lots of people sat here. He wondered briefly who they all were. A policeman in his blue uniform looking grave sat there, too. All of them were looking at him. A cold shock ran through his body. He saw his Mum and Dad and Malcolm. His little brother sat on a seat in between them. They were all dressed in their best clothes. Henry and Ivy avoided looking at their third son. They just sat silently staring straight ahead. He willed them to look at him but they didn't. With desperation he tried to catch Malcolm's eye. He loved his little brother and missed him very much. Malcolm was sitting very still which was very unusual for him. Eric hoped that would change. But it didn't. Reluctantly he turned back to face the front.

There was a rustle of expectation as a door opened and an important looking man walked in. He bustled to a large table in front of them, drew out a chair and sat down. The man put on a pair of horn rimmed spectacles and gazed around the children's court. First of all his gaze fell on Eric. The boy sucked in his breath and trembled with fear. Miss Abraham patted his knee. She whispered, "Don't worry."

The man's gaze fell on Henry and Ivy. They both wriggled slightly in their seats under his look. Ivy looked acutely embarrassed. Henry stared stonily at the opposite wall.

The magistrate cleared his throat and asked.

"Is Doctor Amos in court?"

A man behind them stood up and agreed that he was, indeed here.

The doctor spoke at great length. Eric kept hearing his name being mentioned. He didn't understand all that was being said. Then a policeman stood up, then another lady. It went on for some time. And they were all talking about him!

The magistrate pushed his chair back. He swept out of the room clutching a sheaf of papers.

Miss Abraham whispered to Eric.

"He will be back soon. You just sit there."

She left her seat and went over to one of the ladies who had stood up and spoke.

Eric felt exposed. He could feel his father's eyes drilling into his back. His body trembled once more.

At last Miss Abraham returned to her seat. He felt safe again.

Then the magistrate returned.

He addressed the frightened little boy in a kind voice.

"Come here, Eric."

He looked worriedly at Miss Abraham. She helped him off the chair and led him over to the magistrate.

He told him, "Now we have discussed your case at great length here today. We think it will be much better for you to go and live in the country where you will have plenty to eat and lots of other children to play with. You may sit down."

Eric returned shakily to his seat.

The magistrate addressed the court matter of factly.

"I am authorizing a fit person order to be effective immediately for it is obvious Eric is in need of care and protection."

A sigh rippled around the court.

Children and Young Persons Act 1933
A court has power to commit a person brought before the court to the care of a fit person. The appropriate local authority shall for the provision of this Act relating to the making of orders committing a child or young person to the care of a fit person be deemed to be a fit person willing to undertake the care of him.

Impulsively, Miss Abraham took Eric's hand in hers. Startled, he flinched and pulled away.

"Don't you worry," she said. "It's all over now. How would you like to go for a ride in my car?"

A ghost of a smile flitted across his face and his eyes lit up.

"Yes, Miss I would. What make is it?"

She led him by the hand to the edge of the kerb, to where a small black car was parked.

"Here it is. I believe it's a Wolsley Eight. I am not much of an expert on these things. It's obvious to see you are."

He nodded happily.

"Yeah I am. I used to stand and watch them when I was...at.....home."

His voice tailed off. The light in his eyes died.

She helped him into the passenger seat. He slouched deep in its depths, until he was barely visible. Small feet clothed in battered plimsolls stuck up in the air. His hands gripped the edges of the seat tightly, showing whitened knuckles.

Sadly, she shook her head. Sometimes, she wondered if she was doing the right job? It was very difficult. She wanted to scream and shout at the people that could cause a small child such pain. Her colleagues were always telling her not to wear her heart on her sleeve. They told her that she would get used to it. She reflected as the car slid away that she hoped she never did.

As they drove from Southwark to Sidcup she noticed his interest in all the car's workings.

Gradually she managed to engage him in conversation. He told her he liked animals as well.

Soon, they had arrived outside a large red brick house. She noticed the panic on his face as the car stopped. Reluctantly, he climbed out onto an asphalt path. He slid his hand in hers and held on tightly. Miss Abraham rang the brass bell on the wall. There was a pleasant aroma of cooking wafting through the closed door.

A short lady in a flowered wrap around overall opened the door. She smiled at Miss Abrahams.

"Hallo, I'm Miss Lang, housemother of Rowan Cottage."

The young Welfare Officer propelled the little boy forward.

"This is Eric. I think you are expecting him. I am Miss Abrahams."

Miss Lang smiled down at the boy. He didn't smile back. She shrugged her shoulders regretfully.

Miss Abrahams explained, "He has had a very bad time. I am afraid it will be a long road to recovery."

Miss Lang nodded sympathetically.

She said lightly, "At least he has come at the right time. It will soon be lunchtime."

Miss Abrahams ruffled Eric's hair.

"Yes. And I am afraid I have to go now, Eric."

Panic rose in his face again.

A jet black kitten appeared in front of them.

Eric bent down to stroke him.

Miss Abrahams slipped away with moist eyes.

Diplomatically, Miss Lang slid the big glass door shut.

She spoke kindly to him.

"Did you know, Noggin is new, too."

She picked the kitten up and handed it to Eric.

He wrapped his thin arms around the kitten and buried his face deeply in its soft fur.

PART THREE: GROWING PAINS
1953-1958

Chapter Eighteen: Rowan Cottage

October 1953

My life had changed overnight. I had got up gingerly on my first day to find that for the first time in my life I was dry! And that continued forever after. That particular nightmare was over.

And at long last we were together. Me, Bernard and Bobby.

And I had a friend. Her name was Caroline. She was two years younger and also a bright girl from a large family. All of her siblings would eventually end up in Rowan.

Of course a new place meant we had to get used to a new routine. And a new set of rules.

The Hollies was a big place.

There were sixteen houses, which were called 'cottages'. Each one held twenty children. Each child was given a number as a means of identification. The cottages were staffed by single women. At that time they would have been known as spinsters and were often on the wrong side of forty. The person in charge was called a housemother. She was helped by an assistant housemother and two assistants. They all lived in.

There were four 'blocks'. These were towering four storey houses holding at least thirty five children and were staffed by a married couple with the help of various assistants, who also lived in. There was another large house which was actually called The Hollies, although no 'insider' ever knew it as that. To everyone it was simply 'the big house' or 'the office'. The Superintendent, Mr Irving, who was boss over everyone and everything, lived here with his family. There was also a laundry, a bakery, a haberdasher's, a cobbler's, a food store, a gymnasium, a swimming pool, a farm and a sickbay at one time. There was a school as well, but The Hollies had been the forerunner of changes by London County Council. The school and its playing fields were turned over to the Education Department. It had been renamed Burnt Oak. (This was part of radical thought by L.C.C. to integrate the 'insider' children into 'normal' life)

There still remained sweeping grounds of large fields and an area of woodland. The largest field was called the 880, a smaller one was known as the 440, whilst another was the 'bottom field'. There were lots of other areas of grass, with air raid shelters on them, which were reminders of the recent war. They were boarded up and strictly out of bounds, which naturally made them an inviting target for some children.

The woodland was known as Mr Irving's wood. This too was officially out of bounds but it didn't stop the boys from going in there, even if they did run the risk of getting shot. One of Mr Irving's pastimes was shooting wood pigeons.

All of this was enclosed by wall, fences and gates. It was like living on a private island.

Rowan was like all the other 'cottages', a sprawling building.

Upstairs it had four dormitories and four staff rooms, two bathrooms each with two baths in. And two separate toilets. There was a connecting door from one side of the house to the other although, technically speaking the sexes were segregated at bedtime. Another connecting point was a long veranda at the back of the house. It was possible to see into the windows of two of the staff rooms from the veranda. A fact the older boys took advantage of.

Downstairs, at the front of the house was the 'Esse' room. It was so called because it housed a large range, fuelled by anthracite, on which all the food was cooked. One wall curved into a bay with square paned windows that looked out onto the front lawn and gave a good view of 'the big house'. The room was used for other purposes as well. There was a very large square table in the middle of the room where all the food was served up. By the side of the table was a glass fronted cabinet. This stays in my memory especially because it was here all the post and the newspapers were kept. I was an avid reader. I couldn't believe it when I was actually allowed to read them all. One memory I have is reading horrific stories about Kenya. This was the time of the Mau Mau. In the corner was a bureau where all the 'paperwork' was done and more importantly all pocket money was paid out. Visitors were usually invited into here.

Through a connecting door was the dining room, which was filled with enough tables and chairs to seat everyone at one sitting. This too had a bay window.

On either side of these two rooms were identical hallways leading to front and back doors. Wide, highly polished staircases rose to the upstairs rooms from the hallways on each side of the house. My favourite hallway was by the Esse room. There was a full length mirror fixed to the wall. I often gazed in this as I was growing up. It was the only one in the house. Opposite the Esse room was the playroom. Books and toys were scattered everywhere. There was a battered wireless perched on a narrow windowsill. It was hampered by severe atmospherics, which, coupled with the loud din coming from the room anyway, made listening to it impossible. Despite that, Caroline and I tried. We never missed 'Journey into Space'. We used to sit cross legged on the table which was directly under it and put our ears right on it.

Down the passage was my most hated room. This was the scullery. All the washing up was done here. Its only saving grace was the window that looked out onto the yard.

The hallway then led to the 'bootroom'. All shoes and wellingtons, plimsolls and sandals were kept and cleaned here. Next to that was the larder, which was a large walk in cupboard lined with shelves. An alcove housed a large fridge. On the tiled floor there was a milk crate full of quart bottles of milk. It was delivered daily by milk lorry. This was by the back door which led out to the yard.

On the other side of the house, the hallway led to one front door which to my knowledge was little used. At the foot of the stairs was the door to the staff sitting room. We weren't allowed in there without permission.

Opposite that was the boiler room. A big cast iron pot bellied boiler, fed by coke, dominated the room. Anything that needed burning was thrown into it with great glee. Swimming costumes and wet towels were hung in here to dry.

Down the passage, under the stairwell, was the communal washroom. There was a row of sinks along two walls with a wooden rack above them. All the toothbrushes were kept here, each one being marked with its owner's number. On the other two walls were rows of numbered hooks, with differently coloured wash bags and small towels hanging from them. Each child had a bar of soap, flannel, brush, comb and a tin of powdered pink toothpaste.

The cloakroom was next door to that. Two racks held all the coats. Another back door led out into the yard.

Each cottage had its own back garden area. There was a small square between the back doors. Washing lines criss crossed from one wall to the other. A wide tarmacked area led to a large outhouse. The middle part had a high ceiling. Large sacks of vegetables, the children's bikes and any other bulky items were stored here. Old black bikes were supplied if a child wanted one.

At either side of the outhouse were coke, coal and anthracite cellars. At the back were obsolete outdoor toilets from long ago. The girls loved playing 'shops' in here. There was also an area of grass. We were encouraged to garden. Those that were interested were given a small piece of the grass. One of the gardeners dug them up for us. That must have been the start of my interest for I can remember having one and laboriously sowing seeds. By the garden gate there was a low twisted tree. Nasturtiums grew along a rattan fence.

The 'front' garden was a neat circular lawn which wrapped around the front and sides of the house. There were several flower beds apart from the monkey puzzle tree in the centre. It also had a Rowan tree by one front door, which of course is where it got its name.

On every child's arrival at The Hollies they would have to be outfitted with clothes. Each one would have to go to the haberdashers to collect a bundle of clothes. The cobblers was in the same building located under the trees behind 'the big house'. The haberdashers was upstairs. It was full of sewing machines and cotton threads and shelves full of clothing. The cobblers was downstairs. From there we would collect shoes and sandals, from the kindly old cobbler. The clothes and shoes had previous owners. It would be unusual to be supplied with new clothes for when a child left the clothes had to be handed in. They were used until they were worn out.

We wore uniform. It was unique to the 'Homesie Kids' and set us apart from the 'outsiders'. (They were anyone who lived outside the gates). The girls wore pin striped dresses, white socks and brown sandals in summer and navy pinafore dresses, white blouses, and black lace up shoes in winter. The boys wore short grey trousers right up to the time they left at the age of fifteen. With these they wore grey shirts, grey jackets, red ties, long grey socks with red bands and black lace up shoes in winter. The only difference is summer was that they could leave off their jackets and wear sandals.

We rose every morning at 6.30am. It was a mad scramble to get to the washroom as quickly as possible, dab a cold flannel around our faces gingerly and clean our teeth with the spearmint flavoured powder. The girls were usually washed first as we were nearer to the washroom. Our dormitories were on the same side of the house. We scrambled quickly into our clothes. Then we had to make our own beds.

We would all meet in the dining-room for breakfast. This would consist of a dish of cereal followed by a cooked item such as a boiled egg. There would be a plate of bread and butter on every table. Most children came from poor backgrounds. They would never eat as well ever again.

After breakfast we would disperse to carry out our allotted jobs. Every child had one. Mine was always washing up. Another was putting away. I grew up to hate anything that went on in sculleries. These jobs had to be done before school so it was a bit of a rush. It didn't do to dally in the dining room. Eric's job was usually getting in the anthracite for the Esse. There were lots of other jobs. Someone had to clear the dining room and relay the tables for the next meal. There was coke to collect, tidying up the bootroom, washroom and cloakroom. The fires in the playroom and sitting room had to be cleaned out. Laundry had to be collected. Some boys had to 'bumper' the wooden floors. (A bumper was a long-handled, heavy floor polisher made by Ronuk). Only the boys could handle it. There were numerous other jobs that had to be done.

All this was in spite of every cottage employing a daily help. These came in weekdays and usually lived locally. Ours was Mrs. Sphantum. She was plump and old with grey hair. Her legs and feet were permanently swollen. The first thing she did was to change her outdoor shoes for down at heel slippers. Then she would put on her wrap around pinny and tie a scarf around her hair. She was a kindly woman who called everyone ducks and dished out sweets when no one was looking. Often she could be heard muttering under her breath.

"Poor little mites."

Once a month we had Mr.Irving's assembly to go to before school as well. This was held in the gymnasium. He would hold court on the stage at one end. And he insisted that his family support him. His sour faced wife would sit unwillingly to one side of him with her older children, Sandra and Patrick. Only the babies' cottage, which was away from the main home by the Halfway Street gate, was exempt. Every other child had to attend, unless they were in the sick bay.

Despite first impressions, tall grey-haired Mr Irving who shot pigeons for fun and chain-smoked untipped cigarettes was a kindly man who cared very much for the children under his care. But it was also his job to make them behave. So he would bawl them out when he had reports of bad behaviour. He would also mention by first name any child with a birthday, which was quite a feat considering the number of children in The Hollies in total.

My brothers and I attended our first assembly the very next day after we arrived.

With trepidation we knew that going to a new school would be our next hurdle.

Chapter Nineteen: School

I stood in the hallway with my little brother. We had sat together in the dining room.

He had whispered to me at the table that he didn't want to go to that school.

I held hands with Bobby in an effort to reassure him. It was his first day at Halfway Street infant school. There were five other infants in our cottage. They were used to the route to school. Bobby gripped my hand so tightly that the skin had turned white.

"I want to go with you," he moaned softly.

Miss Lang appeared from the Esse room.

"Now then, Bobby," she rebuked him. "You are holding everybody up. Let go of your sister. You will make her late. Caroline is waiting for her."

She was not very tall and was inclined to slight plumpness. Still she crouched down to the same level as the little boy, who also had a tendency to be well covered, unlike me.

Her tone softened. It was obvious she liked him. That wasn't true of all the children in her care.

"Come on now," she said. "I am sure it won't be that bad. And you will see your sister this afternoon."

She straightened up. Reluctantly Bobby let go of my hand.

He went with the others looking back all the while. I stared after him until he was out of sight.

Later that day he told me that he had, with the others, walked past the big lawn in front of the gymnasium and along the path beside the 880 field, passing the haberdashers and cobblers on the way. They had walked past the farm next. He told me with great excitement that there was a donkey called Neddy, eating the grass. All the children had patted his neck, with the permission of the farm hand.

He said that there was a small gate which they all went through. Just across the road was the school. They had run fast until they reached the playground.

Bobby had a young teacher, named Miss Simms. She called all their names out. He sat next to a little blonde-haired girl, who was an 'outsider'.

Miss Simms desk was right opposite them. The little girl whispered to him.

"Will you show me your thing at playtime?"

Miss Simms did her best to stifle a giggle.

The day passed quickly. He worked hard at his schoolwork. Like me, he was happiest when he was busy learning.

There was some more excitement on the way home. Neddy had gone but there was a giant chocolate poodle running up and down the road. This was Kim, who belonged to the Irvings. He was always escaping. One of the farm hands eventually caught him. The story was that he was bought for Sandra, the Irving's daughter. They had mistakenly thought they were ordering a miniature poodle.

I set off with Caroline and other junior school age children. Just across the road from Rowan there was a path which cut through the grass which surrounded Mr Irving's woods. This was called the 'cinder path'. Everyone used it to get to the set of gates which led out of The Hollies. After we passed Larch Cottage we turned right out onto proper pavements into Burnt Oak Lane. It was a short walk to the school. With my heart in my mouth I entered the playground wishing at least I had the support of Bernard. But I didn't. He was now eleven. I *did* have Caroline. She was as opposite to me as she could be, being a natural extrovert by nature. Then the bell rang and we separated as we were in different classes.

My teacher was a man. His name was Mr. Hills. He seemed kindly enough until he singled me out. Staring over his glasses he asked me.

"Have you got a lisp?"

I replied.

"No."

To his horror, I burst into tears.

In reality, I didn't know what a lisp was. I *did* have a slight speech impediment at the time. By the end of the day he made up for any upset he had caused. He told me in surprise.

"You are a bright girl."

I didn't really know what this meant either, but it seemed good.

He knew that it was unusual for children from our circumstances to be academically bright. Very often the reverse was true. It was usually caused by poor background and lackadaisical upbringing. Very occasionally intelligent genes were inherited and would shine through, no matter what. I have always attributed mine to my mother. This isn't a criticism of my father. He would have been the first to admit he wasn't any good at 'book learning'. I was born with a natural ability to spell and a thirst for books, just like Mum. Bobby inherited these qualities as well.

Bernard unfortunately, didn't.

He managed to get by in Rowan. All the staff liked him. He was a happy-go-lucky, likeable character, who was easy to control. Very quickly he had formed a friendship with Eric and some of the bigger boys. The boys of Rowan linked up with the boys of Pine cottage, which was next door. Together they made a formidable gang.

Again, like me Bernard was going to be alone.

At eleven he was the youngest member of the gang. He had to go to Alma Road School until he was thirteen. The rest of them had reached that age.

Although it was my wish to be with my brothers, I didn't actually see much of Bernard. He was too busy enjoying himself with his new found friends.

It was disappointing for him to realise that he would have to go to school without them. He consoled himself with the fact that they could walk part of the way together. Their route would be down Burnt Oak Lane, into Station Road, past the entrance to the Glades, past the Holy Trinity church, which stood on the corner of Hurst Road. Once across the road the large crowd of boys would dawdle past Spicer's the newsagents. The lucky ones who had pocket money left could buy a few sweets. Most of them didn't. They would continue under the railway bridge to the next parade of shops. The pet shop and the bakers would be the pull here, especially on the way home. The ladies in the bakers shop would take pity on the Homesie Kids. Often they would get given stale cakes which would otherwise be thrown away. Bernard and his cronies would continue along Alma Road. Here they would part company. Eric and the older boys would continue on to until they reached Bexley Lane. They would attend Sidcup Secondary Modern for boys, although it was known as Bexley Lane.

The boys told Bernard not to worry for at least he didn't have to walk as far as them to school. Their journey was actually a good three miles long.

They urged Bernard to join the lunchtime photography club, with totally straight faces. The teacher was Mr Carson, who was close to retiring age and seemed kindly.

Bernard was shocked when the man put his hands down the front of his short trousers in the darkroom, whilst he had his hands encased in rubber gloves and immersed in the developing fluid.

Droves of children streamed through all the different gates, positioned at the outer perimeter of The Hollies, at four o'clock. They attended a variety of different schools. There was Halfway Street Infant School where the children came in the small, metal gate, which was a new innovation to allow the young five to seven year olds quick access to school. Then there was Burnt Oak, Alma Road and Bexley Lane for Boys, whose nearest entrance and exit was in Burnt Oak Lane. Another school was Blackfen School for Girls. All who attended this school would enter by the gate in the bottom field. They would have a long walk to do too. The other gate was by Linden Cottage, where all the babies lived. This gate was used to ferry the Catholic children to school. They lived apart in several cottages. Visitors would also use this gate as it was close to a bus route.

The grounds would be filled with noise. All the children had to make their own way back to their particular cottage. Some would hurry whilst others would dawdle, even diving into the forbidden woods.

On arrival at each cottage there would be jobs to be done.

Some could be carried out at once and some were done after tea.

One job was 'buttering' bread which was overseen by an assistant. Another was getting the dining room ready. This included laying the tables and putting a dish of jam on each table from large tins kept in the larder.

It was lucky if you had these jobs for after tea you were free to play or listen to the radio.

Another job that could be got out of the way was fetching fuel for the Esse, boiler and fires. Well it would have been quick! These jobs were always given to the boys and inevitably a lot of rivalry caused coke fights between Rowan and Pine. God help the boys who caused either Miss Lang or Miss Bowen the Pine housemother to come out to stop it. She had a reputation! Compared to her, Miss Lang was a pussy cat.

Miss Lang did the cooking. (Unless she was off duty) She would often be red faced and bad tempered as she struggled to cook on the Esse. It had four large plates on the top of it whose temperatures was unpredictable, to say the least. The food she had already cooked in large tins she would put in one of the ovens. They were so fierce it often got ruined, especially things like sausages. Whilst this was going on an assistant would hustle everyone else into the washroom to wash their hands.

Then everyone was expected to sit down to tea. This was a cooked meal such as scrambled egg and baked beans or tinned spaghetti, followed by bread and jam and even thin slices of Madeira cake on certain days. All of the children would have had the opportunity to eat a full dinner at school. Nevertheless, all the food disappeared at teatime in double quick time.

In later weeks, I would scan the rota on the wall in the Esse room anxiously hoping I wouldn't have to wash up in the afternoon. The baking tins were really difficult to get clean. We would have packets of soap flakes to swish around in the big metal sink. A lot of the time they would sink to the bottom of the greasy water in a sludgy mess.

The dining room had to be prepared again, for breakfast the next day. This was alright in the winter, but it sometimes caused problems in the summer. For breakfast instead of jam we had marmalade. This was kept in big tins, too. It was put out on dishes with a saucer cover. One was placed on each table. All the places were laid and cereals were put ready in dishes. I can remember on some hot summers armies of ants having a ball with the dishes of marmalade.

Miss Lang and her assistants ate with us. She had her own food. There was always a packet of Energen rolls by her place. She ate them every day for breakfast for the five and a half years I was there, but I never saw any change. She remained stout.

Once all the jobs were done we were allowed to play or carry on with any other activities we might have. I joined The Brownies with Caroline. The weekly meetings were held in the gym. As were Cubs, Scouts and Guide meetings.

In the summer we were allowed to go swimming in the Hollies pool which was nearby. I loved swimming. It was the only physical activity I would ever enjoy.

Bobby joined the Cubs. I persuaded him to, for I felt extremely guilty going off to Brownies and leaving him, knowing I wouldn't be around to say goodnight to him.

The cooking wasn't over for Miss Lang. She would heat up large round pans of milk into which she would stir cocoa and sugar. Each child would have a cup of cocoa before bed. And we would each be given a desert spoon of malt and cod liver oil, which I hated. I can still taste it now. Eric loved it, though.

Every other night it was bath night. They were supervised for boys as well as girls by the assistants. On wash night we would have to strip wash in the freezing cold washroom. The only consolation was the assistant who was supposed to be supervising us often disappeared and left us to it. So our washes were sketchy to say the least.

There were six beds in one dormitory and four in the other on each side of the house. I slept in the big dormitory with Caroline.

We were all in bed by eight o'clock.

Miss Lang and her staff retired to their sitting room with cups of coffee.

Of course that was the normal weekday routine. However, sometimes there were differences.

Occasionally there would be picture shows in the gymnasium. These were always on Thursdays. This would be a welcome change from normal routine and a good reason to hurry through the chores. We all sat on green canvas chairs watching hoary old films such as Will Hay or Bulldog Drummond. But we loved it. For several hours we were transported into another world.

Until we came down to earth with a bump. that is.

Chapter Twenty: Weekends.

Of course at weekends the routine changed.

On Saturdays, getting up, washing and making our beds was the same. But there was no school so things were more relaxed. Carrying out our various jobs was done at a more leisurely pace. Breakfast was slower and more argumentative. It was over at last and all the dirty dishes were washed and put away and the dining room re-laid by Susan Taylor for the next meal. (She was one of the big girls, and responsible for making sure all the dirty crocks were cleared and all the places correctly laid.)

Firstly, Miss Lang carried out a cursory inspection to make sure all other jobs had been done.

There were some exceptions. Poor Derek Izzard for one was unable to make his bed. He slept in the big dormitory with Eric, Bernard, Daniel Shaw, Freddy Wilde and Kenny Master. Every morning he rose from a steaming bed. His wet sheets and nightshirt were packed hastily into a laundry basket and his bed was left open to air. It was his shame for the red rubber sheet to be exposed to all and sundry. Only bed wetters had these rubber sheets. He was the butt of many practical jokes. Only I could understand how that felt.

Once she was satisfied that everything had been carried out satisfactorily Miss Lang seated herself at the bureau in the Esse room.

The twenty of us (unless there were any vacancies) formed an argumentative line from where Miss Lang sat to the door of the Esse room, out into the passage past the scullery, ending up by the fridge room and the back door. She opened a ledger and checked the list of names and birthdates. Once she was certain that all was correct she would begin doling out pocket money to each impatient child. Every week she would remind each child of the need to save. To every child's disgust she took back a portion of what they were due. This would be put into a Post Office savings book. We didn't care about that not just then. A grumble rumbled down the line about how much she had the cheek to take. It didn't do any good. She took it anyway. Later we would be glad.

It was a great thing to have a birthday. It meant a rise in pocket money. Every one was envious of the child who had recently had a birthday. Eric was the source of that envy in October. We were all summer born children. Bobby and I had birthdays in May, Bernard's was in July. We would have to wait for the thrill of extra money until next year. Just having pocket money for the first time in our lives was a wonder in itself, so we didn't care.

Little groups of children stood around chattering, much to the disapproval of Miss Lang and her assistants. They made it abundantly clear that we had to go out. And stay out until dinnertime.

So we had no choice. Even in the winter, when the weather was bitterly cold or there was snow on the ground. Our only protection from the weather was a faded mackintosh which had many previous owners before us.

Children appeared from all cottages, making for the Burnt Oak Lane gate once again. This time there was a mass exodus for the Odeon cinema in Station Road. This was just opposite the Glades and Church.

A large crowd of children (all outsiders) were already gathered outside. Hurriedly we joined them. It would cost us a precious one shilling and three pence to get in to Saturday morning pictures. To some of the Homesie Kids this was too much. While the rest of us queued up, bought our tickets and chose our seats, they had a plan. They didn't worry about missing the usher standing at the front with the tray of sweets and ice creams. They crept around the side of the cinema through the rough grass and waited. One of them would pay to go in. He would take his seat innocently and wait for the lights to go down and the ushers to disappear. This didn't take long for they were unable to stand the din. Then he would open the emergency exit and let the others in. Together we would all sit and watch a continuous round of films which included Flash Gordon, Roy Rogers, Gene Autrey, Bulldog Drummond, The Lone Ranger and Lassie. If you were lucky and managed to hear anything, it was a good morning's entertainment. If you didn't then at least it whiled away the time. It finished around noon.

We would all dawdle back to wash our hands for dinner. This was a two course meal, comprising dinner and pudding, all of which had been prepared and cooked while we were out.

On Saturday afternoon we were expected to disappear again, though issued with a veiled warning to be back by four o'clock.

This time we went to Sidcup High Street. It was a long walk. The total length of Station Road until it joined the High Street. Most of us took a short cut through Hatherley Road, stopping off, of course, at the pet shop on the way. They had live animals in here which were an added attraction. But nothing had the lure like Woolworths! This was where we were attracted like moths to light. It was a veritable Aladdin's cave. Inevitably pocket money didn't stretch far enough to buy little dolls, rings, forbidden makeup or stamps, dinky toys, batteries for bike lamps, penknives. Eventually everyone succumbed to the temptation. Usually we were in pairs. One would egg the other on. The adrenaline rush of stealing was terrifying. Some of the children, though, were without fear. Once the things had been spirited away in mackintosh pockets we would walk quickly to the glass doors, hurry through them and run like hell around the corner to Hatherley Road. As far as I know no Homesie Kids ever got caught. Once we were far enough away we would examine our wares with some delight and a large measure of guilt.

As we were winding our way down Hatherley Road we would often bump into Smokey Joe, the local tramp. Us girls found him a bit scary. I think even Bobby did. He had a bike with no tyres, with all sorts of things hanging from it. Winter and summer he wore an old army trench coat and a woolly hat. Rumour had it that the local police would take him in on Christmas Eve and bathe him, put him in a cell and give him a hot dinner.

And then there was Skinny Lizzy! She had short grey hair, a long green coat, and the thinnest legs you have ever seen, sandals and white ankle socks.

The boys made her life a misery. They would follow her about, shouting obscenities.

Eventually the fun was over and it was time to go. Drifts and drabs of children clutching Woolworth paper bags would be winding their way back to their cottages, where tea would be waiting for them.

After the usual routine of eating and carrying out jobs and a measure of time spent in the playroom, Saturday would be over once again.

Sunday was another day.

Of course, getting up, washing and breakfast routine was the same.

It differed slightly because we had to wear our best clothes. Sunday was church day.

Out of respect the girls had to wear coloured berets.

With the exception of the Catholic children, we all went to the Holy Trinity in Station Road, which was a high Anglican order. Nothing or no one interfered with us going to church. No exemption was allowed.

Each cottage formed a double crocodile in the company of the housemother and one unlucky assistant. Mr Irving and his family were at the head, whilst all the different cottages brought up the rear. Every cottage had its own pews. It always started with a procession of the choir and the silver-haired vicar. He walked slowly swinging an orb on a chain. We wrinkled our noses up at the smell of the incense it released. He would continue to spray it around throughout the service, except when he was giving his sermon. This was often directed at us. The service seemed to go on and on although I enjoyed the singing, there seemed to be endless prayers. It was a good opportunity for the girls and boys to eye each other up. This was one of the occasions when we were altogether, all the cottages and all the blocks. Many a romantic seed was sown after church.

It was expected of us to put a penny in the collection bag which was handed round at the end of the service. Miss Lang usually furnished us with a penny each. She frowned heavily on those who kept the penny back. It was one of the worst crimes you could commit.

We had to go for a walk after church. Sometimes this would be in the Glades. This was a park with a large lake in the middle. In the spring it was beautiful with large swathes of daffodils and spring bulbs. Beds of roses gave it colour in the summer. There were always graceful swans and ducks on the lake. One part of it was out of bounds to the public. Boys always got in there and broke down branches of trees. The Homesie Kids got the blame. Mr Irving periodically banned everyone from going in there unless they were with an adult. He would say over and over, looking over the top of his glasses, "I know it's not our boys doing this." A sea of innocent faces stared back at him.

There was something else special about Sundays. Every other week, it was visiting day. Our Mum and Dad always came, rain or shine. I would have a letter two days before telling me they would be there.

We would, after lunch, wait impatiently by the front door in between the Esse room and the playroom. Still dressed in our best, with tidy hair we would stare along the cinder path for any sign of them. Usually we would be much too early, for they weren't allowed to come until two o'clock. It didn't matter.

Of course we didn't appreciate the difficulties they had to overcome in order to visit us. They had to write in every time for a pass which would only last for one day. Considering that they were not very well educated this amounted to a form of cruelty. Below is an example of an actual letter obviously penned by Mum.

6 Abbey Terrace
Abbey Wood
12th October 1953

Dear Madam
Will you please forward to me a visiting pass for Bernard Joyce and Robert.

Yours Faithfully
Mr and Mrs Randall.

Note: Spellings and grammar are as they were on actual letters.

Below is a reproduction of a copy of an actual letter from the Children's Dept to the Superintendent of The Hollies, who would then acknowledge it. This rigmarole had to be carried *every* time my Mum and Dad wanted to visit us just for two hours.

I hold photocopies of these letters as they form part of my 'file'.

LONDON COUNTY COUNCIL
CHILDRENS DEPARTMENT

In any reply
please quote

CH ACO/6 VJC

CONFIDENTIAL

Dear Sir
Bernard Joyce & Robert Randall
Following my consultation with you a permit has been issued to Mr & Mrs Randall to visit above named children on 18/10/53 between the hours of 2 and 4

The holder of the permit has been informed that the visit may not last longer than 2 hours; that the permit (which should be handed to you immediately on arrival at your home) is intended for the use only of those named thereon; and that, if the visit takes place at other time, or on any other day or exceeds the permitted time, or if the permit holder is accompanied by any person who is not named on the permit, the privilege of visiting may be withdrawn.

The Superintendant   Yours Sincerely

The Hollies   Children's Officer.

We were not aware of the problems. We were just glad to see them. Nor did we understand the complications of Mum's illness. Sometimes they came together and sometimes they did not. This put us in terrible agony, for we didn't know which one to go with. We wanted to be with them both.
Dad had craftily got hold of the pass. So as usual Mum didn't have a leg to stand on. They too were dressed in their best. Dad always had a camera slung around his neck. I am sure it must have been difficult to think of places to take us, especially in the winter. One of the favourite places was a café at Blackfen. We would spend the two

hours there. Every now and then Dad drew out his pocket watch and anxiously scanned the time. It passed all too quickly. Soon we had to go.

Not very many children had visitors. A lot of the children had no one to visit them. Instead they were given 'Auntie and Uncles'. They were usually local middle class couples, carefully screened by the London County Council. Eric's were Mr and Mrs Benfield. He was a pharmacist and an ex Squadron Leader. They already had two daughters of their own. Eric used to visit them at their house in Welling. It gave the children like him a little bit of care and attention that they didn't receive from their own family.

On Sunday afternoons unless you had a visitor, it was compulsory to go to Sunday school. This was run by Mr Standing. He was the assistant Superintendent and lived in Vine Cottage. The gym was used for this. He was a tall, thin weedy man, with a gentle disposition and a timorous wife. Most of the children ran amok, especially the boys, who by Sunday afternoons were totally fed up with singing hymns. Still, every week, he persevered.

Tomorrow a week would begin again.

Chapter Twenty One: Going Home

As soon as I walked in the door after school, Miss Lang handed me a letter. The envelope was slit open but I didn't notice. I drew out the thin piece of lined paper and read the contents quickly. Of course it was from my Mum.

Mrs L E Randall
Abbey Terrace
Abbey Wood

October 8th 1953

Dear Joyce
I hope this letter finds you well and happy. I am glad you like where you are now. Did you get my last letter. We are going to come and see you as soon as we can.
We've been on the housing list for 11 years now so I think we will get a house soon then you will be coming home for good.

Give my love to Bernard and Robert.

Yours Faithfully

Lydia Randall.

A.V.WALKER   S.I.M.T.A. F.1 Hse
HOUSING DEPARTMENT
DIRECTOR OF HOUSING
TOWN HALL
WOOLWICH. S.E.18   Telephone: WOOLWICH 1181

Please quote Ref. 5.1/3/45/1957
All communications to be
addressed to Director of Housing.

Your Ref:
CH/ACC.6/GMA
14TH October, 1953

Dear Sir,
      Re: H.J.Randall,6 Abbey Terrace,Abbey Wood,S.E.2.

I thank you for your letter of the 5th instant regarding
the   above   family,   and   would   assure   you   that   the
information will be treated in confidence.

In   view   of   the   circumstances,   the   feeling   of   the
committee is that it is not advisable to make any offer
of accommodation to this family.
The Area Children's Officer
London County Council

Children's Department   Yours Faithfully
34, Watson Street
Deptford, S.E.8.   Director of Housing.

Harry stroked his chin thoughtfully. He turned to Lydia.
"Well, Missus, you 'ad better get the pad out then and put pen to
paper."
Lydia nodded in agreement.
She sat at the table, opened the lined pad and began the letter.

6 Abbey Terrace
Abbey Wood
Dec 12 1953

Dear Madam
I wish to have the children home from Saturday 19ᵗʰ Dec at
10 am until Jan 3ʳᵈ 6.30 pm.

Yours Faithfully
Mr. H. Randall

The letter landed on the desk of the Area Children's Officer two days later. Thoughtfully she tore open the envelope, recognising the writing. She scanned the brief contents with disapproval, pursing her thin lips.

Leaning forward, she buzzed for her secretary. The door opened immediately, a middle aged woman, with close cut hair, bustled in with pad in hand.

Miss Champion indicated.

"Miss Reed will you please locate Miss Simone for me. I wish to see her now."

The secretary smiled.

"Yes, of course."

She hurried from the room.

Miss Simone mounted the stairs to the upper rooms of 6, Abbey Terrace. She tapped lightly on the door at the top of the stairs. It was opened by a man.

She enquired, "Mr Randall?"

Harry smoothed his thinning hair with a nervous hand.

"Yes, yes, please come in."

She stepped into the room. Lydia sat in the only armchair. She glanced casually at her, but didn't speak to her. Her words were addressed to Harry.

"I am afraid we cannot agree to the children coming home for the whole holiday."

He clapped his hand to his head in consternation, looking around in a worried manner at his wife.

Miss Simone smiled thinly. In a low voice she said reproachfully, "Mr Randall. You aren't on holiday for the whole period are you?"

Shamefully, Harry agreed.

"No I am not. It's 'er. She keeps on badgering me."

Miss Simone nodded sympathetically.

"Well, Mr Randall, I will tell you what has been worked out. You can have the children on the 19th December, in order that they can attend the works party. But they must return on Sunday the 20th by 6pm. We will agree to the children being collected by your wife at 3 pm on 24th December but they must come back on the 27th December."

Distressed sounds came from Lydia.

They both ignored her.

A sheepish Harry quickly ushered Miss Simone down the stairs.

Hoping for some sympathy, he told her in a hushed voice.

"Some new people have moved in downstairs. They've bought the house. We have been told we can't use the garden."

Of course we knew nothing of all this. There was a lot of excitement at Rowan for we were getting ready for the Christmas concert which was going to be held in the gym.

Every cottage and every block had to put on an act. Everyone had to go including the Irving family.

I think Miss Lang dreaded it. I don't think she was very artistic.

This year she was leaving it to her assistant housemother, Miss Cooper. She had come up with a sketch of a hit song at the time, which was sung by Guy Mitchell.

She Wears Red Feathers

(She wears red feathers and a huly huly skirt)
(She wears red feathers and a huly huly skirt)
She lives on just coconuts and fish from the sea
A rose in her hair and a gleam in her eye
And love in her heart for me.
I work in a London Bank
Respectable position
From nine to three they serve you tea
But doom your disposition
Each night in the musical hall
Travelogues I see
And once the pearl of a native girl
Kept smiling back at me.
She wears red feathers and a huly huly skirt
She lives on just coconuts and fish from the sea.
A rose in her hair and a gleam in her eye
And love in her heart for me

This was being presented as a comedy sketch with boys dressed up as hula girls and a girl dressed as the London banker. It was a great success.

We were almost reluctant when we were collected by Dad to go to the party.
And it didn't feel right. Something had changed. We no longer belonged.
It was awful, too, seeing Mum's desperation.

Christmas Eve soon came, she arrived as arranged to collect us. We departed to the envious stares of the other children.

Christmas Day arrived. We had one thing each. Bobby had a train set. Bernard had a lorry and I had a doll. We had a nice time picking out sweets from little glass dishes and eating a few nuts from a wooden tray. Mum was out in the scullery cooking the dinner, which was a chicken Dad had triumphantly bought after work on Christmas Eve at an auction. Great ceremony was made of serving this meal. The table was pulled out and a clean tablecloth was put on. Dad made a great show of turning out the gaslight and lighting the Christmas pudding. (which had been previously made by Mum). He made sure that each of us had a sixpence in our dish. Sadly, the brief time we had passed quickly. I wondered where Mum had gone. It was unusual for her to leave us for long. I crept upstairs. She was lying on the bed, her eyes red from crying. Dad was cuddling her. I knew that we were the cause of it. I crept away sadly.

When we arrived back at Rowan we found that all the children who stayed got more than we did.

Abbey Terrace
Abbey Wood
April 4 1954

Dear Madam
I wish to have my children home from Wed 14 until Sunday 24 from 10am until 6.30. I will be taking the children for a holiday.
Yours Faithfully
Mr H Randall

I wish to leave by not later than 10am Thursday morning

161

The letter was obviously a thinly veiled subterfuge in my Mum's writing to secure a week at home for us without any questions being asked, or any further inspections being carried out.

Dad came to collect us. He seemed worried and anxious. After the tedious journey home on two trolleybuses and one tram, we found out why.

Mum was as high as a kite. I don't know what had gone wrong. It is my guess that Dad wanted to take us to Meopham for the week. This was probably the 'holiday' he spoke about in the letter. By now he had built his own chalet. Unbeknown to the authorities we were regular visitors, there.

Dad probably DID have a week off. He would have had a good holiday allowance as he was a civil servant. Maybe he didn't want her to come.

I still have vivid memories of this particular 'holiday' with our parents.

Dad sat around clutching his head. Every time he moved a muscle she'd rush in from the scullery (where she seemed to be preparing endless meals) and scream abuse at him. She seemed to have eyes in the back of her head. If he made any attempt to touch any of us she would fly across the room like a banshee and scratch his face with her long nails. Nor could he say anything.

This was a complete change to their normal behaviour. Usually he would do all the talking, mostly constant criticism, which because she was such an introverted character, she took without comment. So, it seemed that he got away with it. However he never realised that the resentment *was* building up inside her and beginning to boil like a kettle. Without warning it would boil over.

This behaviour could and usually did last for three weeks. Gradually the gaps between her outbursts would grow longer until they faded away completely, to be replaced with abnormal quietness when it was difficult to get a word out of her. Of course Dad didn't cause her condition, but he didn't handle it very well.

He seemed to aggravate it severely.

She never shouted at us, though.

But all the noise *was* frightening, for he would add to it by trying to reason with her. And of course it didn't work.

Dad decided that we should go back to Rowan. Sadly this meant cancelling our holiday. We were very upset about this.

All he had to do was get us out! That was a lot more difficult than it seemed.

She had a sixth sense where we were concerned. He wasn't allowed anywhere near us. She didn't mind *him* going out at all. It pleased her that he had gone. Unbeknown to her he had phoned the Welfare Office and spoken to the duty officer, who had told him to contact the police. I don't think he really wanted to go to those extremes. There was something shaming about that. It was made more difficult because she insisted I stay close to her. By a stroke of luck he managed to spirit the two boys away. So, three days after they had come home they were back at Rowan. She was so disturbed this time that she continued to cook for five. I can still see her now putting five plates on the table and spooning great mounds of mashed potato onto them. He tried unsuccessfully to get me away from her. Two long days later he did call the police. I like to think that it was as a last resort.

Two policemen took the stairs two at a time. She gave in meekly when she saw them. They were figures of authority. This would have scared her. I can still hear her screaming my name as they dragged her down the stairs.

"Joycie! Joycie!"

I screamed too because I was frightened of what they were doing to her. When Dad grabbed me I backed away. His eyes filled with tears as he weakly tried to explain his actions. I went with him but I was locked in my own world. The natural sympathy I felt for my mother's impossible plight lay heavy on my heart.

Chapter Twenty Two: Summertime

June 1954

It was summer.

Bobby still followed me everywhere I went. It was becoming a little irritating. I had hoped he would make friends of his own, like I had. Caroline and I were firm friends. She could be a bit naughty, though. That was why Miss Lang encouraged our friendship. She thought I would be a good influence on her. It had never occurred to her that it would rub off on me. Nor had she bargained for the closeness of siblings. She hoped Bobby would be closer to Bernard but he wasn't. They were always at loggerheads. Bernard and Bobby were total opposites. One was outgoing and naturally merry, the other one was introverted and serious.

Now that we had balmy summer days we were allowed to play in the back yard in the evenings until bedtime.

Having shaken Bobby off, due to his younger age and earlier bedtime, Caroline and I hung around the side gate in the hope that we would see Mr Irving. We didn't have long to wait for him to appear. Sure enough he strolled by, in his grey suit, puffing an untipped cigarette. He kept it in his mouth the whole time, taking large draws and blowing out gales of grey smoke. As it grew dark all you could see was the bobbing tip. When he drew level with our gate he held out both hands. We ran to him and slid our hands in his. Together, we walked around the grounds.

We craved these little bits of attention, for they were very few and far between. For Caroline they were non-existent and for me they were fleeting. My parents did not show open affection, not even to each other.

I had discovered a new and exciting pastime. Swimming! Normally I hated anything remotely athletic. This was different! All my spare time was spent in the indoor swimming pool, opposite our cottage. I often met Mr Irving and his son, Patrick there, for they were also keen swimmers. Bobby came too, sometimes because he liked to be with me.

Sports Day was held in June. It was usually held at the end of the month, on a Saturday. From every cottage would be athletes were chosen and put into red, blue, green or yellow teams. It began after an early lunch. All the races were run on the 880 and the 440 field.

Parents were invited, but not many came, because few children had any contact with them. The carefully selected Aunts and Uncles came too. The number of watching supporters was made up by London County Council dignitaries.

A queue formed quickly at the gym, where the staff served cups of tea and beakers of orange juice. I can remember my Dad making a beeline for it after he got bored watching other peoples children running races. None of us were the least bit athletic.

He always said, "I'm parched. My stomach thinks my throat's cut."

We would all laugh, including Mum, and follow him in the direction of the tea and refreshments.

After that, we would all find our way to the pool where swimming races were being held.

Small cash prizes were given to the lucky few who had won and a cup awarded to the best team. This was displayed in The Hollies, with a coloured ribbon for the winning team.

Later there would be a special evening of entertainment in the big house. The visitors were entertained on the lovely secluded lawn, with displays of whirling country dancing by the girls and intricate sword dancing by the boys.

July 1954

It was school holidays.

Everyone had their own idea what they would do with their free time.

Some of the boys headed for the farm, hoping they could cadge a lift on the tractor and trailer. They offered to help with the laundry deliveries to every cottage. The trailer was piled high with white linen bags with labels on. This was the worst job. The helpers were thin on the ground for that. Much more to their liking was delivering all the numerous dry goods needed by every cottage like 7lb tins of fruit or jam, large bags of sugar, big packs of tea, packets of porridge and cornflakes. There was a long list of requirements needed by every cottage. Best of all they liked helping to bag up and deliver the fresh vegetables which were grown on the farm. They would stagger out to the outhouses with great bravado and bright red faces, much to the amusement of the driver.

It was also confirmation in July.

This was for the children like Eric who hadn't been christened. Everyone involved had to go to church in the evenings for about six weeks beforehand.

They had lessons in the vestry. When they were ready there was a grand dress rehearsal.

On the day all the girls dressed in white and the boys dressed in their suits.

They formed a long procession to the Holy Trinity church. We all had to go as well to make up the congregation. Again, outside visitors were invited to attend.

After the religious ceremony everyone would wander back from the church. All the children not involved would return to their cottage. The visitors would congregate on the apron shaped lawn in front of the gym, where they were served tea and cakes.

After the visitors had left, a reception was held in the big house for all the children concerned. For once in their short lives the long term Homesie Kids with no one were exalted to an important position for a few short hours.

Another pastime that was popular with the older boys was bike riding. They looked forward to the long summer school holidays. Some of them made elaborate plans for a day out. They were careful to exclude anyone they didn't want along. It was decided by Joe Mays (as the oldest) that Johnny Dandridge and Johnny Wilder could come. It was discussed at great length and agreed that Eric would be allowed, too. At thirteen he would be the youngest. Armed with a packed lunch they set off for the long journey to Eynsford, which would take them up to Sidcup High Street and on to the A20. Several hours later they would arrive at their destination. Hot and dusty, they rode with great glee through the ford, beside the old bridge, and collapsed on the river bank. They walked along until they came to a pile of rotting wood. Sunbathing amongst it in piles of leaves were bright green, black and yellow adders. The boys poked them relentlessly with sticks. Luckily, the snakes slid off into the water, surfacing huffily on the opposite bank. Armed with nets and jars they turned their attention to fishing. Carefully they filled their jars with river water and strands of weed. Soon the jars were filled with sticklebacks and the occasional crayfish. These would be carefully transported back to Rowan.

Always, they would die by the next day.

As they lay in the sun chewing their dog-eared sandwiches, they talked, touching on subjects close to their hearts.

Eric told the others that he wanted go into the Royal Navy. He said his Welfare Officer, Mr Herbert Scows, was going to help him achieve his dream.

Joe wistfully told how, at fifteen, he knew he had to leave soon. He wished that before that date he could meet his parents. It was his conviction that they were rich and lived in a big house and for some reason they were unable to give him a home. He was sure that if only they could bring themselves to meet him then they would like him and welcome him with open arms. He was staggered when he learned that it was his friends dream, too. They all thought the same. The talk drifts to girls.

Johnny Wilder persuaded Eric to tell of any experience he had.

He told them reluctantly about the time when he was eight or nine. Miss Lang had made him stand on the landing outside her bedroom (on the girl's side of the house) as a punishment for swearing at her. This time she forgot him and went to bed. Tired and fed up he went through the girls dormitory to go to bed. He asked if they remembered Marion Daniels? They agreed they did.

He said she dragged him into her bed, saying she would warm him up. She wrapped her thin arms around him and hugged him close. Then she would guide his hands under her nightdress and push his little hands between her legs. She encouraged him to push his fingers deep into her flesh. By return she would play with him, stroking softly between his legs, causing him to have sensations he didn't understand.

After that evening it became a habit for her to come to his dormitory to get him out of his bed, after the lights were out. This went on until she left two years later.

Joe related something similar. So did the others.

They all giggled and sniggered about the times in the past when they had crept onto the back balcony and peered through the cracks in the curtains to spy on Miss Cooper. They all decided that they wouldn't do the same to Miss Jessop, who was ugly with goofy teeth and flabby tits.

The boys grabbed their bikes and set off for home. On the way they passed a wooded area. Joe called a halt. He waved the boys deep into the woods.

Leaning against a tree trunk, he jerked down his khaki shorts and his white pants, exposing his privates for them all to see.

Eric stared goggle eyed at the sight.

Joe pointed at him.

"I want you to help me out," he demanded.

Eric stuttered.

"What me?"

"Yes," hissed Joe. "Why do you think we let you come, you little squirt."

"What do I have to do?" he asked.

The other boys tittered nervously.

"Show him, Johnny," demanded Joe.

The boy stepped forward and demonstrated the action needed, with a sheepish grin and a flick of his wrist.

Joe pushed him away.

"That's enough," he said. "I want 'im to do it."

Shakily, Eric stepped forward.

The other two boys pulled down their shorts, too, and stood in line.

They rode back to Rowan in silence.

August 1954

Everyone was getting ready to go to 'camp'. The farm tractor had delivered large wicker baskets, which sat waiting in the Esse room.

All the children were highly excited. The Randall children were no exception. This was to be a new experience for us.

A harassed Miss Lang was busy preparing lists of clothes which needed to be packed. It was a big operation. God help any wrong doers at this trying time.

She had a habit of stamping her foot, shouting at the top of her voice and meting out nasty punishments. And then there was always the threat that camp would be cancelled!

At last we set off in a Bedford Duple coach, followed by all the others. The whole children's home would be empty as we set off en masse for Walton on the Naze. The journey seemed to take all day! The whole entourage stopped halfway for lunch! This was pre packed sandwiches and orange juice. We drove, at last into a huge field where a sea of enormous tents stood in rows.

Another fleet of coaches were just leaving. Talk buzzed around our coach that the other coaches were boys from an approved school. (These schools were for boys who were too young to go to jail, but had persisted in wrong doing) They looked tough. Everyone was relieved after they had gone. We stared in amazement at the long structure made mainly of glass that was the dining hall. There was a toilet and shower block, too.

The tents acted like dormitories and would become our home for the next two weeks. They had low camp beds in them for the children. The staff tents had single iron beds in them. All the tents had duckboards. The sexes were segregated as they were in the home. After all the arguing had stopped and all the camp beds had been filled we were expected in the dining hall.

The hall was filled with trestle tables and forms. These were for the children.

The Staff sat at one end on proper chairs. There was silence as the hungry children fell on the food which soon disappeared. It didn't last long. Gradually the squeaky voices of excited children rose to join with the high pitched chirping of hungry sparrows waiting for scraps, high up on the metal struts which spanned the roof.

Mr Irving called for everyone's attention. The noise slowly died to silence with the exception of the cheeping of the sparrows.

He would look up and joke.

"You, too."

He gave a happy address, wishing everyone a good holiday. Nudged by his wife, he held up squares of coloured pieces of thin card. He explained that these were tokens which could be bought, from the dining hall after breakfast, on any day except Sunday, to spend in Walton. He waved a dismissive hand and the place erupted into noise.

The next day after breakfast we made our way to the edge of the field. This was the quickest way out and into Walton on the Naze. A deep dyke ran along the bank. There was a large expanse of slimy water coated with bright green algae swirling along the bottom. A rickety 'bridge' just two planks wide stretched across to the outside world. The boys strutted across it with mock bravado, whilst the girls grabbed the flimsy railing and carefully edged over it. Secretly we were all relieved when we reached terra firma on the other side. The boys ran across the road to the boating lake despite Miss Lang's pleas. Eventually they tore themselves away, knowing full well that they needed tokens to go on the various boats. Those that had been before reminisced about the boat they were going to get out, which was the same one as last year.

We walked in an orderly line through the picturesque town to the Post Office.

Miss Lang handed each child their precious savings book. *Now* we realised the point of saving money! It was so we could spend it here! We were miffed when Miss Lang confiscated every child's money and dropped it into an envelope with each name on it. She would keep it, doling out a little each day.

With this we would purchase tokens, at a large discount.

As a gesture of goodwill she handed each child a few tokens, which she had purchased with her own money. She collected the Post Office books as well, stowing them in her large brown bag. We were told to explore the town if we wished, but not to forget to return to camp at lunchtime. It is a mystery how we knew the time as none of us had watches. I guess we must have asked amused strangers.

The girls and boys headed for the pier, where all the rides were. Caroline and I made a beeline for the waltzers, or the big wheel. It was the first stirring of senses for we were both a little in love with the man who swung the circular chairs around and the man who worked the big wheel. The latter would deliberately rock the chair as we passed, making us all squeal and scream. We spent all our tokens on these two rides, screaming loudly at the top of our voices, especially when we were marooned at the top.

The boys would head for the slot machines, the bumpers or the end of the pier. Here they would watch men fishing, usually managing to cadge some sort of equipment, in order to have a go themselves.

On some days we would plead to go swimming. Walton on the Naze had a lovely beach, with the tide way, way out.

Other afternoons we would walk miles along the cliff tops. It was here I saw a slow worm for the first time. Once I remember we walked to the next town which was Clacton on Sea. The weather always seemed hot and sunny.

On Miss Lang's insistence, I sent Mum and Dad a postcard. After that I never gave them another thought.

We didn't escape church, though. It was held in the dining hall and was taken by Mr Standing as usual.

The day always ended with much dalliance in the shower block, for they were a novelty we weren't used to. And we would stretch out on our camp beds and talk and talk until the light faded. Tomorrow was another day.

All too soon our camp holiday would be over.

Then we would be heading back to Rowan, school, and Mum and Dad's unhappy plight.

For just a while we could escape it.

Chapter Twenty Three: Mater

All the children in Rowan have learned that Miss Cooper will be leaving soon, to marry a policeman, which meant she would be unable to stay in her job. It was against policy for married persons to continue a 'career' and was still common for the middle classes to stay home, keep house and have children.

She was fairly unusual and definitely not the stereo-typical spinster of the time, for she was young, pretty and outgoing. It was common for everyone to call by her first name. We all called her Nancy, much to the disapproval of Miss Lang. If she heard us she went mad. It didn't stop us though. And she definitely encouraged the easy going approach. She was friendly to everyone on a casual basis. Any close attachments or open displays of affection were frowned upon anyway.

So we were all very sad that she was leaving because she was very popular.

We were intrigued to meet her replacement. The new assistant housemother was Miss Celia Masters. She was slim and trendy and brought with her a Dansette record player. It was her wish that we called her by her first name, too.

This made Miss Lang angry. She forbade it utterly. Miss Masters came up with a clever compromise. So from then on she became Mater. She had a talent of making every child feel special, by remembering every birthday. It was a thrill to get a brightly coloured card from her, written in her distinctive green ink. She was the only one who ever did that.

There were other talents she had, too.

Eventually the time would come when Miss Lang would be off duty. It was well known that her parents lived in Sidcup. On some Sundays some of the well behaved children were taken to visit them. They were elderly so she would often take several days off at once.

Now, Mater was in charge.

She would set the record player up in the Esse room and play very new records of music hot from America. They came via her brother, Alfred, who had originally brought them back as a present for his sixteen year old son, Jeff.

So, after tea and chores, the children would dance to the tune of 'Shake Rattle and Roll' by Bill Haley and the Comets and 'Its Alright Mama' by the very exciting and very new Elvis Presley, until bedtime.

Not much was known about these singers outside America at the time. The Rowan 'Homesie Kids' had a preview of what would become known as Rock 'n' Roll, thanks to Mater, before the rest of the world caught up.

She was also a brilliant gardener. Her help with our patches was much appreciated.

Her cooking was innovative, too. Not boring scrambled egg for her. The meals she conjured up on the Esse were always different.

She also made her own clothes. Her sewing machine could be heard whirring away in her room, when she was off duty. The things she made were always in fashion and much admired by the girls and boys alike.

Noggin the cat was still around. By now he was getting old. He still had official birthdays, however. One year she made him a birthday cake of tinned cat food covered with pink icing. He licked the icing to one side and scoffed the lot. What she did for the cat she also did for the children. It wouldn't be unusual for that particular child to help make his or her birthday cake.

Whilst Miss Lang preferred the 'good' child, Mater had a particular interest in the naughty child. Her fascination for Eric was obvious. She violently disagreed with Miss Lang's treatment of him. This could be severe. He was constantly being punished for misdemeanours.

Miss Lang and Mater did not get on. They only tolerated each other because of their positions.

Mater was determined to find out more about Eric's background.

She eventually managed this when Miss Lang was off duty. Determinedly she dusted off a large stack of ledgers destined to be moved to the big house in the near future. At the moment they were stacked on the floor of the staff sitting room.

Her hands grasped what she was looking for. She flicked open one ledger and read:

On May 21st 1948 Eric John Shurmer, aged 7, was received into Rowan, directly from the family court at Southwark, which was as a result of a fit person order. There was no record of his early life. There was one letter from his mother, which was just one line telling him to be a good boy. This was pasted into the book. There were no other records of further communication. The ledger stated that he barely ate, despite the fact that he was grossly undernourished. It was observed that he was obviously in a state of shock. His only interest was the cottage cat, Noggin. It was decided that he needed to see a psychiatrist.

In a later ledger she found further reports:

18th September 1949. Eric Shurmer visit to psychiatrist.

22nd May 1950. Eric Shurmer visit to psychiatrist.

Later ledgers reported that it hadn't helped. Despite these visits, Eric remained consumed by a terrible anger. It wasn't even sure who this was directed at. It was stated that it was likely that his anger was directed at his parents.

Another ledger revealed:

July 18th 1951. Eric Shurmer had received a visit from his brother, Gerald. He had turned up without seeking permission or writing in. It was a difficult situation. Gerald was little more than a boy, although he wore a soldier's uniform. The report said that he was obviously doing his National Service. It was decided by Mr Irving that the visit could go ahead on this occasion. An observation said that the visit was a disaster. Eric had become even more upset than he was before. He had been told by his brother that he would be going home soon. When it became obvious that there was NO communication from his parents he had become extremely upset and verbally abusive.

A meeting with Mr Irving had decided that Henry and Ivy Shurmer would receive a letter complaining of the flouting of the rules.

There was a footnote that they had replied indignantly saying they had known nothing about it.

Mater carefully checked every year's ledgers for any more information. Her face flamed at every reported misdemeanour of his and the resulting punishments. She also noted that it was only recently that he had stopped having nightmares. There was a report that he had spent a good night. She was angry. This boy obviously needed help.

Mater was intrigued by Eric. There was no doubt of that. She didn't neglect the other children, though. All the same, to her, Eric was a special case. Why him, no one knows.

The whole cottage knew he was at permanent loggerheads with Miss Lang. They rubbed each other up the wrong way. He suffered the brunt of this because he was continually being punished. Mater was a sucker for a good looking wayward boy. It was her desire to try and help him. She had made it her business to learn all about him. When his Welfare Officer came to see him she made sure she was on duty.

By the end of that day she knew more of his background history than he did,

It was a peculiar feature of being a 'Homesie Kid' in those days that the child concerned knew nothing of their own history. They were always bewildered by this and spent years wondering why they were there. This caused them to weave stories about themselves and their families which were fanciful to say the least. The truth was usually a lot sadder and a lot more basic. It ranged from having a sick mother, to losing a mother and a father unable to cope, to a child not being wanted (as in Eric's case) and there were a lot of other variations, too. In those days you weren't told. It just wasn't done. This caused a lot of anger, resentment and pain.

Mater vowed she would try to help Eric. She started by taking him out on visiting days. First of all she took him to meet her friend, Edna. She declared what a lovely looking boy he was. It was beyond her belief that parents could abandon such a nice boy. Pleased with the success of her first visit, she took steps to arrange a second.

This time she took him to visit her brother, Alfred and her nephew, Jeff. This, too was fairly successful, although Alfred read her the riot act about forming an attachment with one of her charges. He could smell danger, even if she couldn't.

It hadn't exactly escaped her notice that some of the older girls in the cottage joked around with him. She watched them, with narrowed eyes, from the scullery window chasing him and slapping him playfully. This she knew was the forerunner of flirting. To her surprise she felt a stab of jealousy every time she witnessed it. With a supreme effort she told herself not to be silly, surely her brother Alf, was right, things were getting out of all proportion.

Despite her private misgivings, Mater was soon inviting Eric to her room.

This was a sacred place belonging to that member of staff alone. It just wasn't done. They shared the intimacy of a last drink of cocoa, whilst she gave him her latest gift. This time it was a book of naval warships. There was little spare space in these staff rooms; they had to hold all their worldly goods. Soon, Eric was sitting on the bed, close to Mater. They made jokes about practically having to sit on each others laps.

It hadn't escaped her notice how mature his body was growing, when she supervised bath nights. Of course he wasn't the only one. She was less interested in the other boys, except to wonder when this supervision of fully mature boys and girls was going to be stopped by the London County Council.

Of course it was in case of accidents like scalding.

She had noticed strange sensations coming over her whenever he was near.

It was getting difficult to fight them.

Her opportunity came when Miss Lang was off duty and off the premises.

Mater appeared by Eric's bed. Everyone else in the dormitory was asleep, including Bernard. She shook him vigorously. Sleepily, he opened his eyes.

She held a finger to her lips and beckoned to him to follow her. He went to her room. She stretched herself out on the bed and pulled him down beside her. Urgently she placed his hands on her throbbing chest. She scrabbled inside his pyjama trousers. Later, she was surprised to find wetness in her hand.

She whispered to him.

"I didn't know you could ejaculate."

Meeting in her room after lights out on Miss Lang's days off became a regular occurrence. The heavy petting continued. One night when the only sound was soft snoring, Mater and Eric had full sex. He was not quite fourteen.

Chapter Twenty Four: High Winds & Fireworks

Miss Lang beckoned to me.

"Joyce, pop over to the office, there's a dear. Mr Irving wants to see you."

I bit my lip worriedly.

She patted my shoulder.

"Its alright, there is nothing wrong."

I managed an anxious smile. She pushed me gently towards the door.

The big house wasn't far away. I climbed the wide stairs to the arched door. It was always open, winter and summer. He met me on the stairs.

"Ah, hello Joyce," he said. "I was just coming to look for you."

I giggled nervously.

He held out his hand. I slipped my fingers into his large palm. Together we descended the stairs. At the bottom, he rocked back and forth on his heels.

(This was a habit of his)

He drew a deep breath.

"A little bird has told me you are a clever little girl. Is that right?"

I nodded happily, whilst not really knowing what he meant. I was just happy to be getting attention from this lovely man.

He continued.

"It has been decided that you will benefit from being sent to a different school. Do you think you will be up to travelling on the train to New Eltham all by yourself?"

I murmured, "Yes."

He nodded sharply.

"Good."

He let go of my hand.

"You will need a special school uniform for Wyborne. This will be ordered. It should be here in a few days."

He lifted my chin with a forefinger.

"You try it on and come and show me what a smart girl you are, won't you?"

He dismissed me.

"Off you go, now."

I walked off in a cloud. How did I feel about changing schools? I was afraid.

Would I really be able to manage to get on the train by myself? And what about Bobby? He, too would be changing schools. We would have been together. I was curious, though. And the work at Burnt Oak was easy. A bubble of excitement grew inside me. I decided to write to Mum and Dad to let them know my good news.

I didn't know that things had taken a turn for the worse for them. In addition to losing their main bedroom, which had caused them a great deal of anxiety, they had also been forbidden to use the garden for some time. The two rooms they had left seemed more crowded than ever.

This caused severe depression and desperation. It was a dangerous situation for them both.

For any little spark could trigger Lydia's condition.

Things grew even worse when the new owners told Harry that he should look for somewhere else to live. They wanted them out and they wouldn't take no for an answer. Harry bitterly blamed Lydia. Of course the news did have an effect on her. She was becoming talkative and outgoing. This was not a good sign for Harry. But it did give her the necessary courage to go and see the council, once again.

For reasons unknown to her, she met a blank wall, despite the years they had been on the housing list.

Harry, too, had been unsuccessful in finding anywhere new.

They had to leave the next day.

Officially, they had nowhere to go.

My letter arrived just in time.

They had no choice but to put their few sticks of furniture in store.

Harry was nothing if not resourceful.

He decided that there was no option but to move to the piece of land he had purchased the previous year. Luckily, fences had been erected and the chalet was built. The plot even had a name, now. It was called 'High Winds'.

The building had the look of a dilapidated Swiss chalet, without the tiles. It also had a veranda. The furniture was built in. Inside it had a double bed and three bunks. In one corner, just inside the door, was the kitchen area. On a table top, several paraffin burning heaters warmed an oven on a stand. (It worked, funnily enough. I know because I once baked cakes in it.) Next to that, there were several paraffin heaters with rings on the top of them. In the other corner, there was a refashioned table and two chairs, thrown away by someone else. (During the summer months these were outside on the veranda). The walls were lined with metal Brook Bond tea panels. (These were used at the time on hoardings to advertise the company. Auntie Doris, Dad's sister-in-law, worked for Brooke Bond.) As décor they left a lot to be desired.

The amenities were also questionable. There was no electricity, running water or sewage.

A Tilley lamp was used for lighting. This was complicated. Only Dad could do this. It had a glass globe at the top, with a mantle inside it. A pipe ran down to the base tank which was filled with paraffin. A pre-heating torch had to be dipped in methylated spirit and clipped to the pipe. This was lit. Blue flames would run up inside the open ended globe until they reached the mantle. We would watch the process with fascination. Just at the crucial point, a plunger screwed into the base had to be pumped up and down rapidly. This sent air up the pipe. Then Dad would turn on a tiny tap releasing the paraffin. Hey presto there was light. And it was a good one. I could easily read by it.

Water was a problem, too.

Sadly there was no standpipe here like there was outside Uncle Jack's. Along one outside wall there was a long metal bath. Carefully positioned guttering and drainpipes fed rainwater into it. The bath was always full to the brim. With lots of leaves caught in the net curtain fixed across the top. Every bit of it had to be boiled before it could be used.

But I don't remember us ever being ill.

The toilet facilities were basic. We had an outside chemical toilet, which was just a drum with a seat on top of it, inside a small building made of wood and corrugated iron. It stood on its own, away from the chalet. This was just as well because it stunk. The thick, cloying smell of Elsan hung in the air. I dreaded having to use it. Fearfully I would open the door and peer around looking for the large spiders that frequented it. They had great long legs and white button bodies.

All the plots of land up here where High Winds was were uninhabited during the week. The only sound that could be heard on a sunny day was the birds singing. And it was rare to see any other people, even at weekends. Taking on a piece of uncleared woodland and turning it into a habitable domain was a big task. Most people's enthusiasm waned quickly. They came for a while then never came back. The plots were meant for holiday use only. Living there wasn't strictly allowed. But there were plenty of others flouting the law.

Harry and Lydia had no choice.

He wearily led the way up the hill, weighed down by haversacks and cases.

Lydia struggled up the steep incline behind him.

Neither of them wanted to think of the future at that moment.

It was September and the nights were drawing in.

Around the corner was autumn which would inevitably lead to winter.

Tonight at least they had somewhere to lay their heads.

Bernard was thrilled. He was now old enough to go to Bexley Lane with the others.

Eric had a birthday. He was now fourteen.

It was autumn. The leaves on the trees turned to gold. Amongst the boys, the excitement was growing. For the talk that accompanied them on their long journey to school was of nothing else but firework night.

It was a big event in The Hollies.

One day the crowd of Bexley Lane boys poured into Spicer's and bought some bangers and a box of matches.

Between them they conjured up a plan. They would select a certain house along their school route home, light a banger, shove it in the letter box and run away.

It wasn't anything new. Schoolboys have been doing it since time immemorial.

To a boy it was all part of the fun of Guy Fawkes Night.

Of course someone had to be nominated to actually carry out the deed. It was amazing how much hesitance there was when push came to shove. Eric was always up for a dare. What he lacked in stature he made up for in bravado.

They all made the mistake of selecting the house of an old lady living right near The Hollies gates. Eric ran pell-mell up the hard path, stretched up and shoved the lighted banger through the letter box. They all raced away towards the safety of the gates. For good measure Eric lobbed another lighted banger in the post box on the wall. They giggled as they saw thick black smoke billow from it.

What they didn't know is that they were seen by the old lady, who happened to be a personal friend of Mrs Irving. The next day she took the offending remains of the banger and went to see her friend. Unbeknown to the boys, they were being watched from the big house. Soon the old lady had identified them all.

When they got home a few days later, Miss Lang was waiting for them.

Her face was still red from the shame of having to deal with an unusually irate Mr. Irving.

She ranted and raved at the culprits in her cottage, Bernard amongst them.

But the one who took most of the blame was Eric.

She raved at him.

"You callous, unfeeling boy. How could you do that to an old lady? And whatever were you thinking of by setting the post alight. Have you any idea of the trouble you have caused."

Eric stood there sullenly. He didn't answer.

She shook a finger in his face.

"Well I'll tell you, shall I?"

Non-commitally he shrugged his shoulders.

She shook the unrepentant boy and pushed her face in his. He backed away.

"You burnt a hole in that lady's carpet runner. And all the letters in the post box were destroyed."

He had the grace, now, to look a trifle shocked. All the other boys nibbled their lips.

Now she addressed them all.

"Get out of my sight, all of you. Go to bed. Right now. There will be no tea for any of you today."

Sheepishly, they shuffled out of Esse room, Eric included.

Miss Lang grabbed him by the scruff of his neck.

"Not you, my lad. I haven't finished with you yet."

Eric struggled to free himself from her grasp.

She almost spat the words in his face.

"Your extra punishment will be missing the fireworks tomorrow night. And you will lose your pocket money until the carpet runner has been replaced."

Eric's face revealed nothing. He assumed a nonchalant attitude. This enraged her even more. Shaking with anger, she hissed.

"Get out of my sight. Go to bed now. And no talking."

He sauntered casually out of the room.

Bonfire Night had arrived. A clear dark blue sky dotted with stars presented itself to the excited children. The air was crisp and cold.

With the exception of Eric, they all gobbled their tea in record time.

The children jostled each other, fighting to get into the cloakroom to find their mackintoshes. Hurriedly, they spilled out of the back door into the yard, chattering excitedly.

Miss Lang appeared. She stamped her foot to get attention.

"Be quiet! We are not going anywhere until everyone forms an orderly line."

Swiftly, we scrambled for places. (The fear of being sent to bed instead was very real). I shrugged apologetically at Caroline as Bobby slid his hand in mine and stood next to me.

A sudden noise made us all look up to the back veranda.

Eric stood there, in striped pyjamas and blue dressing gown. We all fell silent, feeling sorry for him. I think we all felt Miss Lang's treatment was too harsh.

In the shadows it was just possible to see the shape of Mater.

Then we filed out of the gate and forgot him.

We walked to the big blocks, taking a short cut through the Limes backyard, onto the bottom field. There in front of us was the biggest pile of wood I had ever seen. We had, in the last few weeks, watched it being built. Soon all the cottages were assembled. The field was full of adults and children. Mr Irving appeared, dressed in old clothes and wellington boots. He thrust a lighted torch into the belly of the bonfire. There was a loud roar from the watching crowd, as flames licked at the wood. Mr Irving handed lighted sparklers to some children. He personally supervised lighting the fireworks, which were in a large box at his feet. All the girls screamed at the noise from the large bangers. Everyone oohed and aahed at the pretty ones. Trestle tables had appeared in Limes' back yard. When there was a lull in the fireworks, we joined a long queue which was forming in front of them. Cheerful helpers were doling out mugs of hot, sweet cocoa from a steaming urn. And each person was handed a sausage in a roll. There were more fireworks. The bonfire was almost gone, only the dying embers were left. It was time to go. In a happy daze, we made our way back to Rowan and bed.

Chapter Twenty Five: The Ultimatum

Lydia hated it at High Winds. She was stuck among the trees, all alone most of the time. There was little to do. The chalet itself was low maintenance, but carrying out any other chores such as washing was difficult. She had to use the same chipped enamel bowl for washing clothes and washing up dishes, making continual trips to the metal bath with a saucepan for water. Harry *had* managed to obtain a mangle and he had fixed her up a rope line slung between the trees. It was useless, now, because the weather had deteriorated. She had no choice but to hang it inside the chalet on a string especially fixed up for the purpose.

There was no way of keeping food fresh, so she had to shop nearly every day.

She had few personal possessions. And she owned little clothing. Then it was the custom for women to wear two-inch heeled, lace up shoes. My mother wouldn't have had more than a pair of slippers and one pair of shoes. First, she eased her poor calloused feet into shoes that always pinched. (Her toes were permanently bent due to wearing bad footwear in the past. On each toe was a large corn. Walking was a painful experience for her.) She didn't own any practical, sensible footwear for the country like wellingtons or boots. The only protection from the weather for her head was a beret which she pulled down as far as she could over her forehead. Her thin duster coat was more suited to town wear. It was always her custom to carry a handbag, tucked high in her armpit. From her elbow dangled a fold up woven bag for the shopping.

The nearest shop was Carters General Store. This was several miles away. To get there it was necessary to climb down a narrow track running between a steep hill bounded on both sides by large fir trees. Someone obviously owned the steep tract of land on the right hand side, as a fence had been erected and ran all the way down to the bottom of the hill. As yet they hadn't started clearing it. Lydia managed to use the fence as a hand hold. It scared her greatly slithering down the hill for it was gloomy and dark on her left hand side. With utmost relief, she would reach the bottom. Stretching in front of her was the wide expanse of Rhododendron Avenue, which wasn't bad. Over the years many substances had been added to it by the illegal residents that owned the plots either side of it. Sadly she just had to cross this. She had to walk along two rough tracks, opposite, which were now becoming slippery underfoot. One was known as The Goat Way and the other was Bluebell Walk. (I was never sure whether my father made these names up. There *were* goats at the far end of the track and there certainly *were* bluebells in the spring.) With her only precious pair of shoes coated in mud she would walk the rest of the way along a tarmacked road to the shop. Going back would be worse for she would be further burdened by a bag of groceries, including a glass bottle of sterilized milk.

Incredibly, Harry continued with his job at the Royal Arsenal in Woolwich. It meant him travelling into Gravesend on the first hourly bus from Culverstone, and then catching a train to Woolwich by eight o'clock in the morning. He left High Winds in the dark, negotiating the same hill as Lydia, by torchlight. And he had to do the same when he returned.

She was in a state of terror by then and was often totally distraught.

Living at High Winds did pose another dilemma, close to their hearts, for them both. How were they going to convince the Children's Department to let us go home during the various holidays?

Unbeknown to them, this was to be the least of their worries, for the moment.

It was late October. Leaves were falling off the trees rapidly, and there was a nip in the air. Harry had lit a floor standing chimney paraffin stove for her before he left. Inside the chalet it was warm and cosy.

Lydia had nothing to do.

She sang loudly to the little Bakelite wireless which Harry had left on for her. Today she was almost happy. She had recently had a letter from me. This always cheered her up. And she didn't have to make the long walk to Carters today. She also had a book to read, that Harry had brought her home. It was her favourite pastime.

At first, she didn't hear the knock on the door. Then the music stopped, momentarily. A sharp knock sounded again on the wooden frame. She sucked in her breath noisily and stared wildly at the door. Her feet were frozen to the spot.

Then she heard a voice.

"Open up please. I know you are in there."

Reluctantly she knew she had to face whoever was out there. Her heart thudded loudly in her chest as she stepped across the floor. With shaking hands she pulled the warped wood open. A young man stood there, dressed incongruously in a pin striped suit and green wellingtons.

He eyed her up and down.

Shortly, he said.

"I'm from Strood Council."

Lydia's hand flew to her mouth.

"I'm sorry, sir."

The young man smirked in spite of himself. He was just twenty one and a newly qualified council clerk. He had set out with a formed opinion of these people breaking the council's rules. His life was very different; he lived in a comfortable detached house owned by his parents on the edges of Meopham Green. Before the day was over he would change his opinions.

He asked her baldly, "Are you living here, madam?"

Lydia rubbed her hands together anxiously.

She burst out guiltily, "Yes, sir, we are. We couldn't 'elp it though, we had nowhere else to go. It was them. They made us leave. And we've been onto the Council. They won't give us nothing. I've tried and I've tried."

A small smile twitched at the corner of his lips. Curiously, he craned his neck to see into the dim interior of the chalet.

He asked her bluntly, "Who are 'we', exactly?"

"Me an' my 'usband, sir."

He stabbed a forefinger in the air.

"So..........there is just the two of you living here? No children."

She nodded then burst out painfully.

"We 'ave got three children. They can't live with us, until we get a house. They are in an 'ome in Sidcup."

Understanding dawned in his eyes.

"Ah, I see."

Her eyes shone brightly with unshed tears.

He patted her shoulder awkwardly, feeling inadequate.

"Might I ask you one more question, if you don't mind?"

She nodded in agreement.

"I would like to know where your husband is. This is his piece of land you see. It is in his name and I should be addressing him."

Lydia sniffed.

"'E's where 'e always is. 'E's at work. Always leaving me 'ere all on my own."

The young man stroked his chin, thoughtfully.

"I have no choice then, but to pass on the Council's message to you, I am afraid. I am very sorry for your plight. You are not allowed to live here all the year round. I will give you some notice which I hope will help you. You have six weeks to find somewhere else to live."

The young man stepped off the wooden veranda and picked his way down the flint stone path that Harry had started making recently. Carefully, he pulled the homemade gate closed behind him. Then he disappeared down the hill. Lydia stared dully after him.

London County Council
JWW/EB

Memorandum from   Director of Housing
To: The Children's Officer
                        34 Watson Street
                        S.E.8
Reference   HM/D5/9/635.

13 November 1954

Telephone extension

I am dealing with an application for rehousing from Mr Harry James Randall, late of 6, Abbey Terrace, Abbey Wood, S.E.2.

Mr & Mrs Randall are at present residing in a dilapidated week-end hutment at Culverstone, Meopham, Kent, and report that their children are in the Council's care at The Hollies, Sidcup.

I shall be glad to know if there is any reason why the children should not be returned to their parents if adequate accommodation is provided.

Received
R.J.Allenby
15NOV 1954

Harry held the official letter in his hand. He shook the piece of paper.
"That's what it says missus. Says I have got to report to Gravesend Hospital on Monday."
Lydia looked at him.
"Are they going to keep you in?"
"Why yes, they are."
She fell silent for a moment. Then she burst out, "How am I going to go on, then?"
Harry sighed deeply. He held a hand to his forehead and admitted, "I don't know." He sat on the bed with a bump.
"How long will you be?"
Harry pursed his lips thoughtfully.
"Well the doctor said ten days."
Lydia echoed, "Ten days! Nearly two weeks."
"Yes, missus," agreed Harry.
Lydia lapsed into thoughtful silence. She stared into space.
Harry weakly tried to justify what was about to happen.
He opened his eyes wide and arched his bushy eyebrows.

"Now look here, missus. I can't help it. I *need* this operation. I'm in that much pain. Until it's fixed I can't do any lifting or anything."
Lydia jerked back to the present.
"It's a mystery to me, man, how you got a hernia in the first place."
Harry spread his arms wide.
"It's just one of those things, missus. It 'as just 'appened."

Mrs Randall
High Winds
Rhododendron Avenue
Culverstone
Meopham
Kent

18.11.1954

Dear Madam
I am sending you our above address and as I have been told by Strood Council I must be off here within six weeks being as my husband is in hospital can there be anything done to help me.

Mrs Randall

22nd November 1954

Dear Mrs. Randall

In reply to your letter of 18th November, will you please say to which hospital your husband has gone, and the date, also what is your income at present.
Have you any idea to what address you will be moving when you leave Meopham.

Yours Faithfully

Area Children's Officer.

Mrs Randall, High Winds, Rhododendron Avenue, Culverstone, Meopham, Kent.

Mr H Randall
Rhododendron Avenue
Culverstone, Meopham
Kent.

16.12.1954

Miss D F Champion

Dear Madam

I would like my children to spend a few days with us at Christmas. We are going to friends.

Received 14 Dec 1954
I am Yours Faithfully
Mr H Randall

Above is a letter asking for us to go home for a few days at Christmas. There is no reply confirming the arrangement. I believe the lie of going to friends was too thin for the Children's Office to swallow, this time. We were destined to spend this Christmas at Rowan. As it happens we were amazed that every child was actually given half a pillowcase of toys. We didn't know that they weren't new, that they were donated by well-meaning local people. It wasn't actually that bad spending Christmas there, but we didn't breathe a word to Mum and Dad of course.

MEMORANDUM
From   The Director of Housing
                Mottingham District Office
To   The Area Children's Officer,
                34 Watson Street, S.E.8
Reference   Hm/5/9/635
Telephone   Extension
Date   30 December 1954

Mr. H. J. Randall

With reference to my memorandum of 13th November, 1954, concerning the above applicant. I shall be glad to know if you are yet in a position to let me know whether the children who are stated to be in the care at "The Hollies", Sidcup would be returned to their parents in the event of the Council providing suitable accommodation.

R.J. Allenby.

Received
31 Dec 1954

The reply: note the date.

Children's Department

TIDeway 4275

CH/AC06/EC

MEMORANDUM TO: The Director of Housing
                   Mottingham District Office.

FROM: Area Children's Officer, Area 6

Yr. Ref.   Hm/5/9/635

Re: RANDALL family
High Winds, Rhododendron Avenue, Culverstone, Meopham, Kent.

In confirmation of our telephone conversation today, I write to say that the circumstances of this family remain, as outlined in our letter of 5th October, 1953, remain unchanged.

The mother is considered quite unfit to render adequate care of her children. They have been allowed home on leave for only short holidays, and only when the father was able to be with them all day. This arrangement has been made at the request and with the full co-operation of Mr. Randall, who, himself, has admitted that his wife could not properly care for them.

Therefore, this case still remains one in which we would be most reluctant to discharge the children to the care of their parents.

D.F.C.
3rd February 1955.

Since his operation Harry was home on sick leave. He had just got up. It was early. He had on a pair of long johns and a rough shirt he wore to bed. Lydia was still asleep. Puzzled, he opened the hut door to persistent loud knocking. There were two men on the veranda. The older man waved a piece of paper under Harry's nose. He stared at it and visibly paled, making the pimple on the side of his nose stand out sharply.

The older man said tersely.

"You were warned in October. You cannot stay here any longer. Be off here by the end of the week."

The young man smiled an apologetic smile. Secretly he was glad he didn't have to deal with it alone. The older man grunted, "Come on."

They both headed off.

Harry went inside the chalet and sat down shakily. Strood Council meant business. He knew he hadn't taken Lydia seriously when she told him. Well he had to now. They had to find somewhere else and quick.

Chapter Twenty Six: The Brownie Belt

April 1955

By now Caroline had joined me at Wyborne School. This meant we could travel together. We would leave early, before everyone else and make the short walk to the station, with our satchels banging on our backs. After a short wait, we would get on the train and travel just one stop to New Eltham. At that time I believe we were the only children going there. I was so glad to have her company.

To my horror, it had been discovered that I was short sighted and needed glasses. The ones I was given were the round, pink National Health type, which I hated. I took them off as soon as I could. It was surprising how easy they were to break. They spent a lot of time being mended! Someone eventually came up with the idea that I should have two pairs. So I was foiled again.

Today, I was to be thankful for my new glasses. When we were toiling up the station slope, I spied something glinting on the ground. Swiftly, I pounced on it before Caroline could, which wasn't like me at all.

It was silver in colour and oblong in shape. There was some writing on it. Caroline and I examined it minutely. It read 'Mr. A. Deary' in italic lettering. And it was a cigarette lighter. This time I refused to let Caroline take charge. I told her that I found it and I was going to hand it into Miss Brown, our headmistress. Caroline insisted on coming with me. Instead of going to our class when the bell went, we marched to her office. She patted us both on the heads and gushed profusely that she was glad her girls were so honest. We knew what she was really thinking, though. She didn't expect much of Homesie Kids, so she was surprised. We went off to our classes. As time rolled by we didn't think any more of it.

April turned into May.

Becoming a Brownie was encouraged by all the housemothers. The meetings were held on a week night in the gym. I was a very keen Brownie, and had nearly all my badges. This particular night, I was dressed in my brown uniform with the yellow scarf around my neck, but I couldn't find my Brownie belt. I was quite prepared not to bother about it. Miss Lang sent me upstairs to find it. She said I couldn't possibly go without it. Angrily, I stamped up the shiny wood to my dormitory. I fell to my knees and searched in my bedside locker, where a lot of my clothes were kept. It wasn't there. Then I saw it. It was caught up in the wheels of my iron bedstead. How had it got there? Someone was playing a trick on me. I crawled under the bed and plucked it from its hiding place. I backed out and bumped straight into a boy who was standing watching me intently.

I sucked in a surprised breath.

It was Eric who stood there.

"What are you doing in here?" I asked. "This is the girls' dormitory. You are not allowed."

Eric pushed me against the metal edge of the bed.

Calmly, he said, "I want to do it with you."

I stared at him goggle eyed.

Whilst I didn't really know what he meant, my racing heart told me that it was something bad. That it was something which wasn't allowed. I began to tremble with fear, despite my efforts to control it.

Ineffectually, I whispered, "It's Brownie night, I'll be late. I was only looking for my belt."

He swiftly yanked my brown tunic up and pulled my blue knickers aside. I stood in terror whilst he poked at me with something soft and hot. Then at last, he pulled away, fumbling at the fly of his short grey trousers. I noticed with some detachment that his long grey socks had fallen down and were wrinkled around his ankles.

He whispered urgently.

"Don't tell anyone. You won't tell Miss Lang, will you?"

We both started as we heard a sudden noise on the stairs.

Without waiting for a reply, he vanished through the doorway.

I was alone again, trembling and shaking. Tears sprang to my eyes and coursed down my cheeks. I dashed them away with the back of my hand. With difficulty, I threaded the Brownie belt into the loops at each side of my waist and buckled it up.

Just then, Caroline bounced into the room.

"Whadja been doing?" she demanded. "You've been ages. We're gonna be late."

I didn't answer.

On Monday at school I was summoned to the headmistress's room. There was a man and a woman waiting to see me. It was Mr and Mrs Deary. They thanked me profusely for handing in the cigarette lighter, telling me that it was a present from their only son on Mr Deary's last birthday. It had great sentimental value for their son was killed soon after that in a car crash. They pressed a £5.00 note into my hand. I couldn't resist telling them that it was my birthday soon.

Mum and Dad had managed to find somewhere else to live for the moment.

A scathing previous report from the Children's Office did not think a great deal of their choice.

CHILDRENS DEPARTMENT
OFFICERS REPORTS

05.04.55
Visited 15, Russell Street, Gravesend in answer to Mr
Randall's letter re leave, & saw Mrs Randalls landlady.
Latter did most of the talking as Mrs Randall is
incapable of anything much in the way of conversation.
Apparently Mr and Mrs Randall were turned out of their
home in Abbey Wood-reasons were obscure. They moved to
their own bungalow or hut at Meopham, which is I gather
rather primitive and therefore uncomfortable in winter,
so they met present landlady who kindly gave them 2
unfurnished rooms.
House is very poor and dirty. Landlady is cheerful but
feckless & not very bright.
Landlady and husband are R.C.s, have 4 small children
aged 5,4,3 & 2 (eldest of family died two years ago) who
were sprawling around, dirty, unruly but happy apparently
and adequately fed. While Randall children are here (if
allowed) the other children will go into parent's bedroom
(and bed??)
House is so dirty and overcrowded I feel any leave
granted should be short.

V. O Boyd.

On my birthday, an envelope with beautiful pink and black script writing arrived at Rowan for me. It was a card from Mr and Mrs Deary. He was a calligrapher by trade. I was thrilled and kept the envelope until it fell apart.

Today, I was eleven and I enjoyed all the attention I received. Revelling in the cards I had, any other worries seemed far away.

I had done my best to avoid any contact with Eric. When I saw him coming I would hurry off in the opposite direction, shadowing Miss Lang for protection.

She must have wondered what was wrong, but if she did she didn't say.

His whispered words still echoed in my ears. I couldn't tell anyway. My insides were frozen with guilt and shame. Even thinking about it made me shudder.

I wasn't able to breathe a word to anyone. Not my brothers, my mum and dad, nor even my best friend, Caroline. And the last person I could confide in was Miss Lang.

I was always so surprised, as well, that he had chosen me.

But I didn't want to think about that on my birthday.

I was on my way, alone, to the washroom that evening when Eric stepped in front of me. My heart jumped into my mouth. Despite my care, he had caught me unawares. He put his finger to his lips and led me into the cloakroom next door. He dragged me behind the bulging racks of coats. Soon we were completely hidden from sight. He pressed his face close to mine. I flinched away, banging my head on the wall. He grabbed my arms and drew me towards him. Earnestly he whispered, "You haven't told anyone have you?"
I shook my head, unable to speak.
Satisfied, he lifted up my dress. He pulled my knickers down to my ankles and pushed my legs apart. His stubby fingers probed inside me. With some relief, I relaxed slightly. Then it changed. I felt that soft warmth again on my bare leg. Urgently he moved against me. I trembled and shook in terror. Then it was over. He stood there holding my arms and listening.
I began to panic when I heard voices of children going in to the washroom next door. He put a hand over my mouth. In an instant he was pulling up my knickers and straightening my dress. He pushed me through the coats, remaining behind them himself.
Shakily, I walked next door to the washroom. Somehow I managed to continue as if nothing had happened. Mechanically, I washed my face and cleaned my teeth. I hurried because I wanted to avoid bumping into Bobby or Bernard.
And I didn't want to talk to Caroline, either. I just wanted to go to bed and bury my head in the pillow.

15 Russell Street
Gravesend
Kent

20.05.1955

Dear Madam

I would like to have my children for Whitsun holidays. From Sat 28th until Tuesday 31

Yours Faithfully
Mr H Randall

Pass issued.   *Received 23rd May 1955.*

Despite the visiting Welfare Officer's obvious disgust at my parents' new lodgings they still issued them with a pass. Perhaps on this occasion they were too busy to care. However, he had no intention of taking us to 15, Russell Street, least of all that we should share the landlady's children's beds. We went straight to High Winds where we spent a happy Whitsun holiday.

In June the pressure was on me again. This time it was different. Somehow I knew everyone had high hopes of me. That was Mr Irving, Miss Lang and all the other assistants. It was rumoured that I would go far.

Apparently, I had to sit the eleven plus. It was somewhat of a mystery to me why it was so important to fill in the endless puzzles correctly. I have always hated any kind of maths.

Still I did my best. I tried really hard.

Eric became more adept at catching me.

One time, I was playing 'shops' in the old outside toilets. It was strange how he always knew where I was. .And he always knew when I was alone.

He stood outside, looking in.

This time he asked me.

"Can I do it with you today?"

For some bizarre reason, I whispered, "Yes."

He lifted my pretend counter from across the doorway and came in.

Afterwards, angrily, I threw all my shop into one of the dustbins. I didn't want to play anymore.

This went on. I lost count of how many times it happened. It was worse during the school holidays which were looming on the horizon. I prayed we could go home for a while. At least for a time I would be safe.

It would be beyond my wildest dreams that a solution would present itself.

Chapter Twenty Seven: The Whist Stand

It was the custom of the Homesie Kids to trawl around locally trying to find things to do. A particular favourite was going to jumble sales. It didn't cost anything to get in and it would while away the hours until it was time to go back to Rowan. Hanging about until the end was a good idea, too, because by then the stallholders would be willing to give away what they hadn't been able to sell.

This was how Eric came by a brass whist stand. It would have stood in the centre of the table whilst a game was in progress. In order for the players to know what suit was being played one of four flaps would be flicked. There was a picture under each one of a heart, club, diamond or spade. He came by lots of other bits and pieces as well. Most of them were useless items, which he had no idea what to do with, but he felt good, going back to Rowan with his paper bag of free goodies.

That evening, in the privacy of her room, he showed Mater what he had acquired. She laughed at some of the things, but showed a keen interest in the whist stand for it had given her an idea.

It was becoming a dangerous business, keeping her liaisons with Eric. She had almost been caught on more than one occasion when she had gone into his dormitory to fetch him. Miss Starr, another assistant had come out of her room, on thinking she had heard a noise. She wondered what Mater was doing in the large dormitory when it was obvious all the boys were asleep. Luckily Mater was very quick witted and usually invented a valid excuse. She had told Eric that they needed to be careful that for some time they must keep their distance. He was extremely disappointed; she had aroused his teenage ardour, and it was difficult to quell. He reasoned with himself that he could try out what he had learnt on someone else.

For some unknown reason, he picked me. I wasn't aware up to that point that he had even noticed I existed.

With, Mater, however it was different. She pursued *him* whenever she could, for she was in love. And she wasn't prepared to give him up yet. Her biggest fear was that she would lose him to some young and pretty girl.

The whist stand gave her hope. Calmly she explained it to Eric. She told him to leave it on his bedside locker with all the flaps turned down. When it was safe she would turn up the heart flap. Then, that night, he could definitely come to her room.

Eric bounded up the stairs to his dormitory to fetch his book of ships which he kept in his bedside locker. It was too precious to him to leave in the playroom. Although the bedside lockers were supposed to be for clothes, it was possible to get away with secreting a few special items underneath. Casually, he looked at the whist stand. His hair almost stood on end as he saw that the heart flap was turned up.

That night, with his heart beating faster he turned the handle and entered her room. She sat on the bed waiting for him, wearing a dressing gown. He could plainly see pink skin through the thin material. She patted the bed, putting a finger to her lips as a reminder to him to keep very quiet.

Carefully, she switched her little portable wireless on low. Popular music tinkled out of it and flowed around the room.

Excitedly, she told him that she had managed to wangle taking him on holiday with her when she had her leave. With trembling fingers she removed his pyjamas and ran her hands appreciatively, over his firm young body. She told him they were going to Cornwall, whilst hastily loosening her dressing gown belt. Shuddering slightly from anticipation, urgently she pulled him towards her. Panting slightly, she told him they would go by train to St. Ives. They would set off next week.

She whispered, "I can't wait for next week. You'll like this place, it's a special favourite of mine."

True to her word they set off, travelling all the way by steam train. Eric was an excited boy, sticking his head out of the window to breathe in the clouds of smoke.

Mater sat primly on the carriage seat, wondering at this boy that enthralled her, who had the body and functions of a man.

They arrived by taxi, after dark. A board outside the bed and breakfast told them they had come to the right place. The landlady showed them upstairs to their rooms which were next door to each other via a connecting door. Mater noticed that there was another landing. She heard the landlady's feet on the stairs going up to it. It meant that she slept upstairs. They wouldn't be disturbed.

It became an essential part of their holiday to spend the night together. Here, they could relax more for there was little fear of being caught. They took full advantage of it, having full sex every night. She also managed to take things one step further, teaching him to experiment a little, in order to achieve the highest possible satisfaction for them both.

By day they travelled about on buses and trains in order to sightsee. Mater indulged Eric, telling herself that someone owed it to him. She bought him several gifts, including a fishing rod. They both hoped the holiday would never end.

It meant several trouble-free weeks for me. I could breathe again. And yet somehow I missed his presence. I no longer had to dodge around corners or go upstairs with my heart beating faster and faster. So why did life seem so flat? I don't know. Perhaps the strange emotionless world we lived in was to blame. Did I crave attention, even when I hated what happened? I never did find the answer.

September 1955

Bobby was keen to get back to Burnt Oak School. Now, for the first time in his life he had a friend of his own. He had met a kindred spirit in clever Martin Boyes, who was an outsider. His mother was very interested in his friendship with Bobby. She was keen to be benevolent to a Homesie Kid. Before long she was inviting him to their home in Old Farm Avenue, to play with Martin and stay for tea. Despite his new standing Bobby was still very attached to me. Not much time had passed before he told Mrs Boyes about me. Soon, I, too, was invited to their home.

I had to go to a new school, called The Gordon, which was supposed to be a better class of Secondary Modern.

I wasn't told how I did in the eleven plus. I knew that if you passed you were sent to a Central or Grammar school. As I wasn't going to either, I assumed I had failed. I felt Miss Lang was disappointed in me for she seemed to be short with me a lot of times. I had always got on well with her in the past. This upset me, for I had tried my best.

Now I had to travel in a different direction. I had to walk to the Halfway Street gate and catch a bus to Eltham Well Hall. No one else from The Hollies caught the bus with me. I was on my own.

My first day was bewildering. I crept into the playground and just stood there, hoping no one would notice me. A lot of the new first years were with friends from primary school. I wasn't. Despite that, they huddled together, very aware of being new. A group of bigger boys spotted me, standing alone. They surrounded me and began firing questions at me.

"Wos yore name? Do they call you four eyes?"

"What school'd yer come from?"

"Where d'you live?"

I tried to stutter answers.

One of them burst out, "You're not a Homesie Kid are you?"

A blonde boy jeered.

"She can't be. She's too quiet."

Mercifully, then the bell rang. The boys melted away. Soon, only the first years were left in the playground.

I was relieved to be in school. Learning, I loved. My form teacher was Mr. Richardson. He made a fat ginger girl called Lynda Page sit next to me. It was, he said, to make her behave. He hoped I would be a good influence on her!

Then came break time.

With my poor bladder control, I was desperate, and made straight for the outdoor toilets. There were no toilets free. Big girls were in each one, standing on the seats calling out to each other. I waited in vain for them to go away. But they didn't. Miserably, I went back to the playground and stood alone. Soon, I was standing in a pool of water, crying my eyes out. To my shame I had wet myself. Again lots of children, including the big girls, crowded around me, which only increased my misery. The teacher on playground duty rescued me. I was taken to the housecraft centre. This was a separate house right next to the school. The third and fourth years did their cooking lessons here. The teacher that ran this took me under her wing. She was kind and understanding and luckily didn't have any classes in the centre that day. I took off my wet knickers and washed them, spending the whole afternoon there waiting for them to dry. My only regret is that I missed double English and my very first lesson in French.

Some good came out of my misery for the girls were never allowed to hog the toilets again.

November 1955

On a visit to the upstairs toilet, I was horrified to discover I was bleeding 'down there'.

I automatically thought it was because of what Eric and I had done. Guilt and shame filled my being. I burst into sorrowful tears and rushed up the four stairs to my dormitory.

Susan Taylor was already up there, in her dormitory next door. She heard the commotion of my noisy tears and hurried in.

She asked, "Joyce, what on earth is wrong?"

I sobbed anew. Still I was unable to talk about my fears that what we had done had caused me harm.

In the end, I did blurt out, "I'm bleeding down there."

She was the plainest girl I have ever seen, being plump, with short cropped hair and glasses. But she was also the kindest, often taking the younger girls under her wing like a mother hen.

Gently, she asked, "Do you mind if I see? Will you show me?"

I nodded in agreement, my sobs beginning to subside. Obediently, I did as she wanted me to do.

She laughed out loud.

"You idiot. Its just a period."

I stammered, "A...a..a...period."

"Yes," she said.

Puzzled, I asked her, "What's that?"

She grabbed my arm.

"Come on. Let's go and see Miss Lang. She'll explain it all."

We went downstairs together to find the housemother.

Miss Lang was cooking the tea. She seemed embarrassed. All she said was that I needed to wear sanitary towels and that Susan would show me where they were kept. She said she would also find me a sanitary belt. (This was a strange elastic contraption which consisted of a wide pink elastic band which went around your waist, It also had two dangling pieces which had clips attached to each end. All the sanitary towels in those days had loops on them. These hooked onto the clips. This was supposed to hold the towel firmly in place.)

Susan very kindly took me into the staff sitting room and showed me the cabinet where they were hidden. She also found a small packet containing a new belt. We went back upstairs. She helped me sort myself out, suggesting that I wash my soiled knickers out and keep my belt in a safe place. Mysteriously she said I would need it again next month.

I still didn't know why this was happening to me.

Miss Lang never explained anything.

On my next holiday at home, my Dad tried his best to explain, for my mother certainly couldn't.

Eventually the mystery of what it was, or why it stopped just as suddenly as it had begun, or why it started again every month, was unravelled by biology lessons at school.

Slowly, week by week it began to sink in. Although it was a small happening, I knew that for me, things had changed. Now, life had taken a different turn.

Chapter Twenty Eight: The Slip-on Shoes

December 1955

Things had changed at Rowan. A lot of the older children had left. They could no longer remain in The Hollies. It was time to make their way in the world. For most of them, even the boys, this was terrifying. The Hollies was all they had known for most of their lifetime. And a lot of them were without any family to run to. The system tried to reunite them with their nearest and dearest. Often Welfare Officers would work hard to locate parents, most of the time without success. Even appealing to their better natures didn't always help. They wanted no truck with what they thought they were rid of. Luckily the children concerned weren't enlightened about that. They entered into their new life hugging the same dreams they had all along-of one day being reunited with their rich parents! It would be a long disillusioned road before they would learn the truth. By that time they would be men and women, with families of their own.

Big children like Joe Mays, Kenny Master, Derek Izzard, Amy Phillips, Winnie Wilder, her brother Johnny had all departed. The exodus had started at the end of the summer and continued until now. Sometimes it was a drawn out process due to whatever the circumstances of the particular child. It depended what their wards, London County Council, had decided they would be capable of doing in their adult lives. Most of them would never achieve what they could have because they were damaged and therefore lacked the necessary staying power needed to thrive in normal life.

Suddenly Susan Taylor left, too. She must have come of age.

I didn't know her history. No one ever knew anyone else's unless it had been brought to the surface by some occasion, like the visit to Eric by his brother Ged, when he found out he had three brothers. Usually a child left at fifteen.

Sometimes, though, in some circumstances it was allowed. It was in Eric's case. This was because he wanted to go into The Royal Navy. If he got in he would serve as a boy sailor. He couldn't do this until he was fifteen and three quarters.

This month was the strangest at Rowan since I had lived there.

Eric was the oldest boy. He was fifteen and two months. Bernard was next at thirteen and a half, along with Paul Cartham and his sister Jennifer.

My strange on/off relationship with Eric had continued. Sometimes when he caught me I was glad. I craved the attention he gave me. He whispered to me that I was his girl, and no one else's. Our meetings were mixed with sadness because we both knew he would be leaving soon.

There were other times when I was angry with myself. I was determined at these times to be better, to be stronger and to resist him. I was upset because I never did.

Later in life I would learn that some of us are weak and some of us are strong. I was weak, with an underlying strength to keep a terrible secret I couldn't disclose. That was because I was afraid of the repercussions.

I had to forget it for the moment. Miss Lang asked me to organise something for the Christmas concert. She wanted me to turn a popular song into a sketch. There were only two proper 'parts'. Although the friction between them continued, she suggested with a sigh that I had to give the starring role to Eric, as he was the oldest boy.

I *did* give him the part and I gave the other part to myself.

On the day, a row of little children standing at the back of the stage sang.

'I saw Mummy kissing Santa Claus underneath the mistletoe last night.'

Eric dressed up, acted out the part and kissed me tenderly. There was thunderous applause!

January 1956

Mr Scows, Eric's Welfare Officer had some news. Miss Lang told Eric that he will be coming to take him to the Royal Naval recruitment office at Blackheath for an interview and a medical. He came back with mixed feelings. Mr Scows tried his best to reassure him, telling him that it was excellent that he had passed the entrance exam, it was just a pity that he had failed the medical.

He had a hernia in the groin and was too short by a quarter of an inch.

Despite his bitter disappointment, all was not lost. Within several weeks, he was soon found a bed in Queen Mary's Hospital at Sidcup.

Miss Lang took a selection of children to visit him after the operation. I and Caroline were amongst them. We had a long walk from the Hollies all the way up to the High Street, past Sidcup Place until we eventually reached the hospital.

We walked along a maze of outdoor corridors with roofs, which were made of wood. They creaked alarmingly when they were walked on. These led to a long hut where Eric was, in an adult surgical ward. He was the darling of the ward and made much fuss of by the other occupants of the beds and all the nurses. A lasting impression of his stay in the hospital was the death of a Polish ex-soldier, who was in terrible pain. No one slept on the night he was dying. This was the first death Eric had witnessed. All the men said it was a shame that he had to at his tender age.

He was pleased to see us all. He joked about with all the other children, whilst I hid at the back as usual. We never really spoke. There was a card on the locker. We all looked at it. The writing was in familiar green ink. It was from Mater.

April 1956
Eric had to go back to the Royal Naval Recruitment office. He had to have another medical. Mater reassured him that this time it would be alright. She was sure that he had grown as well.
He left the Recruitment office on a cloud. This time he had passed the medical. And he had grown by half an inch. As soon as he was fifteen and three quarters, he was going to join The Navy as a junior seaman.

June 1956
The day came for Eric to leave. I had already promised him that there wouldn't be anyone else.
I *did* feel sad. The truth was that I had a strange feeling for him that I couldn't fathom. At twelve years old I didn't understand what those feelings could be.
We all crowded on the front lawn outside Rowan to wave Eric and Mr Skews goodbye.
He was taking Eric to the station and seeing him on to a train for London. From there he would travel to Ipswich. It would be the first time in his life that he had travelled on trains and tubes.

I sort of knew deep down inside that his promised visits that he would come back to visit would not materialize. Most children who left never came back.

I was miserable at The Gordon School. I came to dread playtimes. Usually I hid in corners on my own as I hadn't made any friends. Or I would take a book down to the playground to read. Despite being forced to sit with Lynda, she didn't want to know me outside of the classroom. I dreaded the line up to go back into class. The boys would tease me continually about my clothes and in particular my shoes. They would laugh and say they thought I had my brother's shoes on. Whereas most of the girls were now into the new fashion of permanent pleated circular skirts, that swished when they walked, mine was an old fashioned box style that was too long. My shoes were heavy brogue type brown lace ups. All the other girls had neat slip-ons which were the latest fashion. And it didn't do me any favours reading in the playground either. I got called 'bookworm' amongst other nasty things. And none of them forgave me for coming top in everything, even maths. Things got even worse when I won a composition competition for schools in South East London sponsored by Brooke Bond Tea. There were set titles to write about. I picked one and wrote what was apparently a very mature story. It is to my shame that I cannot even remember what it was about. At the time I wished fervently that I hadn't entered it, for the bullying got even worse.

However, at last, things had started looking up at school.
A new girl had arrived. Her name was Hazel Covington. Mr Richardson introduced her to me. I believe this was because her background was sad, too.
Her mother had died recently of T.B. She was living with her Aunt Nellie in New Eltham.
We became firm friends. I shared an affinity with her, for her clothes were old and unfashionable as well. She suffered more at first because her Aunt had decided to give her a home perm before she started school. It was not a success. Her fair hair was a giant ball of frizz. We became the joint butt of everyone's jokes. Now I didn't care because I had Hazel to back me up. We stood against them together.
Soon I was invited to her Auntie's house for tea.
This became a regular occurrence.
Aunt Nellie got to hear that my dearest wish was to own a pair of slip-on shoes. She told me that she would make a sacrifice for me. Instead of treating herself to a new nightdress she would buy me a pair of slip-ons instead. On one visit we travelled to Eltham High Street and selected a pair. They were gorgeous. They were blue suede with velvet bows on the front of them.
I was utterly thrilled until I was told I mustn't wear them to school. Desperately, I pleaded with Miss Lang to relent. She wouldn't budge, nor could she see that the whole point of owning the shoes *was* to wear them to school. I was only allowed to wear them in the evenings and at weekends.
By now, though, I had learned to be devious.

I smuggled them into my satchel.

When I reached the Halfway Street gate, I changed into them and wore them to school. All went well until I forgot to change them back one afternoon. I even think the bullying had turned into respect. I couldn't believe I had made such a mistake.

Miss Lang confiscated them. I appealed tearfully to Mater to see if she could get her to change her mind. Miss Lang was adamant. The lecture I received was long and reproachful.

"I cannot believe it of you, Joyce. How could you be so deceitful? I trusted you. How dare you approach another member of staff to try and persuade me."

She went on and on and on.

I ended up in bitter tears.

And my beautiful slip-on shoes were gone.

My troubles weren't over.

Another new girl had come to our class. Her name was Irene Berry. She became friends with Hazel. This was because they travelled on the same bus home as Irene lived in New Eltham, too. She had long brown hair, fashioned into the newest hairstyle of a ponytail and she was well dressed and attractive.

I knew it was going to be a struggle, but somehow I had to hold onto my friendship with Hazel.

One day, the headmaster, Mr Michaels, summoned me to his office. He put an arm around me and hugged me to him. I stared mesmerised at his stained black teeth and the cigarette ash all over his jacket and trousers.

He asked me if would like a chance to go to a grammar school. I didn't know how to answer him. Then he asked me what I would like be when I grow up. At twelve I didn't actually know. I mumbled that I would like to look after children. Disappointed at my answer, he dismissed me. I lost the only chance I would have to go to the Bluecoat School.

I tried really hard to get back into Miss Lang's good books. At last she said Hazel could come to tea.

On the day, she relented and returned my slip-on shoes to me.

Chapter Twenty Nine: The Lodgings

A man in a pin striped suit stood staring out of the Esse room window. Bernard ambled into the room. He was a trifle reluctant for he was mystified why this man wanted to see him.

For the most part he was a follower rather than a leader, with an extremely genial disposition. He liked to get on with everyone and fall out with none, including Miss Lang. That's why he was here.

The man turned around and smiled, holding out his hand.

"Hello, Bernard. I'm Mr Rollins, your Welfare Officer. It is my job to look after you from now on."

Realization dawned on Bernard's face.

Mr Rollins laid his bulging leather briefcase on the big table which stood in the middle of the room. He opened it and withdrew a buff folder. Feeling in his inside pocket he drew out a pair of gold spectacles which he placed on his nose. He rifled through the folder until he reached the page he wanted.

Bernard waited patiently, unconsciously twisting a forefinger through his fringe.

Mr Rollins smiled encouragingly at him.

"You know that you will be fifteen this summer."

Bernard bristled slightly with indignation.

"Course, I know. I'm fifteen in July. That's when my birthday is."

Mr Rollins swallowed.

"You are aware that you will have to leave Rowan and that you will have to find a job?"

Bernard sighed softly in exasperation.

"Yes. Of *course* I know. All the boys talk about it."

Mr Rollins regarded him seriously over his spectacles.

"Have you got any idea what you want to do?"

Bernard considered the question carefully.

Lessons in school had been a trial for him.

He shrugged his shoulders non-commitally.

The man sighed slightly. He had known from reading Bernard's notes that this wasn't going to be *easy*.

He continued somewhat hopelessly.

"And have you any idea where you are going to live?"

To his surprise, Bernard said cheerily.

"Yes, of course. I'm going to live with Mum and Dad."

Harry fussed around Lydia pulling her dress straight and smoothing down her hair.

"Now don't forget, missus. Let me do the talking."

Lydia was in her quiet mood. She was happy to oblige.

He coached her again.

"When we get to the Kent Children's Office, we'll explain what we are after. We want the children moved nearer. They'll understand the travelling is murder. Besides we can tell them the whole story from start to finish. And we can say that we have put our names on the housing list here."

Lydia looked at him alarmed.

"But we haven't, have we?"

Harry waved an impatient arm in the air.

"I know that. They won't though. We will as soon as we get around to it. It stands to reason that we should. We can't stay in that place forever, living in someone else's house, with no where to call our own."

He shot her a warning look.

"Just don't put your foot in it, will you."

Lydia muttered inaudible agreement under her breath.

The Duty Children's Welfare Officer smiled perfunctorily at them both. She leaned her elbows on the desk and nodded sympathetically whilst Harry poured forth his story. Lydia sat quietly beside him. She didn't utter a word either to back up his story or dispute it. His voice, too, eventually petered out into silence.

The woman began to scribble on a large pad in front of her.

She confirmed the details again with Harry, her pencil poised above the paper.

"Did you say you were staying at number 15, Russell Street, Gravesend, Kent? And that your children are in the care of the L.C.C. at the Hollies, in Sidcup? Your Children's Office is in Deptford?"

She reeled off all the other details she had written as well.

Harry nodded in agreement.

She stood up. A dismissive smile wreathed her face.

Harry and Lydia staggered to their feet.

Politely, she told them as she ushered them out of the door.

"It was *so* lovely to meet you both. We will be in touch."

Memorandum
To   Miss.West.
From   MLS

Kent County Council telephoned re Randall case. They wondered if you had visited the Randall's address at 15 Russell Street, Gravesend. If not, they thought you would be interested to know this house is in very bad condition to the extent that the landlord's own children are in the Care of K.C.C. on account of that. They understand that there is a possibility of the Randall's moving into a caravan.

K.C.C would be grateful if you would write them re the Gravesend address as they would be interested to know your views. Apparently Mr and Mrs Randall called in at their Gravesend office and had a long talk with the C.W.O. about their future plans etc. I checked with the Hollies that the children returned from their holiday on time.

K.C.C. Propose to confirm their telephone conversation in writing.

M.L.S.
4.1.57.

Lots of post dropped through the letterbox of No 15, Russell Street, landing on the bare floorboards with a clunk. Casually, Harry picked up one buff envelope with his name on. It was a letter he was expecting, but he wasn't worried. It would be the same answer as usual. He slit it open and scanned the contents. His eyes narrowed as he took in what it said.

He burst out incredulously, "What the blazes?"

In disbelief he read it again.

22nd February, 1957

MM

Dear Mr. Randall

As a result of our officer's visit to your home, I am unable to grant leave this weekend for your children as the sleeping arrangements are not adequate now that Bernard, Joyce and Robert are getting older. I am sorry that I am unable to grant leave but as the children are getting older they do need more room. I hope that as soon as you are able to provide more bedding for the second bed and if possible, another bed you will let me know so

that my officer can visit you, and reconsider the
question of again granting home leave.
If you would like to have a talk about this, I shall be
pleased to see you if you will make an appointment.

Yours sincerely,

D.T. Champion

Area Children's Officer.

Harry groaned loudly.
"Cor Blimey. That's torn it. It 'as an' all."
Lydia wrote in, on Harry's behalf, applying for Easter leave. For the
first time since their children had been in the L.C.C's care they were
very worried that this would not be granted.

Lydia was terrified of continuing to live at 15, Russell Street.
The landlady had been taken ill. It was soon confirmed that she had
contracted T.B. She confronted Harry whilst the landlord was out of
the room.
"What are we gonna do, man? I 'eard T.B's catching."
Harry scoffed.
"Don't be so daft, woman."
A wild expression filled her eyes.
"It is I tell you man. You ask anyone. What if *they* find out? They
won't ever let us 'ave the children again."
Harry pursed his lips thoughtfully.
"Hmmm. You might 'ave something there."
Relief flooded her face. She shook his arm.
"Can we find somewhere else."
He sighed deeply.
"Yes. Yes. We'll see what we can do."
The both fell silent as the landlord bustled into the room.

They got a guarded reply from The Children's Office which *didn't*
confirm that we could go home. Again, it queried whether they had
managed to get another bed and more bedding. Harry did his best to
fob them off, knowing full well that none of us would ever spend ANY
time in that house.

As far as I can remember we only set foot in it once. On that occasion,
I remember seeing a woman sweeping down the bare staircase with a
broom and going down to the kitchen which was in the basement.
There was a large table which was filled with open packets of food

and dirty crocks. The landlord sat at the table eating a pigs head. I can remember vividly that I felt really sick and couldn't wait to get out. It was a relief never to enter it again.

The huts at Abbey Wood had been pulled down. New housing had been built not far away. Gran and Grandad, Uncle Ronald and his daughters, Joanie and Pauline were rehoused. Auntie Elsie and Cousin Rose were all that was left in their hut. Cousin Bill had taken everyone by surprise by marrying an Irishwoman, Lena. He was now in his forties. Afterwards her children kept popping up, like rabbits out of a hat. It became a family joke. Eventually it transpired that she had six. Auntie Elsie and Cousin Rose were given a brand new council flat. Bizarrely enough, it was just a few yards from Gran's new house. So the feud continued. We often visited them both. On the allotted days we would travel to Abbey Wood. Mum and Dad would split up. She would go to her mother's. He would go to his sister's just like old times. We had to divide our time between them. Firstly we would go to Gran's, see her and our cousins, Joanie and Pauline. Grandad was there in the flesh, but not so you would have noticed. He was as silent as ever. Again we hoped Uncle Ronald would be absent. Then Mum would begrudgingly send us to Auntie Elsie's. I always had this feeling that Auntie Elsie didn't like me. I think I irritated her because I was so softly spoken. Later I had to concede that I must have been mistaken. Amongst my papers I found this letter.

1 Dianthus Close
Abbey Wood
S.E.2.

Dear Joyce

Just a few lines to let you know that I will meet you at Welling Corner Friday night at 6 O'clock. I won't be able to come right to the house for you as I won't be finished very early.
I expect your Dad has told you that you are coming over for the weekend.
Well that's all for now so I will close.
Love from Auntie Elsie and Rose.
P.S. Give love to Bobby & Bernard.

Xxx

Sending you an envelope in case you want to answer.

I never knew of this letter's existence.
There *was* a scrappy report which read as follows:

```
                    London County Council
Memorandum
To:          Mrs Hassall

The Randall children have an Aunt (paternal) living at 1,
Dianthus Close, Abbey Wood, S.E.2. She wanted to have
Julia this weekend but Miss Simone said no, as the whole
thing would have to be 'looked into'.

Phoned Hollies.

MPO
```

*Whoever she was, she couldn't even get my name right!

Bernard was devastated to learn that he couldn't go to live with Mum and Dad. He would have to go into lodgings.

Eric was on leave. He turned up at Rowan in his Royal Navy uniform. His training was complete. I heard on the grapevine that he was off to Malta next week. I didn't get a chance to speak to him. Mater monopolised him all the time. My disappointment was great.

Lydia was relieved that they had found another place. They would move across the road to live with Mr and Mrs Tranter. By now she had given up hope that she would ever have her children home again permanently. She did feel they would have more chance of having them home for holidays at No 11, Russell Street.

Harry and Lydia had heard that their old landlady had died. She was 37.

They wrote in again to ask for leave for us in August. To their relief Mr Rollins gave the house the all-clear when he called to check it over. And a reply from the Children's Office confirmed that we can go home.

Two days before we were due to go, I fell ill with tonsillitis. I had to stay in the sickbay. Bernard and Bobby could go home as planned. I burst into floods of tears when Mr Irving did his rounds. In a rash moment, he promised me that if I dried my eyes he would take me personally in his car, as soon as I was better.

In a few days I was declared fit enough. Mr Irving came to collect me. We set out for 11, Russell Street, Gravesend.

That part of Gravesend was very poor. Mr Irving looked down his nose when he got out of the car. He banged on the peeling door with a large fist, with me by his side. Mrs Tranter opened it. She was young and dolled up to the nines. Her hair was dyed jet black and she wore heavy makeup.

She shook her head.

"No luvvy," she said. "They're not 'ere. They are all at the 'ut at Meopham."

Mr Irving stared at her in distaste, noting the applied beauty spot by the side of her mouth.

I was desperate and very afraid that he would take me back to Rowan. I tugged on his arm.

"I know where it is," I told him.

He looked at me with narrowed eyes.

"Are you sure?" he asked.

Frantically, I nodded my head.

He smiled.

"Come on, then. Show me the way."

Somehow we found it. Dubiously, he parked his car in a convenient niche at the side of Rhododendron Avenue. He laboured up the hill, after me, in his smart suit. We arrived at the gate of High Winds. The first person we met was Dad, in boots, old trousers at half-mast, braces and a tattered vest.

He exclaimed in dismay, "Dear oh dear! That's let the cat out of the bag."

Bernard and Bobby were dressed in just shorts and were filthy dirty. Mum lay on one of the beds reading. After refusing a cup of tea, Mr Irving disappeared down the hillside.

Later, he sent a note to the Children's Department to say Mr Randall had been fibbing.

Bobby and I said a tearful farewell to Bernard. He was going to live in lodgings in Lewisham. Bravely, he promised us that he would come and visit us when he got settled in.

Like, Eric, he had become an outsider now.

A worried Harry wondered why he hadn't had a reply to his latest letter asking for weekend leave for us. He rang up in desperation, but was frustrated to find he couldn't speak to the Duty Welfare Officer.

His call was blocked by a clerk.

He received a scathing letter telling him that he did NOT have permission to take us to High Winds. It was suggested that he go to the Children's Office to discuss the matter. When he did, he was asked to supply a list of amenities available at High Winds.

Desperately, Harry pleaded for us to be allowed home for the weekend. He was told that we could go as long as we stay in Gravesend. The Welfare Officer warned him that they would check to make sure we were there. We had no choice but to stay at 11, Russell Street.

I worshipped Mrs Tranter. I thought she was beautiful. I was now thirteen and desperately growing my hair so that I could have a ponytail, which was the height of fashion. She suggested dying my hair, and making up my face. My hair ended up a bright auburn. I had a great weekend.

On my return to Rowan, Miss Lang was irate. She made me wash my hair repeatedly until the rinse was all gone.

The Housing Department had written again to the Children's Dept. enquiring whether they could offer the Randall family accommodation yet.

London County Council

```
17.12.57
CHILDRENS DEPARTMENT

OFFICER'S REPORTS

Visited  Mr  Randall  at  his  chalet  at  Meopham  re  Xmas
holiday at this chalet for Bernard and his and sister who
are at the Hollies.
Found it to be satisfactory-ideal for children's holiday-
situated on top of a wooded ridge. Warm and comfortable.

G.H.R.
```

Some sort of approval at last.

Hooray for Mr Rollins!

Chapter Thirty: The Wind of Change

I was *so* impatient to grow up. I listened to Radio Luxembourg with Caroline, so I knew what was in the hit parade. Mum and Dad bought me comics so I had a rough idea what was fashionable. I had some special clothes secreted away. I was saving them for a special occasion. They had been given to me last year.

We all used to be envious of Elaine Peters.

She left last summer.

It seemed like she always wore her own clothes. They were nice as well. Such as the rest of us could only dream about. She used to wash and iron them herself. I was one of the girls who used to watch in envy as she pressed transfers onto the legs of a bright yellow pair of pedal pushers. The steam rose from the iron as she pressed the flimsy paper hard. Carefully, she peeled it away to reveal perfect italic lettering of singing stars names. There was Cliff Richards, Elvis Presley, Buddy Holly, amongst others.

```
MM
8 January 1958

Your Ref. 5.1/3/45/1957

Dear Sir.
H.J.Randall and family
11 Russell Street, Gravesend, Kent
```

Thank you for your letter of 24 December about the above family.

Joyce and Robert are still in the care of the L.C.C. under section 1 of the Children's Act and are at Rowan Cottage, The Hollies, Lamorbey, Sidcup, Kent. Bernard Randall aged 15 is also in the care of the L.C.C. and is in approved lodgings supervised by my After Care Officer. Joyce is expected to leave school in the summer of 1958.

Mr and Mrs Randall have accommodation in Gravesend in the home of a young couple with a number of small children. This house is very crowded and there is no room for Mr and Mrs Randalls children. They also have a small hut on a piece of waste land at Meopham in Kent which they have furnished with beds so that the children can spend short holidays there. Mr and Mrs. Randall have therefore had their children on leave from The Hollies for short periods over the last two years.

At one time Mrs. Randall's mental condition gave cause for concern. She appears to be much improved and has not been in need of hospital care for some time.

Both Bernard and Joyce are old enough to care for themselves and to be of some help in the home and the youngest child Robert is a bright capable boy. The children are very closely attached to their parents and the Randall family is probably one of our most closely knit families. The older children are conscious and unhappy about the separation from their parents and they attribute this to the lack of housing. As you know Mr. Randall continues to make efforts to get his family a home and both parents frequently express despair about the possibility of making a home for the children.

In view of Mrs. Randall's past history we cannot be certain that she can run a home but I feel that in view of her improvement she may, given a chance, prove a capable mother. It is apparent that she will not continue to improve if she has no hope of fulfilling her very strong wish to make a home for the children. As the children are so much older they can obviously do a lot for themselves and I feel this family has some considerable chance of re-establishing itself if it is re-housed. By midsummer two of the three children will be working.

The separation continues to cause unhappiness to the family.

If you feel that you can either now or in the near future consider re-housing this family I shall be grateful if you will notify us so that my welfare officer can see that the rehabilitation is closely watched to ensure its success. We shall be glad to co-operate in any effort to rebuild this family.

The Director of Housing	Yours Faithfully
Housing Department	
Town Hall	D.F.C.
Woolwich, S.E.18.	
Area Children's Office	

Footnote: Even they made mistakes sometimes! I was actually still thirteen at the time the above letter was written. I would be fourteen in May, not fifteen. I wasn't due to leave school until summer, 1959.

The whole cottage was agog. We were getting our own television set. In the past only the office had one. Each cottage was allowed an hour of television a week! Ours was at five o'clock, on a Thursday, to watch Ivanhoe. We would file into a large sitting room and sit cross legged on the floor. The reception was awful, but we didn't care. The threat of the treat being cancelled was very real. Most of us were careful to behave for ever after.

Now, every cottage was getting one.

It meant we could watch more, hopefully.

The small black and white set was of course in the staff sitting room. It only gave Miss Lang more leverage to get us all to behave. And we didn't get to watch any more, either. It was highly frowned on, even then!

METROPOLITAN BOROUGH OF WOOLWICH

A.V. WHITE. A.I.M.T.A.   FI Hsc
Housing Department
DIRECTOR OF HOUSING
TOWN HALL
WOOLWICH, S.E.18
Telephone No Woolwich 1181

All communications   5.1/3/45/1957
To be addressed to the
"Director of Housing"

Your Ref: MM   20th January, 1958

Dear Madam,

Re: H. J. Randall & Family
11, Russell Street, Gravesend

I thank you for your letter of the 8th instant, and are very grateful for the information you have supplied concerning this family.

I will communicate with you immediately a decision has been reached by the appropriate Committee of the Council.

Yours Faithfully,

V. White

Director of housing

The Area Children's Officer,
London County Council,
34, Watson Street,
Deptford,
S.E.8

I had been ecstatic when Elaine had thrust the yellow pedal pushers under my nose before she left last year. And a tiered deep pink skirt and a layered net petticoat. I had stroked the skirt lovingly, fingering the names around the bottom flounce.

"Go on," she beamed. "Take them."

"Oh, I couldn't," I told her in feeble protest.

To my relief, she insisted.

Hurriedly, I put them away in my bedside locker.

Since then I had tried them on again and again, hoping that I could pluck up the courage to wear them. Always, I took them off and put them away again.

The Hollies was changing. The bakery was closed. Soon the haberdashers and cobblers would follow suit. Now, each child was allotted a clothing allowance per year instead. We were going to be able to buy our clothes from the shops. Mine and Caroline's hopes of being able to wear proper clothes were dashed when we found out that Miss Lang would be doing the shopping.

<u>METROPOLITAN BOROUGH OF WOOLWICH</u>

```
A.V.WALKER A.I.M.T.A   F.I.R. Hsc
HOUSING DEPARTMENT
DIRECTOR OF HOUSING
TOWN HALL
WOOLWICH,S.E.18                    TELEPHONE WOOLWICH 1181
```

```
5.1/3/45/1957
Your Ref:
CH/AC06/MM
25TH March, 1958
```

Dear Madam
Re: Mr .H.J.Randall & Family
11, Russell Street, Gravesend, Kent

With reference to previous correspondence, I am pleased to inform you that approval has now been given for accommodation to be provided for this family.
I must stress, however, that there is no immediate prospect of assistance, but I will communicate with you again when an offer is to be made to Mr. Randall.

Yours Faithfully

A.V. White.   Director of Housing

Leave to go home was granted more liberally, now. Dad (or rather Mum) still had to write in but there was no quibble about us going, even for a weekend now that High Winds was an approved place. And Dad noticed this and was quick to take advantage of it, writing in at every opportunity to have us home.

I was now fourteen, and considered responsible enough to make the journey with Bobby to Gravesend unaccompanied. We would meet Mum and Dad at Mrs Tranter's. It was great. It meant I got to see her again.

In May, there was a bus strike so we travelled by train. When we got there Dad was still at work and Mum was out shopping. Bobby and I got a little worried when we heard this. It wasn't like Mum not to be waiting anxiously for our arrival.

Mrs Tranter's jet black hair tumbled to her shoulders in a wavy mass. She was getting ready to go out. I watched her apply thick pan-stick to her face and lashing of mascara to her eyelashes. Delicately she flicked a brush over her cheeks until they turned the hue of pink she was happy with. In amazement I saw her rub makeup on her legs. With an eyebrow pencil she drew a line down the back of her legs. In a casual cockney voice she said, "Oh I think your Mum is luvly. She don't get treated right, though. Your Dad could be better to 'er. E' keeps 'er short of money for a start off. She is bloody amazin'. I 'ave *never* known a woman who could make a pound stretch so far as she can. She goes to Bovey's on the corner an' she comes back with so much stuff an' she *still* 'as change. I wish I could. I do an' all. 'Ere you are, that's yer Mum, now."

We had broken up from school for the summer holidays.

At last I plucked up the courage and put on my pink skirt and petticoat.

I roamed around Sidcup, delighting in the way the skirt floated along with me. I had abandoned my glasses long ago, except when I was made to wear them.

Through long sessions of practice I had perfected the latest American hairstyle of the large wave over the forehead and high ponytail on the crown.

Normally I was with Caroline or Bobby. But, Caroline and I were no longer such close friends. I had Hazel and Caroline was always with Linda. She had come to Rowan in 1956 and was younger than Caroline.

Things had changed for Bobby as well. He was always at Martin's house.

So, today I was alone.

I turned in amazement as a boy wolf-whistled at me.

It was my first!

He crossed the road to join me. We chatted for a while and arranged to meet later, in a park down the road.

I was beside myself. He was an outsider. And he liked me!

Racing back to Rowan, I wondered how I could get out later that day. We were allowed out to play after tea, but leaving the grounds was forbidden.

I rushed upstairs to change into my yellow pedal pushers. They were a beautiful fit! Skin tight! I just *had* to check in the full length mirror by the scullery. Standing before the mirror I admired my reflection. I frowned a little at the school blouse I was forced to wear with them. Never mind. I stood the collar up, pulled the body of it tightly over my flowering bosom and tucked it neatly into the waistband of my jeans. With narrowed eyes, I buckled a wide belt around my middle. (This had been a purchase from Woolworth and had cost three weeks' pocket money)

I was ready to go!

Miss Lang stepped out of the Esse room. She had a face like thunder. Someone had upset her and it wasn't me.

"Joyce Randall," she said, placing a lot of scandalised emphasis on my name. "I *hope* you are not thinking of going out in those."

She pointed an accusing finger at the pedal pushers.

I didn't answer.

Her voice rose dangerously, her face growing bright red.

"They are *disgusting*. I can see every crease of your backside."

I blurted out.

"They are supposed to be like that."

She wagged her finger.

"You are *not* to go out in them. Do you hear? I absolutely forbid it."

Sulkily, I turned on my heel and stalked into the playroom. With rising frustration I waited until she disappeared to the other side of the cottage. I had no intention of not going out. Wildly, I dashed out the back door and ran for the gate. With my heart thudding I hurried to the park. I feared I would be too late. The seat where we had arranged to meet was empty. I sat down shakily. I waited for ages. The sky changed colour. He didn't come. I crept back to Rowan biting my lip, wondering how I was going to get in without being seen.

The post had arrived at 11, Russell Street. Mrs Tranter handed a buff envelope to Lydia.

"Ere are. This one's for you."

Lydia stared at it dubiously.

"It's got 'is name on it."

Mrs Tranter turned it over.

"It's got a stamp on the back. Looks like it's from some Housing place."

Lydia snatched the letter.

Two bright spots of colour marked her cheeks.

She ripped the envelope open and drew out a folded sheet of paper.

Her eyes opened wide as she stared at its contents in disbelief.

Incredulously, she whispered, "They're giving us a house. Woolwich Borough."

"Oh Lydia," squealed the young Mrs Tranter. "How wonderful!"

She hugged Lydia tightly.

They sat down on the settee and studied the letter carefully.

Lydia's face fell as she took in the entire meaning of the letter. It stated that the house had to be viewed immediately, that it would be assumed that the person or persons named were not interested in taking up the tenancy if there was no response. There was more. It seemed that a week's rent had to be paid in advance before tenancy could be taken up.

Wildly, Lydia turned to Mrs Tranter.

"What am I going to do? I haven't got any money."

Softly, Mrs Tranter said regretfully, "I wish I could 'elp you, love. I'm skint until Sonny gets paid."

Bitterly Lydia spat out, "Trust the bloody old man to be down *that* bloody 'ole when 'e's needed here."

She lapsed into agonised silence, her chest rising and falling sharply.

Mrs Tranter probed gently.

"Whadja mean, ducks?"

Unshed tears shone in Lydia's eyes.

"That 'ut at Meopham."

Mrs Tranter shrugged.

"Never mind. Perhaps 'e'll be back tonight."

Lydia observed, "He's been down there all the week."

A shaft of sunlight streamed through the window and lit up her face.

She blurted out excitedly, "I've 'ad an idea. I'm gonna phone me Mum."

Mrs Tranter encouraged, "That's it, luvvy."

Lydia explained, "There's a phone box right outside her new house. If I keep ringing it someone will answer it and go and get her."

With Mrs Tranter's help, Lydia managed to scrape up the train fare to Woolwich.

They chuckled as they raided her children's piggy boxes.

Mrs Tranter observed, "I wouldn't do it only in an emergency."

A happier Lydia set off for the station, bemused at the bag of change she carried in her handbag to meet the return fare.

She travelled to Woolwich to meet her mother.

Together they viewed the new house. Gran paid the first week's rent Two sets of keys and a brand new rent book were handed to Lydia Her eyes shone as she noticed that it said on the front, Mr. H.J & Mrs L.E. Randall.

Her name was on there, too.

Now all she had to do was to wait for Harry to return.

Chapter Thirty One: 61, Purneys Road

With trepidation, Harry turned the corner into Russell Street. He wondered how things would be. Going to High Winds was his bolthole. That was one of the reasons why he had bought it of course.

Now, he had a feeling in his bones that there was something up.

The door shot open before he could put his key in the lock.

Lydia stood there, hands on her hips. Her face was flushed and her blue eyes glittered.

"About time you showed your face," she cried.

Harry muttered under his breath.

"Oh no. Don't tell me she's still at it."

Mrs Tranter appeared on the doorstep, too.

She waved her hands excitedly.

"You've got a house. You lucky sod. You've got a council house."

In a bewildered daze Harry entered the crowded house, where everyone seemed to be screaming and shouting.

"Whis-t! Whis-t, you lot. I can't 'ear meself think."

Lydia handed him the well-worn letter.

He ran his eye over the contents.

In dismay, he said.

"But it's too late. This is dated last week."

Mrs Tranter burst in.

"You wanna think yerself lucky you got such a good mother-in-law."

"Eh?" queried Harry.

Mrs Tranter explained what had happened in every detail.

Harry muttered softly.

"Thank God for that. Good job the old bitch is worth something."

Lydia shot him an indignant glance.

"We will 'ave to pay 'er back."

He waved a dismissive arm.

"Never mind about that now, missus. There is something I want you to do for me, later."

She looked at him.

"What's that?"

"Well, I want you to pen a letter for me. I think I 'ad better pop out, first."

Lydia tutted noisily.

"*Now* where you goin'?"

"Well, now. I might just catch the removal place before they shut. See how much they want for taking our stuff to Eltham."

9.9.1958

Dear Madam

You will be pleased to know that we have a 3 bedroom house at 61 Purneys Road Eltham. We are moving in on Saturday 13 and I wish to have Robert and Joyce on Sunday 14th from 10am until 7pm also for Friday 19th until Sunday 21st.

Yours Faithfully
Mr H. Randall

Despite the above letter, things did *not* go according to plan. Harry was aghast at the amount the removal company wanted to charge. Fruitlessly, he searched for a cheaper alternative. Sickeningly, the move was put off for that weekend.

Finally on 22nd of September, they moved in.

I walked out of my school gates and bumped straight into my Dad. He stood there in a tatty sports jacket, collarless shirt, braces and boots. I am ashamed to admit I was embarrassed. Girls and boys out of my class were walking behind me. They were laughing and giggling. I hoped it wasn't at us. He grabbed my arm.
"We're in at last. I want you to come and see it."
I pulled away.
"I can't Dad. I'll be late. I'll get into trouble."
Angrily, he waved an arm in the air.
"Oh, bugger them. They can wait. Just this once they can."
I was desperate to see it anyway,
On the way, he extolled the virtues of our new house.

We arrived at a middle-terraced pebble dashed house. Dad unclipped a wooden gate into a small front garden, with a square of grass, flower borders and a large tree. He opened the green front door and ushered me down a passage with a concrete floor, which was painted red. There were a few mats dotted about that I recognised. One was in front of a door. Dad pushed it open to reveal a decent sized room with a bay window.

Mum was in here. She was singing softly to herself. On her lap, were large swathe of material she was turning a hem on. Her eyes shone with happiness.

"'Ello, love," she said simply.

The room had been newly decorated. The centrepiece was the tiled fireplace with an odd shaped chimney breast above it. I giggled slightly when I saw the wooden clock on the mantelpiece. I remembered that, too, and the mirror with gold patterning at each side, which hung above it. There were just floorboards in here. The homemade mat I remembered from Abbey Wood was on the floor in front of the fireplace. In just a few days, they had, somehow, managed to buy and put up net curtains. Next to the fireplace was a built in cupboard, which filled an alcove from floor to ceiling. The old wooden table was there, too, with a few chairs. There was little else in the room.

I smiled at Mum, suddenly shy.

Dad beckoned to me urgently, distracting my attention from her.

"Come on, girl, this way."

The bright expression faded in Mum's eyes. She bent her head down and carried on with her sewing.

Dad led me into a narrow room. Somewhere since the war the scullery had disappeared from ordinary people's lives. This room would be known in future as the kitchen. There was a built-in cupboard here, too, just behind the door. Next to that was an electric cooker. Opposite, under the window was a white sink with a wooden draining board. Sitting under that was a squat grey electric boiler.

He opened a door with a flourish to a walk-in larder. The shelves were already filled with numerous things. And there was all manner of things on the floor. Triumphantly, he led me to the back garden.

What I saw was a small oblong of overgrown garden with a narrow concrete path and a little green shed at the end.

Dad rubbed his hands gleefully.

Obviously, what he saw was different.

"Told you it was alright, didn't I."

I gave him a bemused glance.

The fence was in a bad state of repair. Next door's garden was clearly visible through the open slats. There was a large pigeon coop, which took up most of the space. Loud cooing sounds came from deep inside the structure, although no pigeons could be seen. There was no pretence at any kind of cultivation. What garden remained was mud. We both stared curiously at this spectacle. Just then, the back door opened and a dark-haired lady stepped out. She began removing washing off a rope line suspended between a rickety shed and the pigeon coop.

"Hello," she said to Dad and me.

We murmured a greeting back to her and escaped back into the house.

Mum was in the kitchen, now. She held a kettle in her hands and remarked casually.

"Thought I'd make us all a cup of tea."

Dad flapped his hands about agitatedly.

"Yes. Yes, missus. Let me finish showing Joycie around first."

We squeezed past Mum. I shot her an apologetic glance and followed Dad.

He led the way out into the passage rubbing his hands again.

Fiddling with a broken handle, he opened another door.

"And this is the bathroom."

I stared at the room. It had a lavatory and wash basin as well as a stained iron bath. The floor in here was concrete, too.

He confided to me.

"And I made sure I 'ad the first bath. I did, too."

He waved his fingers in the air.

"Don't worry about that broken handle. I can soon fix that. You'll see."

I smiled at him.

He pulled open a little door, which was under the stairs.

"That's the coal 'ole," he stated. "Right up we go! Up the wooden hill!"

We clattered up the uncarpeted stairs.

He opened the first door.

"This is your room. See! Your bed's already there waiting for you."

There indeed was the little bed I had always had with the wooden headboard. It was made up as if they were expecting me to sleep in it, complete with the mauve candlewick bedspread I remembered, with the flower in the middle.

We perused the other two rooms which were very sparsely furnished. There was nothing at all in the second room.

Downstairs, Mum and I sat in a companionable silence, either side of the table sipping our tea. I was determined to give her something of me. Now, I ignored Dad's attempts at getting my attention until I was satisfied she was content.

Reluctantly, I knew it was time to return to Rowan.

As I journeyed back on the single-decker bus I had time to reflect. This was our dream come true. Okay so it wasn't *quite* how I pictured it. The starkness of it all hadn't been a part of it. But to them it was luxury unrivalled. The nightmare of living in one room in someone else's house, sharing cooking and toilet facilities and having little space to call their own was over at last. And it was a place where we could all share the dream.

And we couldn't wait.

Mrs Moran perched on the edge of the chair she had been offered.

"And what do you think, Mrs Randall of your new home."

Lydia sucked in a breath.

"I waited long enough for it. We were on the housing list for sixteen years."

Mrs Moran looked down at the floor.

"Yes, it's most unfortunate."

Lydia added, "I want Joycie and Bobby home. They've been away from me for eight years."

Mrs Moran soothed.

"Yes, I know. Unfortunately all we can allow at the moment is daily visits at the weekend. You haven't enough beds or bedding, have you?"

Lydia admitted bitterly.

"No, I suppose not."

Mrs Moran stood up.

"I am afraid I must go. I will try to do what I can to help you. I will get in touch with the Family Welfare Association to see whether they can help with lino etc."

Any distraction would have done for Bobby at that time.

His eleventh birthday was in May. He had to leave his beloved Burnt Oak. His friend Martin Boyes went to a local grammar school. They were split up after five years. Bobby had to go to a comprehensive called Crown Woods in Eltham. At that time even the concept was new. It would eventually have 2000 children. Even after the first few days my brother was miserable.

Bobby remained friends with Martin Boyes. They planned to go to the firework display as it had been thrown open to outsiders now. He told Martin's mother of the family dismay that they couldn't go home for good because they didn't have enough beds. She told Bobby that they had a spare double bed and mattress if that was any help. It was being stored in their loft.

Harry was definitely interested. He went to visit Bernard at his lodgings.

He admitted, "I need your help, son. Can you come over for the da
at the weekend?"

Pushing a borrowed handcart, they both walked with it to Sidcup
which was a distance of about four miles. With help from the Boyes
family, they loaded the bed and mattress onto the cart and wheeled i
carefully to Purneys Road. Bernard helped him to get it upstairs
Together, they assembled it.

Harry waited until Lydia left the room.
He beckoned urgently to Mrs Moran, whispering hoarsely.
"I would like Joycie and Bobby home but I am still paying back loans I
had to move here. I can't afford to have them at the moment."
He put his finger to his lips and whispered, "For God's sake don't let
on to my wife. She'll have my guts for garters."
Mrs Moran nodded understandingly.
Lydia appeared.
Mrs Moran smiled at her.
"I will give you Mrs Christie's address. She is at the Council for Social
Services. Ask her to get you some new bedding."

In November, a parcel arrived at 61, Purneys Road. It was new
blankets.

Miss Lang studied the memo she had received. She went to the door
of the playroom and called me. Bobby wasn't there. He was at Scouts.
She ushered me into the Esse room.
"I have just received a memo. Is this right you are going home for
good?"
I nodded happily.
We went home every Sunday, so I knew.
Crossly, she said, "I wish I had known sooner. I could have used your
clothing allowance to buy you a new winter coat."
I just shrugged my shoulders and didn't answer. At that moment I
didn't care.
She continued, "According to this you and Bobby are going home next
week."

On the 1st December we left The Hollies and Rowan for the last time.
I knew I would never go back, unlike Eric.
Fleetingly, I wondered where he was and would I ever see him again.

Together Bobby and I caught the bus to Eltham, carrying our clothes in bags. Grinning widely at each other, we dawdled through Kidbrooke Park Road swinging the bags between us. We were in no hurry for we were going home. Forever.

Endnote

Lydia suffered from Manic Depression (now called Bipolar Disorder.)

*There was **never** any indication that she would harm us, her children.*
Manic Depression consists of cycles of behaviour.
These are usually:
* Depressive symptoms.
* Manic symptoms
* Cycle of these moods.

No one knows the cause of this illness, but it is suggested by doctors and nurses specializing in the subject that it may be genetic or can be triggered by trauma in teenage or early adulthood.

We have no knowledge of what might have triggered Lydia's condition as she was unable to tell us anything about her early life. Harry believed in a rumour he heard that she was raped by one of her brothers. However, it cannot be substantiated by fact.

The depressive part of her illness caused her to be blank, vague and very quiet. She would sleep a great deal. Some of this was caused by the drugs she took which were much more aggressive then. But undeniably some of it would be the normal pattern of behaviour in this cycle. This could last for weeks.

The manic part always seemed to be triggered off by something bad happening to her. Or sometimes it could be something she had to face up to doing, which for such an introverted person such as her would be a considerable ordeal. She would react by being very talkative, need little sleep, shouting and screaming at her imagined aggressor. (In our case, this was always my father). It usually lasted for about three weeks, but she rarely got physical. During these times she would never take her medication.

My last thought is that the illness could have been managed better by all those around her.

That it wasn't, was our loss.